More Praise for *Market Leader Through Service Excellence*

»*Customers expect state of the art digital solutions, end-to-end, along the whole customer journey. But only human interaction can exceed customers' expectations in the financial services industry. This book offers great insights and valuable advice.*«

Sandra Ickinger, Head of Global Customer Experience Management,
Mercedes-Benz Mobility AG

»*'Market Leader Through Service Excellence' book is educational and useful for everyone who is involved or interested in the services industry. It is rich and deep in many core issues that service practitioners encountered; and offers future-oriented perspectives to explore 'what's else.' Ideas sprouted as I read the book, shifting perspectives for how I view service challenges and finding value in the big picture and the finer details the book offers. The real organisational cases offer provoking thoughts to enhance customer experiences and build a customer-centric culture. Thank you for the comprehensive service excellence pointers all in one book.*«

Dr. BeeLeng Seow, Facili-Trainer and Service Excellence Evangelist,
Continuum Learning Pte Ltd

»*This book is the perfect companion for anyone looking to convince board-level executives to implement customer-centric practices and strive for service excellence. A thoroughly comprehensive guide from strategy, to employee and culture, to application-oriented tips on how outstanding customer experiences are created.*
Dr. Gouthier is spot on: in service excellence, 'standing still is taking a step back.' A big thanks to him and his team for this comprehensive Service Excellence gem.«

Denisa Spinkova, Leading Service Excellence at Qatar Tourism

Service Management | Services Marketing Series

Edited by
Prof. Dr. Matthias Gouthier

Volume 8

Matthias Gouthier [Ed.]

Market Leader Through Service Excellence

World-Class Approaches to Managing Excellent Services

The Deutsche Nationalbibliothek lists this publication in the
Deutsche Nationalbibliografie; detailed bibliographic data
are available on the Internet at http://dnb.d-nb.de

ISBN   978-3-8487-7520-0 (Print)
         978-3-7489-3370-0 (ePDF)

British Library Cataloguing-in-Publication Data
A catalogue record for this book is available from the British Library.

ISBN   978-3-8487-7520-0 (Print)
         978-3-7489-3370-0 (ePDF)

Library of Congress Cataloging-in-Publication Data
Gouthier, Matthias
Market Leader Through Service Excellence
World-Class Approaches to Managing Excellent Services
Matthias Gouthier (Ed.)
237 pp.
Includes bibliographic references.

ISBN   978-3-8487-7520-0 (Print)
         978-3-7489-3370-0 (ePDF)

Onlineversion
Nomos eLibrary

1st Edition 2023
© Nomos Verlagsgesellschaft, Baden-Baden, Germany 2023. Overall responsibility
for manufacturing (printing and production) lies with Nomos Verlagsgesellschaft mbH
& Co. KG.

Service excellence: A cross-industry attitude that may also be tasty for a patient!

Carsten K. Rath

Do you remember your last exceptional service experience? I hope so for your sake because it means that you were positively surprised by a service or, better yet, by the warm attitude of the person performing it and the processes behind it. In my capacity as a service expert and a frequent guest in unique hotels and resorts around the world, I have experienced service in many forms, on a grand scale and in the many detailed intricacies that differentiate true excellence from standardized processes. To truly wow me with services is certainly challenging, yet the diverse teams in hospitality succeed in doing so time and again.

Of course, I still remember my last experience of service very clearly: It was a holiday in 2021. The hotels in Germany were still closed mainly due to the pandemic, while I was already experiencing personal hospitality again in Switzerland. I was sitting in the Grand Resort Bad Ragaz, perhaps the best resort in the Alps, jotting down initial ideas for our article and placing my breakfast order while still half lost in thought. I ordered the usual, including a freshly brewed tea from Ronnefeldt and a soft-boiled egg. Nothing unusual, really, but this meal was placed on my table as neatly as a pin. The egg was neatly, almost symmetrically, cut and meticulously closed again so that I did not have to break it myself and eat it half dented. It was a small but fine detail that thrilled me like a hungry guest and even prompted me to mention it here as a positive episode.

The rest of my breakfast at the Grand Resort Bad Ragaz was also a delight. It sweetened my day even before I got to know the actual perks of the resort. I usually only find such attention to detail in the 101 best hotels in Germany (www.die-101-besten.com). In any case, the Grand Resort Bad Ragaz is mentioned in the new edition of the hotel rankings among the luxurious neighbors of the best 101. The wonderful nuances make a noticeable difference in the processes and, ultimately, for the guest.

Service excellence has been my passion for over 25 years. From my experience as a traveler and as a management consultant, I know that interpersonal relationships and the service attitude that is implemented every day distinguish a company that is successful in the long term from mediocrity.

This is true without exception across all industries and is becoming even more relevant. Since 2020, the global economy has been dominated by the coronavirus crisis. Innovations or new ideas seem to have taken a back seat. Everything is focused on health, medical technology and efficiency. But especially when it comes to the sensitive and complex topic of health, the human factor is the only one that really counts, because only what shines healthily on the inside can shine vibrantly on the outside.

In a hotel or resort, excellent service begins even before the guests arrive for their stay. This constitutes exceptional service; the customers and guests always receive a little more than expected.

The team at Helios Hospitals also starts with healthcare services long before an actual stay in hospital. Since the beginning of their corporate history, they have combined medical care with the highest quality standards, extensive preventive measures and a pronounced understanding of service in everyday hospital life. The project presented, "6 Chefs, 12 Stars," puts culinary arts on the list of priorities at Helios Hospitals. Together with six star chefs, tasty and healthy dishes are designed for inpatients and they are implemented by Hofmann Menue-Manufaktur. Since 2020, we have been combining culinary experiences with the often painful stays in hospital and making the patients' time as pleasant as possible. This is precisely the goal of lived service excellence: to make the lives of customers and patients more convenient and more pleasant. In our article, you can read the detailed background to the project and an outlook on the future of everyday hospital life at Helios Hospitals.

I hope you enjoy it!

Foreword

"Customer service is a permanent construction site!" This is probably the best way to describe my personal experience with various service providers in recent years. While the companies communicate their service with full-bodied advertising promises, in practice, the customer often experiences a completely contrary situation: faulty services, incorrect billing, absent callbacks and much more. It is precisely in such deficient service markets that differentiation is best achieved by offering an above-average level of service. However, the problem is that excellent service does not just happen by itself. Sole proprietors, freelancers and micro-enterprises have a relatively intuitive feeling for what it takes (or should take) to provide an above-average, i.e., excellent, service. By contrast, medium-sized companies and, in particular, large enterprises require structured concepts, measures, and tools to successfully implement and live the idea of service excellence in the long term. Large companies, in particular, have their company-specific approaches. However, to raise all companies interested in providing excellent services to a higher level as a whole, a general, inter-sectoral approach was needed. Therefore, in March 2018, the Technical Committee ISO/TC 312 was initiated, which I have been leading as Chairman since then. With ISO 23592:2021, the first globally valid standard was published in June 2021 to define the principles of service excellence and a corresponding model. This provides companies planning to implement or optimize service excellence with a general guideline. However, what is missing and cannot be identified in such a standard are concrete and detailed best practices and how they work in practice.

The publisher's volume "Market Leader Through Service Excellence – World-Class Approaches to Managing Excellent Services" is dedicated to the exciting question of how service excellence is implemented and lived by and in successful companies. The book's structure is based on the model of service excellence as anchored in the new ISO standard 23592:2021. The model identifies four dimensions with nine elements that must be fulfilled to meet the holistic requirements of service excellence. To this end, proven experts from a wide range of industries present best practices, concepts, and a variety of methods and tools that show readers successful ways to implement service excellence.

The book, which was published as volume 8 in the series "Service Management | Services Marketing" by Nomos Verlag (www.nomos.de), comprises a total of 14 application-oriented articles by experts which, in addition to providing more general explanations of the concept of service excellence, focus on the four dimensions of the service excellence model. After an introductory presentation of the relevance and the model of service excellence based on ISO 23592:2021, the book examines the strategic dimension first. This is followed by a closer look at employee and cultural perspectives as the second dimension. The third dimension focuses on how outstanding customer experiences are created. Finally, the fourth dimension is devoted to operational service excellence.

I want to take this opportunity to thank my research assistants, Ms. Nora Kern and Ms. Carina Nennstiel, who actively supported me during the compilation process. Furthermore, I would like to thank Mr. Carsten Rehbein from Nomos Verlag, who made the realization of this edited volume possible. Finally, I would like to thank Nomos Verlag directly for publishing this book.

This edited volume is aimed at top decision makers, specialists and managers, and academics looking for sound advice, concepts, recommendations for action, and best practices on how service excellence can be successfully implemented in companies.

Now, above all, I hope you enjoy reading it and that you can derive maximum value from the various best practices it presents.

Koblenz, June 2022   *Matthias Gouthier*

Contents

Employee engagement

Understanding customer needs, expectations, and desires

Designing and renewing outstanding customer experiences

Service innovation management

Managing customer-experience-related efficient and effective processes and organizational structure

Monitoring service excellence activities and results

Outlook

Introduction

Managing service excellence: Introduction and overview of the contributions

Matthias Gouthier

Management summary

This article, which opens this edited volume, describes, on the one hand, the genesis of this specialist book, which has ultimately been shaped by the development and appearance of the ISO standard 23592:2021. On the other hand, it provides an overview of the various articles of the experts. The best practices described in the individual contributions offer substantial self-help to companies in implementing the concept of service excellence in all its nine elements.

1. Service excellence is on the rise worldwide

Competitive pressure, which has been further intensified by the corona-virus crisis, the transformation of value chains, and the blurring of industry boundaries, has never been as intense as it is today. Customers have never been as demanding and willing to switch providers as they are today (Lesonsky, 2019). The demands on companies' ability to transform have never been as high as today. All of these factors favor the shift toward service excellence.

After more than 15 years of intensive personal involvement with the topic of service excellence, I can make the following basic statements based on my own experience:

- The term "service excellence" is becoming increasingly popular, not only in Germany but also worldwide. Related job titles, e.g., head of service excellence or director of service excellence, are also found more and more frequently in practice.
- The Asian region, in particular, is showing great interest in the concept of service excellence (see also Thirumaran et al., 2021). In addition, there is growing interest in the Arab countries in promoting the service sector through the use of service excellence. For example, Qatar Tourism, as the official government agency responsible for the development and promotion of tourism in Qatar, has launched a service excellence program that, in addition to a vision and mission, includes

eight different large-scale initiatives to improve the quality of tourism services (Qatar Tourism, 2021).

- After years of defining the content of the concept and the corresponding development of a service excellence model as well as its implementation in an official standard, the elements of service excellence are now being differentiated in terms of content, and relevant aspects such as measurement and implementation are being explored in greater depth (see also the last article "Outlook: New developments in service excellence" in this volume).

Therefore, service excellence is no longer an exotic topic but has become firmly established in practice. In 2007, a Google search returned 1,830,000 hits when the term "service excellence" was entered, and the current figure (September 2021) is more than 12 million hits. However, one should not assume that this is a topic suitable for the masses. That is not the case at all, and it never will be. Service excellence aims to place a company among the top five to ten percent of companies in a market regarding its services.

For this reason, the concept is not suitable for every company. It can only be applied in a meaningful manner and is of value to a company if customers perceive outstanding customer experiences that lead to delight through the provision of excellent services. This step goes hand in hand with positive positioning in the market and differentiation from competitors (see Figure 1). At the same time, it requires appropriate alignment of a company's corporate strategy and service excellence strategy.

Fig. 1: Triangle of market leadership

2. History of the international standard ISO 23592:2021 "Service excellence – Principles and model"

Excellent service does not arise by itself. It requires the consistent and sustainable implementation and continuous further development of a structured approach, which has become firmly established in recent years under the term "service excellence" in both business and academia. In the past, however, opinions differed widely as to what exactly is meant by service excellence and how service excellence can be systematically implemented and lived in companies. For this reason, a global standard was developed at the international level by the technical committee ISO/TC 312 (https://committee.iso.org/home/tc312) chaired by the editor of this book. ISO 23592:2021 defines a corresponding standard and was published in the summer of 2021 (Naden, 2021). However, this standard did not appear from nowhere but has a long history of eleven years. Back then, its starting point can be seen in the two questions of what service excellence is and what needs to be done from the business perspective to implement service excellence systematically and sustainably. The first question, what service excellence is, may sound all too trivial at first glance, but the opposite is true. Very different understandings of service excellence can still be found both in academia and in business, which can be assigned to the following six conceptual understandings (see also Giese, 2016):

1. The term service excellence is used without defining it clearly, neither implicitly nor explicitly (see, e.g., Bitner, 1997; Bates et al., 2003).
2. While there is no clear definition of service excellence, references are made to specific companies and their services (see, e.g., Ford et al., 2001; Heracleous and Wirtz, 2010).
3. Service excellence is understood as a synonym for high service quality (see, e.g., Wiertz et al., 2004; Yu et al., 2013; Zeithaml, 2002).
4. Reference is made to various management systems (see, e.g., Kumar et al., 2013; Voon et al., 2014).
5. An explicit definition of service excellence exists, but it is rather sweeping in nature (see, e.g., Johnston, 2004; Lytle et al., 1998; Prabhu and Robson, 2000).
6. An explicit definition is given, defining service excellence as an organizational capability of a company (see, e.g., Edvardsson and Enquist, 2011; Asif and Gouthier, 2014; 2015; Gouthier et al., 2012; Khan and Matlay, 2009).

The latter understanding forms the basis of the definition found in ISO 23592:2021. According to this, service excellence is understood as the "capabilities of an organization to consistently deliver excellent services" (ISO 23592:2021, p. 1). The primary goal of service excellence is to continuously provide excellent services that create outstanding customer experiences, which should lead to customer delight and ultimately to greater customer loyalty (Gouthier et al., 2012). Since these derived objectives primarily concern so-called "soft factors," creating a uniform understanding and handling of the relevant topics is necessary. Service organizations can benefit from aligning their business strategies to provide excellent services to customers. As a result, customers and society can also benefit from an increased and outstanding level of service.

And the second question of "how" also remained unanswered for a long time (Gouthier et al., 2012). The basic idea for the ISO standard 23592:2021 goes back to the German specification of DIN SPEC 77224:2011, which was published in 2011 (see Figure 2). Convinced of the need to generate a standardized model of service excellence that could be used by all kinds of organizations, the editor of this book launched an initiative in 2010 in order to create an implementable and officially recognized standard. This standard was intended to provide companies with valuable guidance on implementing service excellence. The initiative, which involved around 20 renowned German companies at the time, was financially supported by the German Federal Ministry for Economic Affairs and Energy (BMWi) and coordinated by DIN, the German Institute for Standardization. The result was the generation of the first official standard for "Achieving customer delight through service excellence," DIN SPEC 77224:2011. This standard is still valid today and has found broad acceptance in the German market. One of the advantages of DIN SPEC 77224:2011 is its easy-to-understand and transparent service excellence model.

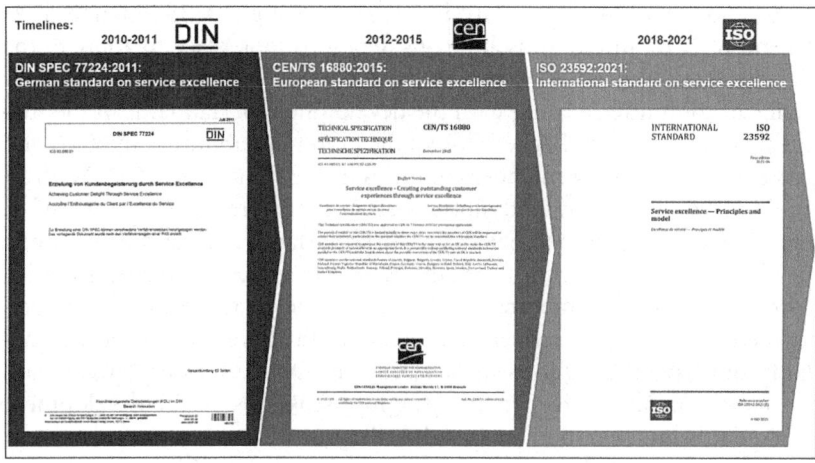

Fig. 2: History of the development of the service excellence standards

During the development process of DIN SPEC 77224:2011, the internationally oriented companies within the German working group communicated their desire to raise such a highly relevant and innovative topic to an international level. At the end of the project, it was therefore decided to develop a European standard after a certain trial period. Accordingly, with the editor's support, DIN submitted a project proposal to the CEN, the European Committee for Standardization, which resulted in a positive evaluation by its member countries. After that, a corresponding project committee, the technical committee CEN/TC 420 "Service Excellence Systems," was established in October 2012. Germany chaired the committee. Thus, DIN took over the coordination of the project committee with the function of its secretariat. The editor of this book headed the European project committee as chairman and was also responsible for the German mirror committee. Over a period of almost two and a half years, nine European member countries have continuously contributed to developing this standard. The result is the technical specification CEN/TS 16880:2015 "Service excellence – Creating outstanding customer experiences through service excellence." This specification serves companies as a guideline for action and assistance at the same time. Since both DIN SPEC 77224:2011 and CEN/TS 16880:2015 are technical specifications, they can exist in parallel on the market. Due to the topic's high relevance for all types of service organizations worldwide and the fact that the provision of excellent service represents a global challenge that can lead to enormous benefits for all stakeholders, the European standard was also only a stopover on the way to a worldwide standard in the sense of a global ISO standard. At the end of 2016, initial ideas and considerations took place to apply to the ISO, the International Organization for Standardization, to establish a new technical committee dealing with the development of standards in the subject area of service excellence. This application was submitted in 2017, and a vote was held among member countries in the summer of 2017. With 21 votes in favor, six against and nine abstentions, the project was approved in total. The committee then began its work in March 2018 and held its first meeting at DIN in Berlin, Germany. The committee comprises so-called "P-members" and "O-members." P-members or "participation members" are member states that actively participate in the development of the standards and have the right to make decisions. O-members or "observation members" can also actively participate in discussions on the development of standards but have no voting rights. At present, the body consists of 17 P-members and 18 O-members and, consequently, has 35 member countries that participate in developing the standards. More information on the work of ISO/TC 312 can be found on its official website at https://committee.iso.org/home/tc312. The guiding principles followed by the ISO/TC 312/WG 1 working group responsible for the development of the standard were, on the one hand, to update the contents of the European standard CEN/TS 16880:2015 and, on the other hand, to simplify the model wherever possible. In particular, new findings on customer experience management, service design (thinking), and digitalization were incorporated into the revised document. After just over three years of work in two working groups, the first two standards were published: ISO 23592:2021 "Service excellence – Principles and model" and the technical specification ISO/TS

24082:2021 "Service excellence – Designing excellent services to achieve outstanding customer experiences," which is specifically dedicated to the design of excellent services. Both standards are aimed at all organizations that provide services, such as commercial organizations, public services, and non-profit organizations. Following the completion and publication of these two standards, the committee is now focusing on the development of an international standard for measuring service excellence performance (ISO/TS 23686 "Service excellence – Measuring service excellence performance") and the analysis of use cases for service excellence best practices. The results will be published in a technical report (ISO/AWI TR 7179 "Service excellence – Practices for achieving service excellence"). Further information on the current and future work of ISO/TC 312 is provided in the last article in this book ("Outlook: New developments in service excellence").

3. Overview of the contributions

Providing excellent service means producing significantly above-average services. Consequently, service excellence is not understood as a concept suitable for the mass market. Still, it aims to catapult a company into the top five to ten percent of companies in a market in terms of its services. Accordingly, it is not enough in the long term to turn individual adjusting screws; the company must develop comprehensively in the direction of service excellence. While the relevance of excellent services is already known and established among leading service companies, there is still no fundamental knowledge in many service markets of how these "soft" factors can be defined and shaped. This publication, therefore, presents concepts, methods, recommendations for action, and best practices from a wide range of industries on how a concept of service excellence can be successfully implemented.

Following this opening chapter, which provides an introduction to the topic and an overview of the contributions, the first two articles, written by Prof. Dr. Matthias Gouthier, take a closer look at the concept of service excellence as a corporate success factor. The first article, entitled "Relevance and benefits of service excellence," describes the various benefits of the concept. The general relevance of service excellence is also discussed. The second article, entitled "The concept of service excellence according to ISO 23592:2021," focuses on the core content of the ISO standard 23592:2021 "Service excellence – Principles and model." Overall, the service excellence model consists of four dimensions with nine elements. This structure of the model forms the basis for the subsequent articles written by various experts from practice.

Even a brief look at the service excellence model will show you that the model focuses on permanently achieving customer delight. To achieve this goal, the service excellence model defines four dimensions. The first dimension comprises "Service excellence leadership and strategy." Consequently, a corresponding "Service excellence vision, mission, and strategy" must be defined, and various "Leadership and management requirements" must be met. Accordingly, the article "The strategic anchoring of service excellence at WISAG" by Michael Moritz deals with the strategic anchoring of the service excellence concept at a facility management company. In doing so, it highlights hard and soft factors in implementing a suitable approach and discusses in more detail why "relationship, participation, and delight" are crucial for success. Christian Polenz and Sabine Börnsen then answer the two questions of what role a company's management plays in the context of service excellence and what management requirements need to be met. Their article is entitled "Living service excellence: A secret to success at TeamBank AG," in which they present a best practice approach of establishing a proper mindset in the sense of a management philosophy that focuses on the customer. The article also addresses the need for an economic evaluation of customer and service orientation, e.g., in the form of the Net Promoter Score (NPS).

In addition to strategic orientation, a company that wants to implement service excellence must pay attention to the second dimension, "Service excellence culture and employee engagement." In his article "A highlight in the hotel industry: Creating a vital service excellence culture and anchoring it for the long term," Philippe D. Clarinval describes very clearly how a service excellence culture can be sustainably established in a company. To this end, the author provides an overview of the value of service excellence for the hotel industry and comprehensively describes managers' importance in improving the guests' experience. Subsequently, Prof. Dr. Matthias Gouthier and Matthias Raquet explain how employee engagement can be increased through the use of blended learning in their article "Employee engagement requires motivation and qualification: The use of blended learning to implement service excellence." In this context, they present the Service Excellence Academy, which was set up expressly for this purpose, and describe how e-learning as a component of blended learning contributes to the establishment and implementation of service excellence.

To meet customer expectations and systematically exceed them and thus delight customers, outstanding customer experiences must be continuously created, which is the third dimension of the service excellence model. Understanding customer needs, expectations, and desires thus play an essential role in service excellence. It is by no means sufficient to focus only on the actual core service promise in the sense of basic service, such as a train journey. Instead, all contact points ("customer touchpoints") at which there is interaction between the customer and the company must be included in the evaluation. This requirement refers to analyzing the customer's journey, i.e., the journey that a customer experiences with a company as a provider. Respectively, "Customer experience management: Insights and recommendations from CX leaders" focuses on the observations of Juliane Köninger and Prof. Dr. Matthias Gouthier. They report on key findings from a qualitative–explorative best practice study. In this contribution, specific success factors in creating a positive customer experience are identified and explained accordingly. In addition, it is crucial to design and renew outstanding customer experiences, which is another element of the service excellence model. In his article "Hospitality 4.0: How digital services improve the travel experience," Dr. Björn Becker reports on how digital services can ensure such experiences. The author focuses on the airline industry, which is primarily characterized by automation, standardization, and high price pressure. In this article, the author describes how the Lufthansa Group can still successfully position itself in such a competitive environment by using various digital services in a customer- and service-oriented manner. In addition, Carsten K. Rath and Enrico Jensch present their article "A healthy future that tastes good! Culinary excellence as an innovative customer experience at Helios Hospitals." They explain how to implement surprising customer experiences, even in a specific industry such as the hospital sector. The topic of health especially has taken on an even more critical position during the COVID-19 pandemic. Hence, the authors draw attention to an essential part of customer centricity, presenting their project on culinary excellence as a USP of Helios Hospitals. Since delight must always be aroused anew, a company's innovative strength is also a critical success factor. In order not only to meet customers' expectations but also to systematically exceed them and thus to delight customers, a form of "Service innovation management" must be established. Dr. Ferri Abolhassan shows how this can work in mass markets in his article "Best practice Deutsche Telekom – Reinventing service: How we turn customers into fans." The managing director of Telekom's service division succeeds in presenting a kind of "reinvention" of customer service that follows a day-one mentality and focuses on more customer proximity and even more professionalism.

Finally, the dimension "Operational service excellence" addresses the operational level (just as a short remark: this term should not be confused with operational excellence; see Found et al., 2018). Here, "Managing customer-experience-related efficient and effective processes and organizational structure" and "Monitoring service excellence activities and results" must be ensured. The subsequent two articles in this specialist book provide an in-depth look at how leading companies deal with these aspects concretely. Best practices from both business-to-consumer and business-to-business industries are addressed. The question "B2B, B2C, or rather H2H? Service excellence in the B2B environment using Brenntag as a success example" is addressed in more detail by Svenja Daniel. In the comparatively fragmented market environment of chemical distribution, she presents a concrete approach to managing customer expectations. She describes why feedback is the key to success and how a survey tool can help achieve a continuous improvement process. Dr. Kristina Rodig and Christopher J. Rastin write about "Service excellence in customer experience at E.ON SE: The role and use of the Net Promoter Score." In their article, they explain the specific use of the Net Promoter Score (NPS) in the corporate environment. In-depth customer insights meet the need for clear measurability and support the company's brand and marketing communication.

Finally, the last article is written by Prof. Dr. Matthias Gouthier. In his contribution entitled "Outlook: New developments in service excellence," he looks at seven developments that will shape the discussion on service excellence at the international level in the coming years.

4. Conclusion

The edited volume "Market Leader Through Service Excellence – World-Class Approaches to Managing Excellent Services" is dedicated to the exciting and highly relevant question of how service excellence is implemented and lived by and in successful companies. The book's structure is based on the model of service excellence as anchored in the new ISO standard 23592:2021. The model identifies four dimensions with nine elements that must be fulfilled to meet the holistic requirements of service excellence. To this end, proven experts from a wide range of industries present best practices, concepts, and a variety of methods and tools that show readers successful ways to implement service excellence.

At the end of this article, it should be pointed out that no company has a fully comprehensive service excellence concept in all its facets. Nor can this be the claim when a company ventures into the topic of service excellence. However, a company must also not start with the idea that a one-off impulse, such as a one-day employee workshop, is all that is needed. Implementing service excellence requires investment in people, infrastructure, and research. Service excellence's implementation and sustainable realization is a demanding and long-term process, which should usually be designed for one and a half to three years to lay stable foundations for service excellence. Establishing service excellence thus represents more of a marathon than a 100-meter race. Nevertheless, the establishment phase can be approached in small but continuous stages. The concept of service excellence in a company must be continuously advanced over time – in the sense that "standing still is taking a step backward." In particular, each company has to find its way to initiate and sustainably realize this implementation process successfully. The following articles provide structured information, valuable suggestions, experiences, recommendations for action, and present best practices on implementing such an approach with lasting success.

Bibliography

Asif, M. and Gouthier, M.H.J. (2014). What service excellence can learn from business excellence models, Total Quality Management & Business Excellence, 25(5–6), Special Issue on "Excellence Models, TQM, and Performance", pp. 511–531.

Asif, M. and Gouthier, M.H.J. (2015). Developing a self-diagnostic framework for assessing service excellence, International Journal of Services and Operations Management, 20(4), pp. 441–460.

Bates, K., Bates, H. and Johnston, R. (2003). Linking service to profit: The business case for service excellence, International Journal of Service Industry Management, 14(2), pp. 173–183.

Bitner, M.J. (1997). Introduction to the second special issue services marketing: Perspectives on service excellence, Journal of Retailing, 73(3), pp. 299–301.

DIN SPEC 77224:2011–07 (2011). Achieving customer delight through service excellence, Berlin.

Edvardsson, B. and Enquist, B. (2011). The service excellence and innovation model: Lessons from IKEA and other service frontiers, Total Quality Management & Business Excellence, 22(5), pp. 535–551.

Ford, R.C., Heaton, H.P. and Brown, S. (2001). Delivering excellent service: Lessons from the best firms, California Management Review, 44(1), pp. 39–57.

Found, P., Lahy, A., Williams, S., Hu, Q. and Mason, R. (2018). Towards a theory of operational excellence, Total Quality Management & Business Excellence, 29(9–10), pp. 1012–1024.

Giese, A. (2016). Delighted and satisfied customers through service excellence, dissertation, EBS Business School, Wiesbaden/Oestrich-Winkel.

Gouthier, M.H.J., Giese, A. and Bartl, C. (2012). Service excellence models: A critical discussion and comparison, Managing Service Quality, 22(5), pp. 447–464.

Heracleous, L. and Wirtz, J. (2010). The Globe: Singapore airlines' balancing act, Harvard Business Review, August 2010, pp. 1–11.

ISO/AWI TR 7179 (2022). Service excellence: Practices for achieving service excellence, Geneva.

ISO/TS 23686:2022 (2022). Service excellence: Measuring service excellence performance, Geneva.

ISO 23592:2021 (2021). Service excellence: Principles and model, Geneva.

Johnston, R. (2004). Towards a better understanding of service excellence, Managing Service Quality, 14(2/3), pp. 129–133.

Khan, H. and Matlay, H. (2009). Implementing service excellence in higher education, Education + Training, 51(8/9), pp. 769–780.

Kumar, S., Choe, D. and Venkataramani, S. (2013). Achieving customer service excellence using lean pull replenishment, International Journal of Productivity and Performance Management, 62(1), pp. 85–109.

Lesonsky, R. (2019). Customer service expectations are rising — Is your business keeping up?, Forbes, https://www.forbes.com/sites/allbusiness/2019/04/10/custo mer-service-expectations/?sh=1326926d14e5, accessed 12/30/2021.

Lytle, R.S., Hom, P.W. and Mokwa, M.P. (1998). SERV*OR: A managerial measure of organizational service-orientation, Journal of Retailing, 74(4), pp. 455–489.

Naden, C. (2021). Excellence in customer service – New international guidance makes everyone a winner, https://www.iso.org/news/ref2702.html, accessed 12/29/2021.

Prabhu, V.B. and Robson, A. (2000). Achieving service excellence – Measuring the impact of leadership and senior management commitment, Managing Service Quality, 10(5), pp. 307–317.

Qatar Tourism (2021). Service excellence, https://www.qatartourism.com/en/indust ry-resources/service-excellence, accessed 05/09/2021.

Thirumaran, K., Klimkeit, D. and Tang, C.M. (eds.) (2021). Service excellence in tourism and hospitality – Insights from Asia, Cham, Switzerland.

Voon, B.H., Abdullah, F., Lee, N. and Kueh, K. (2014). Developing a HospiSE scale for hospital service excellence, International Journal of Quality & Reliability Management, 31(3), pp. 261–280.

Wiertz, C., de Ruyter, K., Keen, C. and Streukens, S. (2004). Cooperating for service excellence in multichannel service systems: An empirical assessment, Journal of Business Research, 57(4), pp. 424–436.

Yu, T., Patterson, P.G. and de Ruyter, K. (2013). Achieving service-sales ambidexterity, Journal of Service Research, 16(1), pp. 52–66.

Zeithaml, V.A. (2002). Service excellence in electronic channels, Managing Service Quality, 12(3), pp. 135–139.

Service excellence as a corporate success factor

Relevance and benefits of service excellence

Matthias Gouthier

Management summary

Service excellence is on the rise internationally. This article shows the relevance of service excellence in general and the benefits that a service excellence approach can bring to companies. Its specific focus is on companies' benefits when they deal with the ISO 23592:2021 standard.

1. Relevance of service excellence

To explain the relevance of service excellence, the term must first be broken down into its two components and the relevance of each highlighted. Accordingly, the relevance of services and the service sector will first be discussed in more detail.

According to the World Bank (2022), services account for around 75 percent of GDP and employment in the most developed countries. But even in many emerging economies, services still account for more than 50 percent. According to a 2020 study conducted by the Western Union Company (2020), 68 percent of global GDP was generated in the service sector, the equivalent of around US$57.49 trillion. Furthermore, it can be seen that international trade in services has also been steadily increasing. For example, in 2018, the service sector accounted for US$59.67 billion of Germany's foreign direct investment (FDI) outflows, almost four times the amount from 2013 (OECD, 2021).

As the most dynamic segment of world trade, services also have the fastest-growing exports worldwide. In 2020, the volume of services exports stood at US$6.04 trillion, while services imports recorded a volume of around US$5.56 trillion (Knoema, 2021). This trade in services covers a wide range of activities in which people from one country provide services to people or companies from another country.

Overall, jobs in the service sector are the primary driver of future employment growth; worldwide the service sector produced around 1,622.2 million workers in 2020 (ILO, 2020). As a crucial sector in economic terms, the service sector creates approximately 50.9 percent of all jobs (ILO, 2020). Additionally, the service sector's share of the world's gross value added increased from 51.8 percent in 1995 to around 64.3 percent in 2019 (The World Bank, 2022).

Thus, in sum, it can be stated at this point that services dominate the economy in developed economies and will continue to grow (Lambert, 2016). To summarize the core aspects:

- Services account for around three-quarters of GDP in the most developed countries and two-thirds of GDP worldwide.
- All developed economies have a significant service sector.
- Most new jobs are created in the service sector.
- The service sector is considered the most substantial growth area in developed economies.

And the service sector will continue to develop positively in the future, as various studies forecast (e.g., Western Union Company, 2020). This is due to the following factors, among others (Wirtz and Lovelock, 2018; see also Lambert, 2016):

- Regulatory developments, e.g., advancing privatization, new rules to protect customers, employees, and the environment.
- Social developments, e.g., an aging population, more affluence with simultaneously rising demands and expectations.
- Market developments, e.g., the blurring of sector boundaries and a growing focus on industrial service provision.
- Technology developments, e.g., artificial intelligence, machine learning, predictive analytics, the Internet of Things, blockchains, location-based services and software-as-a-service.
- Globalization, e.g., increasing internationalization and rising foreign direct investment in the service sector.

Developed economies with a strong service sector and/or a high share of service exports consequently show a strong interest in their service companies improving from average to excellent service levels. In general, services are critical for growth and success and offer new market opportunities in a constantly growing environment. The globalization process of services, service industries and companies worldwide has increased the need for companies to improve their competitive position and build long-term customer relationships. Those who understand services in general and excellent services in particular can create corresponding competitive advantages (Gouthier and Schmid, 2003; Naden, 2021). This enables companies to cope better with structural change in global service markets.

One of the most significant challenges for service companies are the permanently growing and continuously changing customer requirements, needs, and expectations. Additionally, fueled by the globalization and digitalization of society as well as the economy and the increasing variety of available products and services, customers today have more freedom of choice than ever before. This, in turn, leads to declining customer loyalty. Consequently, every purchase and every customer contact is a moment of truth. As a result, companies are increasingly focusing on optimizing customer touchpoints and finding innovative, excellent service solutions that create outstanding customer experiences to delight customers. Through this shift in focus, the goals of creating outstanding customer experiences and achieving customer delight offer promising opportunities. This requires providing excellent services that exceed customer expectations. Delight as an emotional response to excellent services can strengthen customer loyalty to a service provider in this respect (Gouthier et al., 2012).

Nevertheless, there are also opposing voices. For example, Dixon et al. (2010) postulate that companies should solve their customers' problems instead of senselessly delighting them. This is also true in terms of the basic idea: If customers are dissatisfied or even annoyed, their problems must first be solved. However, the bottom line is that it is inappropriate to do without customer delight altogether, which leads companies in a completely wrong direction. Ultimately, a company should implement the following three customer management activities:

1. Complaint management: to turn dissatisfied customers into satisfied customers
2. Satisfaction management: to make the normal customer touchpoints run smoothly and to the (complete) satisfaction of the customer
3. Delight management: to delight customers in critical situations ("moments-of-truth")

The second word in the term "service excellence" also indicates this. According to Martín-Castilla and Rodriguez-Ruiz (2008, p. 136), excellence in the business environment can be understood as "an outstanding practice in managing the organization and achieving results." Hsu and Shen (2005, p. 358) define the concept of excellence even more specifically: "Excellence is achieving results that delight all the organization's stakeholders (this includes employees, customers, suppliers, society in general, and those with financial interests in the organization)." This understanding goes hand in hand with the definition of service excellence set out in ISO 23592:2021. According to this, service excellence is defined as "the capabilities of an organization to consistently deliver excellent services" (ISO 23592:2021, p. 1) that serve to delight the customer.

In the meantime, more and more companies worldwide have internalized the idea of service excellence and have set up corresponding programs. In addition to the companies included in this edited volume, there are many other well-known companies that, according to their statements, have a running service excellence program. These include, in addition to the companies already identified in research literature such as Amazon, Four Seasons, IKEA, Singapore Airlines, Southwest Airlines, The Ritz-Carlton, and Walt Disney Company (see, among others, Edvardsson and Enquist, 2011; Solnet et al., 2010; Wirtz and Zeithaml, 2018), e.g.:

- Cleveland Clinic, one of the world's leading hospitals
- ISS, a global facility management company
- MEWA, a textile management company operating throughout Europe
- Mister Spex, an optician company, operating throughout Europe
- OTIS, a global manufacturer of elevators, escalators, and moving walkways

Interestingly, however, service excellence is not only aimed at commercial organizations. In principle, the concept can be applied to all kinds of companies that provide services, including public services and nonprofit organizations. For example, service excellence approaches can be found in cities like Vaughan (City of Vaughan, 2018). This is a city north of Toronto in the province of Ontario in Canada. It is one of the fastest-growing cities in Canada and has more than doubled its population since 1996. In addition, service excellence is one of the top priorities in the 2018 to 2022 strategic plan in the Canadian city of Burlington (City of Burlington, 2019). And the Canadian capital Ottawa also launched a service excellence program in the past (Patwell et al., 2012).

2. Benefits of service excellence

When asked about the orientation of their own company, most top managers claim that their company is customer-centric. However, if one asks the customers or has even had experience with the company as a customer, one all too often experiences the exact opposite (see also Allen et al., 2005). However, especially in highly competitive markets, aligning the entire company and the products and services offered on the market with the customer is essential. It should be noted that a high level of customer satisfaction can no longer be achieved by providing a basic product and/or service quality that just fulfils the customer's expectations. To be successful and one step ahead of the competition, it is essential to delight customers by offering outstanding and varied experiences. This is the goal of service excellence. But not only companies and customers benefit from service excellence. Society also benefits from an overall increase to an excellent level of service. Generally speaking, two categories of benefit can be identified in this respect. On the one hand, a company benefits when it typically embraces the concept of service excellence. On the other hand, companies have a further benefit when they deal specifically with the official standard ISO 23592:2021. These two groups of benefits are discussed in more detail below.

2.1 Benefits of service excellence in general

As already described, customers today are becoming increasingly demanding and, with their increased requirements, are presenting companies with ever more significant challenges. But not only the requirements, expectations, and wishes of customers have grown. As a result of advancing digitalization and the associated increase in market transparency, caused, e.g., by price search engines, online reviews, and opinion platforms, customers also have greater power to act and negotiate in the markets (keyword "customer empowerment"). Merely satisfactory offers are punished accordingly by a quick switch to an alternative provider. Satisfaction thus represents, at best, an "entry ticket" to a new business relationship. Still, it is by no means sufficient to successfully bind a customer to a company in terms of a "permanent subscription" and to be able to build up a lasting bond. In the past decade, companies have therefore begun to consider how they can retain customers over the long term if this no longer works adequately through the objective of customer satisfaction. Consequently, customer delight has become more and more established as one of the main objectives of marketing and as a corporate objective, not only nationally but also internationally. The intention is that a customer establishes a business relationship expressed in an inner, purely rational, and emotional conviction toward the provider. Such a high personal commitment from a customer requires outstanding customer experiences, perpetuated in customer delight that lasts as long as possible in terms of brand delight.

Consequently, the goal of creating customer delight through the use of service excellence is increasingly becoming the focus of corporate interest. This raises the question of how the pursuit of sustainable customer delight can be achieved in reality. This is where the concept of service excellence comes into play, as it represents a structured approach helping companies to provide excellent services in a targeted and continuous manner. The customer perceives these excellent services and enjoys unique moments that stick in the memory as outstanding customer experiences (Berman, 2005). Such memorable experiences delight the customer and thus promote loyalty as an emotional bond to the company. Ultimately, this stronger customer loyalty results in better financial and non-financial outcomes, which can be reinvested in the continuous development of the service excellence program (see ISO 23592:2021). The corresponding chain of effects is shown in Figure 1.

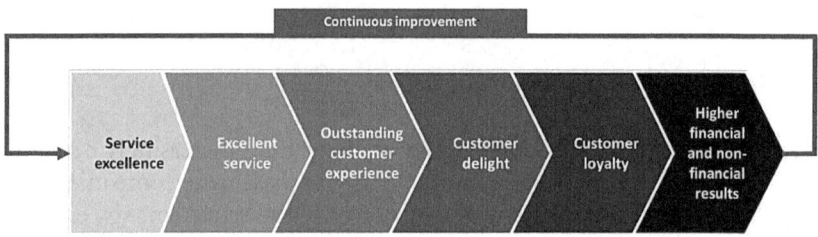

Fig. 1: Positive effects of service excellence (source: based on ISO 23592:2021)

As shown in the figure, several "soft" results and "hard" results can be achieved. One of the soft effects of service excellence is that outstanding customer experiences are created via the sustained provision of excellent services. Another impact is that such outstanding experiences trigger delight. As shown in various studies, customer delight, in turn, results in increased customer loyalty (see, e.g., JD Power and Associates, 2011). This promotes loyalty-related customer behavior, such as sustained repurchasing behavior, increases in purchase frequency and purchase intensity, recommendations, and a greater willingness to pay. Overall, delighted customers also exhibit a higher level of customer engagement, e.g., a greater willingness to actively participate in company programs such as idea competitions and customer advisory boards (Donsbach and Gouthier, 2015).

The positive but primarily psychological and behavioral effects outlined above ultimately pay off to achieve higher financial and non-financial results (Bates et al., 2003; ISO 23592:2021). This is accompanied by the achievement of other primarily market-oriented objectives, such as establishing a customer-centric and service-oriented reputation. This, in turn, goes hand in hand with better competitive differentiation and, conse-quently, with the raising or lowering of barriers to market entry. All in all, the effects described above lead to an improvement in success-oriented corporate objectives, expressed, e.g., in terms of higher sales and profits (Bates et al., 2003; ISO 23592:2021; Naden, 2021).

In addition to the customer- and result-related effects, the use of service excellence can also positively impact labor markets. A company that is perceived as excellent is also more attractive as an employer and consequently has a better chance of attracting better applicants and strengthening employee loyalty and employee engagement. Increased employee engagement, in turn, results in numerous positive effects for a company (Gallup, 2021; ISO 23592:2021).

Apart from customers and the (labor) market, service excellence also leads to various positive effects within the company. These include reducing errors and thus costs, e.g., through a lower error rate and less waste. In addition, costs are reduced due to lower churn rates, more convincing sales activities, and reduced advertising expenditure for new customer acquisition. Agile organizations can also increase their efficiency and sustainably deliver excellent services (ISO 23592:2021).

This list of benefit components does not claim to be exhaustive. Only central, significant effects have been listed. It is undoubtedly possible to record various other benefits that have not been explicitly mentioned here.

2.2 Benefits of using ISO 23592:2021 "Service excellence – Principles and model"

Now that the general benefits of the concept of service excellence have been discussed in more detail, this section will show the specific benefits that a company, and if applicable also the environment in which it operates, can derive from dealing with and implementing ISO 23592:2021:

- A significant, general advantage of standards is that the relevant terms are clearly defined in the documents, thus creating a uniform language and a clear understanding of the terms (Lambert, 2016). This is particularly advantageous in the case of somewhat "fuzzy" and "soft" constructs such as customer delight and customer experience since these are not characterized by objective measurability but rather by customers' subjective perceptions. This results in the possibility of a uniform, also linguistic, exchange on specific facts to improve communication. Consequently, this also applies to ISO 23592:2021, which defines essential terms such as service excellence, excellent service, and customer delight. Overall, this facilitates discussion within and between companies, e.g., with partners in the value chain, as the scope for interpretation in this regard is minimized. Such clear definitions of terms are also a fundamental prerequisite for developing valid measurement tools (see the article by Kristina Rodig and Christopher J. Rastin on "Service excellence in customer experience at E.ON SE: The role and use of the Net Promoter Score").

- Another advantage of aligning with a model of service excellence in accordance with ISO 23592:2021 is that it creates better comparability between companies, as they can orient themselves on a uniform, structured framework concept. This promotes a systematic exchange with best practice partners to improve in-house practices.
- In addition to the principles and the model of service excellence, which will be explained in more detail in the following article, ISO 23592:2021 also provides various lists of exemplary instruments that can give impetus to and help with the implementation of the individual elements or sub-elements of the service excellence model. Thus, it is based on generally accepted best practices reflecting the international state of the art in this respect (Boiral, 2011).
- In addition, ISO 23592:2021 supports the alignment of networks, such as franchise partners and suppliers, in forming a common brand understanding and customer image.
- Finally, ISO 23592:2021 offers guidance to organizations that want to focus their efforts on implementing or improving individual aspects of the service excellence model. They can refer back to the elements and sub-elements that interest them.

In summary, it can thus be stated that ISO 23592:2021 supports companies in either asserting themselves as market leaders or developing in the direction of market leadership through the service excellence approach.

3. Conclusion

In this article, the relevance of service excellence was first discussed in more detail. To this end, the importance of the service sector was highlighted. As a result of current developments, such as increased customer requirements and increasingly intense competition, the topic of service excellence is gaining further importance worldwide. However, it is essential to reflect on the fact that service excellence is primarily aimed at companies that belong to or want to belong to the top five to ten percent of a market. Irrespective of this, all companies can use the service excellence model to develop their company or parts of it in the direction of service excellence. In general, ISO 23592:2021 is a horizontal standard applied to all types of service-providing companies, regardless of their size or sector.

In this respect, service excellence delivers many different benefit components, which have been outlined in the context of this paper.

Bibliography

Allen, J., Reichheld, F., Hamilton, B. and Markey, R. (2005). Closing the delivery gap, Bain & Company.

Bates, K., Bates, H. and Johnston, R. (2003). Linking service to profit: The business case for service excellence, International Journal of Service Industry Management, 14(2), pp. 173–183.

Berman, B. (2005). How to delight your customers, California Management Review, 48(1), pp. 129–151.

Boiral, O. (2011). Managing with ISO systems: Lessons from practice, Long Range Planning, 44, pp. 197–220.

City of Burlington (2019). 2018–2022 Burlington's plan: From vision to focus, City of Burlington, Canada, https://www.google.com/url?sa=t&rct=j&q=&esrc=s&source=web&cd=&ved=2ahUKEwi494LS2-H5AhXrN-wKHdMBB2oQFnoECAQQAQ&url=https%3A%2F%2Fmariannemeedward.ca%2Fwp-content%2Fuploads%2F2019%2F07%2FCM-15-19-2018-2022-Burlingtons-Plan-From-Vision-to-Focus-Revised-July-8.pdf&usg=AOvVaw2wqCcAcYrKkmhCtnSrsaA6, accessed 09/05/2021.

City of Vaughan (2018). 2018–2022 Term of council service excellence strategic plan, City of Vaughan, Canada, https://www.vaughan.ca/serviceexcellence/Pages/default.aspx, accessed 09/05/2021.

Dixon, M., Freeman, K. and Toman, N. (2010). Stop trying to delight your customers, Harvard Business Review, July–August 2010.

Donsbach, J. and Gouthier, M.H.J. (2015). Customer delight as an ex ante and ex post factor of positive customer engagement behavior: Interactive value creation in customer management, in: Bruhn, M. and Hadwich, K. (eds.). Interactive value creation through services, Forum Service Management 2015, Wiesbaden, pp. 211–234.

Edvardsson, B. and Enquist, B. (2011). The service excellence and innovation model: Lessons from IKEA and other service frontiers, Total Quality Management & Business Excellence, 22(5), pp. 535–551.

Gallup (2021). Gallup's employee engagement survey: Ask the right questions with the Q12 survey, https://www.gallup.com/workplace/356063/gallup-q12-employee-engagement-survey.aspx, accessed 09/05/2021.

Gouthier, M.H.J. and Schmid, S. (2003). Customers and customer relationships in service firms: The perspective of the resource-based view, Marketing Theory, 3(1), pp. 119–143.

Gouthier, M.H.J., Giese, A. and Bartl, C. (2012). Service excellence models: a critical discussion and comparison, Managing Service Quality, 22(5), pp. 447–464.

Hsu, S.H. and Shen, H.P. (2005). Knowledge management and its relationship with TQM, Total Quality Management & Business Excellence, 16(3), pp. 351–361.

ILO (2020). World employment and social outlook, https://www.ilo.org/wesodata/?chart=Z2VuZGVyPVsiVG90YWwiXSZ1bml0PSJOdW1iZXIiJnNlY3Rvcj1bIlNlcnZpY2VzIl0meWVhckZyb209MTk5MSZpbmNvbWU9W10maW5kaWNhdG9yPVsiZW1wbG95bWVudERpc3RyaWJ1dGlvbiJdJmN0YXR1cz1bXSZyZWdpb249WyJXb3JsZCJsZCJdJmNvdW50cnk9W10md29ya2luZ1BvdmVydHk9W10meWVhclRvPTIwMjMmdmlld0Zvcm1hdD0iQ2hhcnQiJmFnZT1bIkFnZTE1cGx1cyJdJmxhbmd1YWdlPSJlbiJ9%3D, accessed 02/09/2022.

ISO 23592:2021 (2021). Service excellence: Principles and model, Geneva.

JD Power and Associates (2011). Achieving excellence in customer service: The brands that deliver what US consumers want, Los Angeles et al.

Knoema (2021). World - Service exports in current prices, https://knoema.com/atlas/World/Service-exports?origin=knoema.de, accessed 02/09/2022.

Lambert, G. (2016). Service with a smile, thanks to standards, https://www.iso.org/news/2016/05/Ref2077.html, accessed 12/29/2021.

Martín-Castilla, J.I. and Rodriguez-Ruiz, O. (2008). EFQM model: Knowledge governance and competitive advantage, Journal of Intellectual Capital, 9(1), pp. 133–156.

Naden, C. (2021). Excellence in customer service – New international guidance makes everyone a winner, https://www.iso.org/news/ref2702.html, accessed 12/29/2021.

OECD (2021). Outward FDI flows by industry, https://data.oecd.org/fdi/outward-fdi-flows-by-industry.htm#indicator-chart, accessed 09/05/2021.

Patwell, B., Gray, D. and Kanellakos, S. (2012). An innovative approach to fostering a culture of service excellence in the city of Ottawa, IRC, Queens University, https://irc.queensu.ca/an-innovative-approach-to-fostering-a-culture-of-service-excellence-in-the-city-of-ottawa/, accessed 09/05/2021.

Solnet, D., Kandampully, J. and Kralj, A. (2010). Legends of service excellence: The habits of seven highly effective hospitality companies, Journal of Hospitality Marketing & Management, 19(8), pp. 889–908.

The World Bank (2022). Services, value added (% of GDP), https://data.worldbank.org/indicator/NV.SRV.TOTL.ZS, accessed 02/09/2022.

Western Union Company (2020). The global services trade revolution – Fuelling post-pandemic economic recovery and growth, Oxford Economics, https://business.westernunion.com/en-gb/p/cmp/2020/the-global-trade-services-revolution/, accessed 09/05/2021.

Wirtz, J. and Lovelock, C.H. (2018). Essentials of Services Marketing, 3rd ed., Pearson.

Wirtz, J. and Zeithaml, V. (2018). Cost-effective service excellence, Journal of the Academy of Marketing Science, 46, pp. 59–80.

The concept of service excellence according to ISO 23592:2021

Matthias Gouthier

Management summary

The statement "service is an attitude" is often heard in the context of service excellence. In principle, this statement is correct, and the relevance of the right attitude or mindset is undisputed. However, it is also a fact that an inner attitude is not sufficient for a company to be able to continuously realize excellent services on the market or, as Philippe D. Clarinval writes very aptly in his article: "If we respect only the standards, the service we provide will appear sterile, and if we show only emotions, we will look like lovable but not very competent improvisation artists." Midsize companies and large corporations need a systematic approach and an action-oriented guideline in the sense of a structured concept that helps them act in a customer-centric way and delight customers. This is where the concept of service excellence, as specified in the international standard ISO 23592:2021, comes into play. This article describes the main content of the ISO standard in terms of its terminology, principles, and model for service excellence.

1. Content and structure of ISO 23592:2021

The standard ISO 23592:2021 "Service excellence – Principles and model" consists of seven chapters plus an initial introduction to the subject. There is an English and a French version of the standard to date. However, a German version is planned to be published in the near future.

In the introduction to ISO 23592:2021, service excellence's particular relevance and objectives are discussed in more detail. As already described in the article "Relevance and benefits of service excellence," growing and changing customer requirements, globalization, and digitalization are increasing the demands on companies if they want to survive in the market and want to remain or even become a market leader. Therefore, companies must position themselves in a customer-centric way in this demanding market environment. In this context, it is no longer sufficient to satisfy customers but rather to delight them (Ludwig et al., 2017; Parasuraman et al., 2021). This development requires offering excellent services through which customers have outstanding experiences. This is the objective of service excellence.

Furthermore, the introduction to the standard discusses the four different levels that form service excellence. This differentiation goes back to the work of Robert Johnston (2004; 2007). The four dimensions he describes can be ranked and depicted as a service excellence pyramid (see Figure 1).

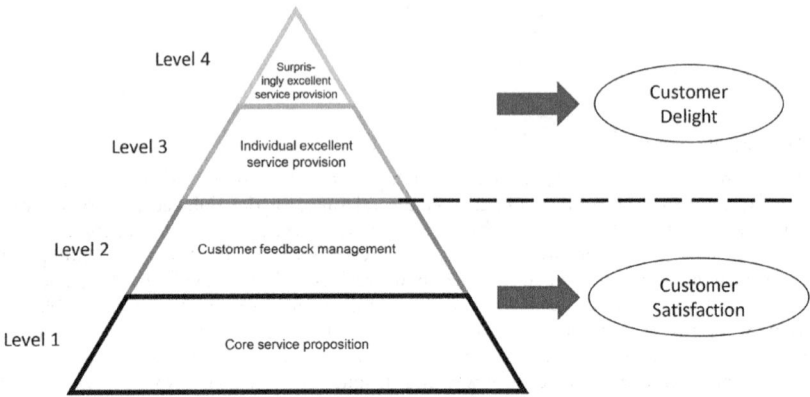

Fig. 1: Service excellence pyramid (source: based on ISO 23592:2021, p. vi)

The two lower levels of the service excellence pyramid form the basis for implementing service excellence, as they are the fundamental prerequisites. Levels 1 and 2 are primarily concerned with meeting customer expectations and keeping promises to customers. Consequently, these two levels typically do not trigger delight but, at best, result in customer satisfaction. Customers perceive the core service proposition (level 1) as the company delivering on its promises. Related to the idea of the Kano model (Kano et al., 1984), services delivered on that level can be understood as the "must-be" demands of customers. Therefore, a company cannot create customer satisfaction with this kind of basic service. At most, customer dissatisfaction can be avoided. Customer feedback management (level 2) leads to good handling of customer queries and problems. With efficient and effective customer feedback management, satisfaction can be achieved and dissatisfaction alleviated. There are already existing standards for these two levels dedicated to handling the challenges described. For example, international standards such as ISO 9001:2015, ISO 10002:2018 and ISO/IEC 20000–1:2018 can be used for this purpose.

For this reason, ISO 23592:2021 focuses on the two upper levels of the service excellence pyramid, which create an emotional bond with the customer and lead to customer delight. These include:

- individual excellent service provision (level 3): Such above-average service provision leads to a service perceived by the customer as warm, genuine, personal, tailored, and value-adding. Consequently, the cus-

tomer experiences a positive emotional response by feeling valued and recognized;
- surprisingly excellent service provision (level 4): This extraordinary service provision results in a customized service that triggers positive emotions such as surprise and delight. It is delivered by exceeding the customer's expectations and adding (subjectively perceived) value. This can be achieved by providing unexpected, outstanding customer experiences. Surprise can be seen as an intensifier because the more surprising an outstanding customer experience is, the more delighted a customer will be (Ludwig et al., 2017). However, there are many different approaches to achieving customer delight (Barnes and Krallman, 2019).

The service excellence pyramid should be used in internal communication, e.g., during the service excellence implementation phase. It explains to managers and employees in a highly understandable manner why a company must focus on both delivering on its promises (levels 1 and 2) and exceeding customer expectations by providing excellent service (levels 3 and 4).

The first chapter of the ISO standard sets out its scope of application. Accordingly, ISO 23592:2021 applies to all organizations that provide services, such as commercial organizations, public services and nonprofit organizations. Therefore, industrial companies that offer industrial services can equally use it. Particularly in the case of industrial companies, where there is no longer much difference between the products on the market, a focus on providing excellent services is a success factor in differentiating oneself from the competition (Ulaga and Reinartz, 2011). In addition, as already described, the standard focuses on the two upper levels of the service excellence pyramid.

As is usual for standards, normative references are named in the second chapter, but there are no relevant ones for this standard.

The third chapter then defines the key terms. As mentioned in the previous article ("Relevance and benefits of service excellence"), a significant advantage of standards is that the relevant terms are clearly defined, thus creating a clear and uniform understanding of these terms. The definitions of service excellence (3.1) and excellent service (3.2) are fundamental here, as this differentiation is often confused in practice. While service excellence is understood to be the "capabilities of an organization to consistently deliver excellent services" (ISO 23592:2021, p. 1), excellent service is the "output of an organization with a high level of service provision performed between the organization and the customer to achieve outstanding customer experiences that lead to customer delight" (ISO 23592:2021, p.

1). Another important term that often leads to confusion, especially in practice, is "customer delight" because of its subjective nature. The term customer delight is understood as "positive emotions experienced by the customer derived from either an intense feeling of being highly valued or by expectations being exceeded, or both" (ISO 23592:2021, p. 2). In addition, the terms co-creation, customer, customer experience, outstanding customer experience, customer journey, satisfaction, service, service provision, service excellence vision, service excellence mission, service excellence strategy, and employee engagement are specified. However, they will not be discussed in detail here.

Chapter 4 deals with the relevance and benefits of service excellence. Reference should be made here to the previous, relevant article, which differentiates between these two aspects of service excellence in its examination of them.

Chapter 5 of ISO 23592:2021 then presents the principles of service excellence, which are discussed in more detail in the following section.

2. Principles of service excellence according to ISO 23592:2021

ISO 23592:2021 has seven principles that are intended to provide companies with essential guidance on what to look out for when implementing customer centricity. The aim is to remove typical barriers to the implementation of service excellence, such as those described by Johnston (2007):

- One of the most significant obstacles is a lack of mindset or attitude. Managers often assess the quality of their services much better than customers do (Allen et al., 2005). In addition, not every manager or every employee has the "service gene" and possesses a pronounced service mentality.
- Another shortcoming in implementing service excellence is that companies are often more internally focused than customer-focused. Often, managers and employees have an inside-out understanding of service provision instead of a necessary (complementary) outside-in perspective.
- A further barrier is inadequate internal coordination and communication between divisions and departments. This refers specifically to the fact that service provision is not designed and optimized from the customer's point of view. Still, seamless service provision often fails due to a pronounced silo mentality within the company.

- Furthermore, existing systems, processes and structures are often not aligned sufficiently with customer needs. In customer service in particular, the focus of objectives is more often on reducing costs and increasing efficiency than on improving customer effectiveness in the sense of increasing customer loyalty.
- Finally, staff shortcomings are also found: a lack of a positive attitude towards service delivery, a lack of knowledge, skills, and abilities for excellent service delivery, or a lack of motivation to go the "extra mile" for customers.

As described above, the seven principles of service excellence (see Figure 2) address these weak points (ISO 23592:2021):

1. The first principle calls for "managing the organization from outside-in." This is one of the core ideas of customer centricity. Accordingly, the company should focus on the needs, desires, wishes, and problems of the customer, and therefore design the desired experience from the customer's perspective. Furthermore, the resources and processes should be continuously aligned in the spirit of customer centricity. This fundamental principle goes hand in hand with the other principles, especially the fifth principle.
2. The second principle calls for a "deepening of customer relationships." In today's economic climate, it is no longer enough to think about individual transactions between a customer and a company; the company must try to retain its customers over the long term. Therefore, a company should strive for a high level of individual attention towards the customer. Additionally, it should focus on the customer's needs and expectations throughout the business relationship. This goal can be achieved in different ways, e.g., through continuous communication and establishing a customer loyalty program.
3. The central insight of "people make the difference" forms the third principle of service excellence. Accordingly, the commitment of all the company's managers and employees, including external partners, is crucial to achieving customer delight. This is true for frontline employees and back-office employees because everyone in an organization provides and consumes (internal) services.
4. "Balanced attention to customers, employees, subcontractors and other stakeholders" is set out in the fourth principle. This step means that customers, employees, subcontractors, and other stakeholders are essential for a company's success. Accordingly, the company should pay balanced attention to all of them. One essential idea behind this principle is that only enthusiastic and engaged employees can delight the cus-

tomer. Another fundamental assumption is that the entire value chain and thus also the integrated subcontractors should show the same high level of attitude and engagement to the customer if a company wants to consistently create delight.

5. A "cross-functional management approach" is the focus of the fifth principle. This is intended to overcome the silo approach or silo mentality already mentioned. It means breaking down the way people think within the company and creating an integrated, cross-functional way of thinking and aligning with the customer's journey.

6. The sixth principle calls for "leveraging of technology." Against the backdrop of the rapidly increasing digitalization of the economy, this principle is becoming much more critical, especially in the case of excellent service provision. Therefore, appropriate technologies, e.g., artificial intelligence, big data, and machine learning, should be used to create excellent service and outstanding customer experiences (Weitzer and Weislaemle, 2021).

7. In sum, the efforts invested in implementing service excellence "create value for stakeholders" is the seventh principle (Antonacopoulou and Kandampully, 2000). This creation of additional sustainable value depends on the co-creation of all stakeholders. Such enhanced value can be both monetary and non-monetary.

After the principles, chapter 6 of ISO 23592:2021 examines the model of service excellence. Chapter 7 then describes the elements and sub-elements of the model in more detail. Both are the focus of the following section.

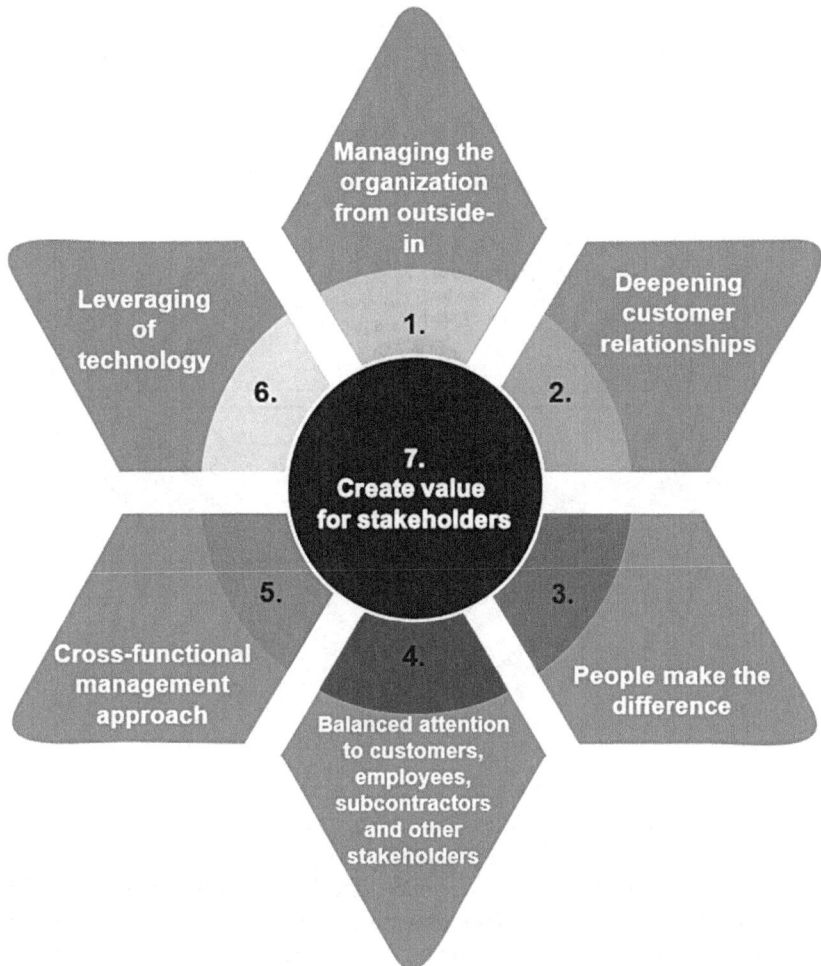

Fig. 2: Principles of service excellence (source: based on ISO 23592:2021)

3. Model and elements of service excellence according to ISO 23592:2021

The model of service excellence according to ISO 23592:2021 consists of four dimensions with nine elements (see Figure 3).

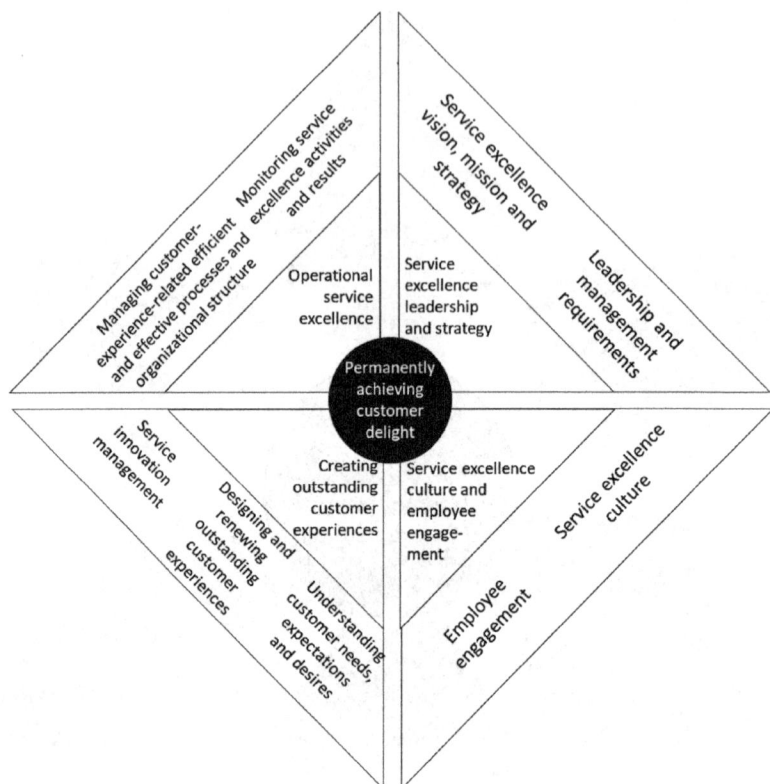

Fig. 3: Model of service excellence (source: ISO 23592:2021, p. 5)

At the heart of the model is service excellence's actual objective: to delight the customer permanently. This objective requires the consistent use of nine elements assigned to the four dimensions mentioned above. It is important to note that this model does not assume a chronological sequence of elements. For example, companies can start by introducing concepts and measures to improve the customer's experience before a service excellence vision and mission are defined.

It is also essential to note that ISO 23592:2021 provides concrete examples of how the elements and sub-elements can be implemented using suitable concepts, instruments, and tools. However, this article does not present or discuss these examples since this book contains a best practice article on the concrete implementation of each of the nine elements; in the case of the idea of "designing and renewing outstanding customer experiences," two articles even demonstrate its concrete realization.

3.1 Service excellence vision, mission, and strategy

The first element focuses on developing and anchoring a "service excellence vision, mission, and strategy." As a general rule of thumb, this is done on a long-term basis, e.g., for a period of three to five years. In this context, the service excellence vision, mission, and strategy provide the framework for the excellent service and the outstanding experience the company aims to deliver to its customers. They have the central role of rendering the principles and design of outstanding customer experiences in all other elements of the service excellence model. To do so, an analysis and clear understanding of the market positioning of a company is necessary. Depending on a company's positioning, e.g., whether it operates in a low-budget, premium, or luxury market, customer expectations vary in terms of level of aspiration and, accordingly, the requirements for excellent service. In sum, this element is defined as a mandatory requirement, which means that if a company wants to be certified to ISO 23592:2021, e.g., it must define its vision, mission, and strategy for service excellence in the long term – and the emphasis here is on the verb "must." The vision, mission, and strategy for service excellence must also be aligned with each other (Crotts et al., 2005) and should be based on the company's overall strategy. The latter is crucial for manufacturing companies, where product and technology orientation often predominate (Lambert, 2016). In this case, the service excellence strategy must be aligned with the company's overall strategy. A strong service excellence vision, mission, and strategy are not created solely by the top managing directors; they should be made and reviewed with input from all stakeholders, including management, employees, and customers.

Furthermore, suppose the vision, mission, and strategy should be understood and lived in the whole organization. In that case, they must also be communicated to all areas of the company and be cascaded throughout the organization. This is a general requirement, which also cannot be achieved through a one-time communication campaign but requires ongoing effort. They should also be implemented throughout the company to build a culture of service excellence. Additionally, it helps to inform all employees about the decision-making process within the company. A look at practice shows that many leading companies have already implemented this requirement and have explicitly anchored the idea of customer delight and service excellence in their vision, mission, and/or strategy.

The first element is thus divided into the following three sub-elements:

1. The first sub-element addresses the vision ("what we want to be;" Collis and Rukstad, 2008). According to this, a company must have a long-term vision of excellent service. In particular, this should highlight that the company is striving to consistently meet and exceed customer expectations, needs, and desires through excellent service. This vision should be aligned with the entire company's strategic direction. Furthermore, it should be based on a sound understanding of the needs and expectations of all relevant stakeholders and the external environment.

2. The second sub-element addresses the mission ("why we exist;" Collis and Rukstad, 2008). Thus, the company must have a long-term mission. This mission enables the development of a service excellence strategy and sets the company's goals for achieving the vision of service excellence. The company should evaluate the proposed mission statements from the customer's perspective and against the backdrop of feasibility.

3. The third and final sub-element relates to the service excellence strategy ("what our competitive game plan will be;" Collis and Rukstad, 2008). This requires a company to translate its vision and mission for service excellence into a coherent strategy. Now, service excellence can be understood as the strategic "sweet spot that aligns the firm's capabilities with customer needs in a way that competitors cannot match given the changing external context – factors such as technology, industry demographics, and regulation" (Collis and Rukstad, 2008, p. 90). This strategy includes solid principles, documented strategic and operational objectives, and actions to realize the goals. The service excellence strategy should be an integral part of the company's overall strategy. However, if it is only a sub-strategy, such as in a manufacturing company, it should at least be coordinated with the overall strategy. In addition, the service excellence strategy should be continuously reviewed and adjusted if necessary.

3.2 Leadership and management requirements

The second element of the service excellence model is dedicated to the role of leadership and management. According to this, all members of the management body and the responsible executives at all company levels play a decisive role in defining, implementing, and maintaining the strategy on service excellence. As a service leader, a manager is expected to exhibit behavior such as recognizing and valuing service excellence, removing barriers to service delivery, and setting clear standards for outstanding customer experiences, among others (Wong et al., 2015). For sustainable implementation of service excellence to be successful, they must be committed to the company's concept and feel obligated to it. One of the critical requirements for the leadership team is to ensure that the service excellence vision, mission, and strategy are developed and implemented in line with the company's overall strategic direction. One approach could be that "each level of management will be the teacher for the level below, becomes the starting point for incorporating [service excellence] strategy into everyone's behavior" (Collis and Rukstad, 2008, p. 90). Management is also responsible for developing the essential purpose and values of service excellence and ensuring that the entire organization, including employees and partners, is committed to achieving these values (Heskett et al., 2015; Testa and Sipe, 2012). The definition of the core values for service excellence can be illustrated very well using the example of Zappos. This company, an American online shoe and clothing retailer and a subsidiary of Amazon, has defined its core value as follows: "Deliver WOW through service." Managers and employees should be guided by the same values, habits, and principles for a company. Furthermore, it is thus crucial for the achievement of service excellence that top executives demonstrate a strong and clear mindset and a commitment to creating an environment that enables employees to realize their potential to deliver excellent service to a full extent (see Hunt and Ivergård, 2015).

This element is consequently divided into three sub-elements:

1. Leadership: Here, the direct link to the introductory remarks becomes apparent. For example, managers at all levels should focus on the service excellence approach. They have to create a culture of service excellence that covers the entire company, including its key stakeholders. They should link the company's performance directly to its performance in terms of service excellence.

2. Sharing efforts, defined responsibilities, and objectives: This second sub-element is about how a company's managers, through strong leadership and role modeling, should create an environment in which employees can deliver outstanding customer experiences. To do this, everyone in the company must know what contribution they are making to achieving the service excellence goals.

3. Employee empowerment and engagement: The third sub-element, aimed at employees, is ultimately directed at managers in an ends–means relationship. Therefore, employee empowerment seen from a

managerial perspective can be understood as a relational construct that describes how those with power in organizations share power, information, resources, and rewards with those lacking them (Fernandez and Moldogaziev, 2013). For example, in an environment of service excellence, employees should go beyond what is expected in order to deliver a superior and personalized experience to customers. However, the responsibility for creating such an environment lies with management (Den Hartog and Verburg, 2002). Therefore, management should share four organizational ingredients with employees. First, they should inform their employees about organizational, team, and individual performance. Second, they should set rewards based on organizational, team, and individual performance. Third, they should share knowledge that enables employees to understand and contribute better to the organizational, team, and personal service performance. Fourth, they should share power to make decisions that influence work procedures and organizational direction at the higher level and transaction-specific decisions at the micro-level (Bowen and Lawler, 1992).

3.3 *Service excellence culture*

The third element addresses corporate culture. It is understood in ISO 23592:2021 as a critical factor in how people think, feel, and act to achieve service excellence, create outstanding experiences, and delight customers. A service excellence culture is thus an essential part of a corporate culture (see Figure 4). It can be defined as a special kind of culture with an appreciation of excellent service. Moreover, it is a culture in which excellent service is taken for granted as a way of life for internal and external customers and as one of the essential norms.

Based on the fundamental work of Schein (2016), there are three levels in a corporate culture that can be adapted to a more specific service excellence culture. As the most general group of elements of a service excellence culture, there are the basic service assumptions, thinking and behavior patterns, e.g., managers and employees' understanding of customers and relationships with suppliers. The espoused service beliefs and values are on the next level up, e.g., service values, policies, and standards. At the top level, there are the artifacts, which can be divided into actively expressed service artifacts in the sense of service communication, e.g., stories, legends, anecdotes about service excellence, and service activities, e.g., service rituals, ceremonies, and habits. Besides all this, there are also passively expressed service artifacts, e.g., architecture and dress code.

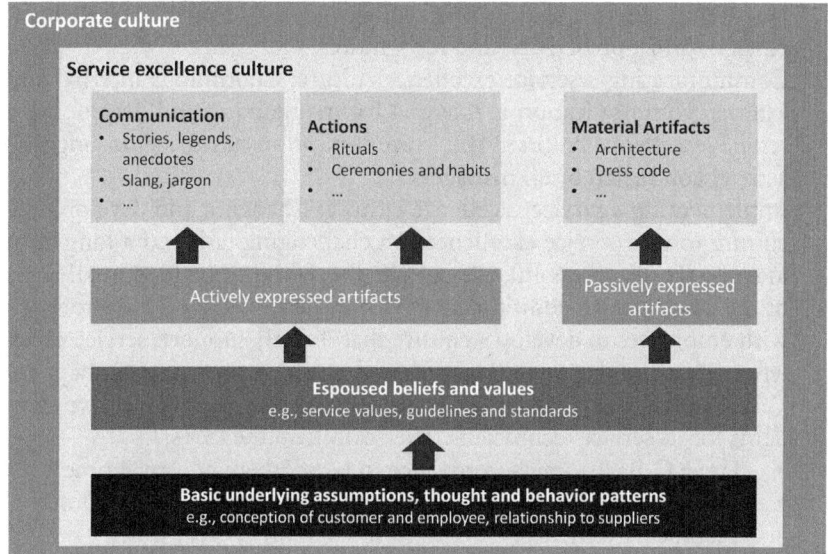

Fig. 4: Service excellence culture as a part of corporate culture (source: based on Schein, 2016, p. 18)

This element is divided into the following three sub-elements:

1. Defining service excellence culture: A service excellence culture should reflect a company's values, attitudes, and behavior. Leading companies define service excellence as a core value of their corporate culture. As an example, Caterpillar, the world's largest construction equipment manufacturer, proclaims its beliefs on product and service excellence in its code of conduct as follows (Caterpillar, 2019, p. 13):

   > *"Excellence – We set and achieve ambitious goals. The quality of our products and services reflects the power and heritage of Caterpillar – the pride we take in what we do and what we make possible. We are passionate about people, process, product and service excellence. We are determined to serve our customers through innovation, continuous improvement, an intense focus on customer needs and a dedication to meet those needs with a sense of urgency. For us, excellence is not only a value; it is a discipline and a means for making the world a better place."*

   Consequently, a service excellence culture enables the implementation of the service excellence strategy, which ultimately leads to customer delight. Examples of such a culture may include: commitment to excellence, empowerment, exceeding requirements, openness to challenges, passion, pride, proactivity, and recognition.

2. Communicating a service excellence culture: Continuous internal and external communication is essential for maintaining and developing a service excellence culture. This communication has to be an ongoing activity conducted by all managers.

3. Implementing a service excellence culture: Changing and developing a culture toward service excellence is a challenging task and a long-term journey. To be successful, the culture should be embedded in all areas of the company. In addition, as service leaders, managers have to work with employees to develop a culture that directly supports service excellence. Behavioral service standards are one way to make this happen. Take Safelite AutoGlass as an example: the company has set five standards for its service technicians. They call them the "5 Ts:"

- Time: Call customers in advance to notify them of arrival time.
- Touch: Shake hands, make eye contact, and engage the customer.
- Technical excellence: Do it right the first time, every time.
- Talk: Tell the customer what we are going to do and do it.
- Thanks: Show appreciation for choosing Safelite.

3.4 Employee engagement

The fourth element of the service excellence model deals with the key success factor of employee engagement. This can be understood as the "extent to which employees are committed to the organization, feel enthusiastic about their job and put discretionary effort into their work" (ISO 23592:2021, p. 3). It involves the employees' willingness to help the organization achieve its goals by showing a positive emotional attachment and commitment to their daily work. The advantage of committed employees for companies is that they are willing "to go the extra mile" for customers and the organization. Based on the profound studies done by Gallup, it is proven that highly engaged teams have significantly more positive outcomes, e.g., 10 percent higher customer loyalty (Gallup, 2022). Especially when customers are delighted by excellent services and outstanding experiences, employees mostly play a significant role (Den Hartog and Verburg, 2002; Heskett et al., 2015). According to ISO 23592:2021, a company must use human resources, processes, and tools in a targeted manner to promote shared values, beliefs, and practices to sustain them and, thus, create outstanding customer experiences as a means to an end (Horwitz and Neville, 1996; Wirtz and Lovelock, 2022). As already explained in section 3.2, management is an essential factor here. It should ensure that employees are enthusiastic, engaged and motivated to go beyond customer expectations to create outstanding customer experiences and thus delight their customers.

This element is divided into six sub-elements:

1. Recruitment and induction of new employees: The recruitment and onboarding phases are essential if the idea of service excellence is to be anchored in the minds of the workforce right from the start. Accordingly, the focus during these two phases should be on the attitude and behavior of new employees concerning service excellence. Thus, it is also about hiring the right people (Wirtz and Lovelock, 2022).

2. Continuous employee learning and development: In this sub-element, employees' passion for creating outstanding customer experiences is emphasized. To this end, all employees, regardless of their level of experience, are expected to have a positive attitude toward continuous learning (Ho, 1999). Due to the ever-changing work environment combined with the permanently evolving expectations, needs, and desires of customers, such an attitude of continuous learning is a necessity to stay up-to-date and thus provide excellent services.

3. Customers' feedback at an employee or team level: A particular feature of companies is that management's ideas about how customers experience service performance and quality typically differ significantly from customers' actual experiences or how customers perceive and evaluate them (Allen et al., 2005). For this reason, companies should regularly obtain reliable feedback from customers and disseminate these customer insights to the relevant departments, teams, and/or people.

4. Evaluation and assessment of employees: Service orientation should be evaluated regularly to improve employee performance. Only if employees know exactly where their strengths and weaknesses are in service provision can they work specifically on improving their service orientation. Additionally, employees should be able to demonstrate that they have consistently provided excellent service and support to their customers.

5. Recognition or acknowledgment system: In terms of creating a positively shaped culture of recognition, this element plays a central role in offering excellent services on a sustained basis (Wirtz and Lovelock, 2022). As is shown in many studies, pride can trigger a positive spiral toward customer-oriented behavior (Gouthier and Rhein, 2011; Kraemer et al., 2020). That is why service champions like the Ritz-Carlton

Hotel Group have implemented company-wide programs to create a positive recognition culture.

6. Employee feedback mechanism: To ensure the continuous development of the company and its workforce, the company should collect feedback not only from customers but also from its employees. This also strengthens employee engagement and improves the level of service excellence (Wirtz and Lovelock, 2022).

3.5 Understanding customer needs, expectations, and desires

After these primarily internal dimensions and elements, customer-oriented elements now become the focus of interest. According to ISO 23592:2021, a company must conduct appropriate research and analysis to adequately understand its customers' current and future needs, expectations, and desires. Only with deep insights can the customers' needs, expectations, and desires be systematically exceeded. Therefore, profound knowledge about customers is a prerequisite for establishing and maintaining a smoothly running service excellence system.

This element is divided into three sub-elements:

1. Scope and depth of listening to customers: Only if the real opinions, experiences, needs, and desires of a customer are obtained can that customer's expectations be exceeded, not only on an ad hoc basis but systematically and persistently (Wirtz and Lovelock, 2022). Accordingly, this sub-element requires companies to have a permanent system that records and tracks customer expectations, desires, and existing and changing customer needs.
2. Organization of data acquisition and use: To gain the most realistic view possible of customers, and their attitudes and behavior, a company should consistently research and analyze customer needs, expectations, and desires using various (quantitative and qualitative) methods. This should be done from a relationship perspective and across all customer journeys. Studies show that performance on customer journeys is more predictive of business outcomes than performance on touchpoints is (Rawson et al., 2013).
3. Adapting to customer needs, expectations, and desires: In the spirit of agility and liquid expectations (Shah and Greene, 2015), customers generally expect products and services to remain adaptable and to be updated in response to changes. This should be done regardless of the

causes of the changes (e.g., legal, social, technological, environmental, fashion, competitive, or innovative developments).

3.6 Designing and renewing outstanding customer experiences

After capturing conscious and subconscious customers' needs, expectations, and desires, this element consequently focuses on translating them into excellent service and outstanding customer experiences. The latter is defined as an experience that is "significantly better than a usual customer experience" (ISO 23592:2021, p. 2). Accordingly, this element requires a company to design, implement, and manage the provision of outstanding customer experiences to achieve customer delight.

This element is thus divided into the following four sub-elements:

1. Designing and documenting the customer experience: On the one hand, ISO 23592:2021 requires the intended experiences to be designed from a customer perspective, including customer needs, customer journeys, and emotional outcomes for customers and employees. On the other hand, customer experiences, those both planned and actual, have to be documented to be able to optimize them consistently.
2. Setting organizational service standards and delivering service promises: This sub-element assumes that the commitment to providing outstanding customer experiences increases if the company explicitly commits to appropriate and required standards. Respectively, it is necessary for the company to set and maintain market-leading internal standards and regularly exceed its service promises. To do so, prominent and service leading companies like Apple (the standard is called "APPLE" for their store employees) and Safelite AutoGlass (the "5 Ts" for service technicians and the "5 Bs" for customer service representatives) have created internal service standards to guide their employees toward excellent behavior in terms of customer contact.
3. Deployment of the customer experience concept throughout the organization: Planning the desired customer experiences in terms of leitmotifs is still relatively easy for a company to realize. The real challenge lies in their implementation. Consequently, this sub-element demands that the customer experience concept should document the implementation requirements.
4. Service recovery excellence: Excellent service should be offered to customers, not only in day-to-day business. Especially when customers have an occurring or existing problem and/or complaint, the company

should help them individually and surprisingly to create outstanding customer experiences and customer delight for this customer group.

3.7 Service innovation management

One of the biggest challenges companies are facing today are the continuously changing needs, desires, and expectations of customers driven by ongoing boastful promises from companies, higher market transparency due to digitalization, and liquid customer expectations (Shah and Greene, 2015). What exceeds customer expectations today may be a standard requirement tomorrow. Moreover, sometimes a customer himself does not precisely know what he expects or wants. Consequently, companies striving for excellent service and customer delight must continuously improve the service they offer (Eisawi et al., 2012). This requires close cooperation with customers but also with other relevant stakeholders. Therefore, a concept like service design that is intensely customer-centric can help companies realize it. For this purpose, the technical specification ISO/TS 24082:2021 can be used as a support. It describes a systematic approach, including principles and activities for designing excellent services that achieve an outstanding customer experience.

As is well known in theory and practice, service innovation can be gradual (evolutionary), improving existing processes and/or services, or groundbreaking (disruptive), developing and introducing new processes and/or services. In this way, service innovation offers customers particular added value, e.g., through new services and promises and improved processes that lead to optimized service delivery and new business models.

Accordingly, this element is divided into the following two sub-elements:

1. Innovation culture: Companies should stimulate and promote a service excellence innovation culture that supports the development of excellent services from the perspective of customers and employees. Therefore, a climate characterized by factors like creativity, inventiveness, and experimentation should be internally fostered to enable a company to introduce new ideas and processes.
2. Structured innovation process: A company should also have a structured innovation process to introduce innovations in service excellence regularly. This process should consist of the following four steps: Idea generation, conception, development, and market launch. These four steps are necessary to generate, manage, and control the continuous

large flow of service excellence innovations from different value perspectives (e.g., new services, core services, service delivery, and complementary services). A slightly more specified approach to developing excellent service is given in ISO/TS 24082:2021. This standard contains the following five core activities: (1) Understanding and empathizing with the customer, (2) defining a design challenge and a unique value proposition, (3) designing outstanding customer experiences with touchpoints and data points, (4) designing a co-creation environment to enhance outstanding customer experiences, and (5) evaluating the design of excellent service.

3.8 Managing customer-experience-related efficient and effective processes and organizational structures

The last two elements of the service excellence model are situated on a more operational level compared to the previous dimensions and elements. The penultimate element of the ISO 23592:2021 service excellence model requires companies to have appropriate processes, technologies, techniques, and organizational structures that enable them to meet the existing and changing needs, desires, and expectations of customers and the external environment. For services especially, a combined process perspective is essential because every service business is nothing less than a network of processes. Combined means that the processes should be analyzed from an internal perspective and evaluated from the customer's point of view. Each service process begins with the customer's requirements and ends with the handover of the results to the customer. To this end, companies should develop, implement, and manage customer journeys that implement the designed customer experience concept and lead to outstanding customer experiences. This requires customer-centric thinking and a holistic service value chain focused on service excellence, including suppliers and other businesses that reflect the importance of exceptional customer focus. In addition, the needs of employees (e.g., employee feedback) should also be included. Generally, it is proven that siloed mindsets and behavior significantly correlate negatively with the economic performance of organizations (Goran et al., 2017). Overall, this element shows various points of connection to the other elements of the service excellence model, so that a breakdown into the following three sub-elements makes sense:

1. Managing customer-experience-related processes: This sub-element calls for a company to align its internal processes and processes with partners to respond appropriately to changes in customer needs, desires, and expectations.
2. Deploying customer-experience-related technologies and techniques: Accordingly, this sub-element calls for technologies and techniques to support the company in generating outstanding customer experiences. These can be digital technologies as a critical success factor today, especially in service delivery, but all kinds of technologies and techniques can help an organization design, manage, and deliver excellent services. They can also help the company manage excellent services and support employees in their daily work.
3. Management of organizational structures and partnerships: Due to the fast changing environment and markets, a company should have a flexible and agile structure, especially concerning the needs and requirements of customers and employees. Consequently, interdepartmental conflicts and poorly functioning interfaces to partners should be reduced and ideally eliminated.

3.9 Monitoring service excellence activities and results

The ninth and final element of the service excellence model is dedicated to measuring the success and examining the task of service excellence. Suppose a service excellence concept is successfully implemented in a company and sustained. In that case, a company must develop and systematically apply a series of internal and external metrics that focus on all elements of the service excellence model. Besides the basic information given in the ISO 23592:2021, the newly developed technical specification ISO/TS 23686:2022 provides companies with a more concrete plan of action for measuring service excellence or, more precisely, service excellence performance. Based on the "OKR" ("Objectives and Key Results") approach, the measurement concepts for each of the four dimensions of the service excellence model are presented in four chapters of this technical specification. This guideline can help top management use these metrics to monitor, improve, and innovate across all business areas. Measuring and monitoring the service excellence approach and performance is not a static approach but a dynamic and living system. The metrics and their application should be evaluated regularly and improved where possible. This element is divided into four sub-elements:

1. Causal relationships: To identify the right levers to optimize service excellence activities and improve their results, a company should understand the key determinants or metrics of the service excellence impact chain elements and their relationships. This should be done along with the entire service value chain organizations, including suppliers, outsourcers, and other partners.
2. Use of performance indicators: Service excellence does not serve as an end in itself but is intended to enhance the financial and non-financial results of a company. Therefore, the company should use a set of appropriate input, process, output, and outcome metrics to manage and optimize the concept of service excellence.
3. Use of measurement tools: A company should use quantitative and qualitative measurement tools continuously and objectively.
4. Use of metrics at the operational, tactical, and strategic levels: Metrics can be seen as a quantitative way to evaluate service excellence. They should be used to support and promote an organization's positive service culture and develop good practices into excellent practices. Furthermore, they should be used to track whether the desired benefits and objectives are achieved and to what extent (ISO/TS 23686:2022).

4. Conclusion

Since June 2021, ISO 23592:2021 has been the first global standard to define the key terms and describe the principles and a model of service excellence. It provides companies with a kind of "blueprint" that they can use as a guide to implementing a concept of service excellence. Additionally, it should be noted that the implementation of service excellence as a holistic approach is not an aspiration that can be realized in the short term, in the sense of a temporary project, but is a longer process – more of a marathon than a sprint. Even after its successful implementation, it is essential to keep the service excellence system running sustainably and optimize it continuously.

In retrospect, the work on ISO 23592:2021 was very efficient and effective because the committee (ISO/TC 312/WG 1) was already able to draw on the intensive preparatory work carried out during the development of DIN SPEC 77224:2011 and CEN/TS 16880:2015. In addition, it was possible to expand the group of participants significantly so that more countries are now increasingly involved in the work. As a result, there is additional capacity to develop further norms and standards in the area of service excellence. More detailed insights and an outlook are provided in the last article of this edited volume, in which an outlook on upcoming developments is given.

Bibliography

Allen, J., Reichheld, F., Hamilton, B. and Markey, R. (2005). Closing the delivery gap, Bain & Company.

Antonacopoulou, E. and Kandampully, J. (2000). Alchemy: The transformation to service excellence, The Learning Organization, 7(1), pp. 13–22.

Barnes, D.C. and Krallman, A. (2019). Customer delight: A review and agenda for research, Journal of Marketing Theory and Practice, 27(2), pp. 174–195.

Bowen, D.E. and Lawler, E.E. (1992). The empowerment of service workers: What, why, how, and when, Sloan Management Review, 33(3), pp. 31–39.

Caterpillar (2019). Our values in action. Caterpillar's code of conduct, https://www.caterpillar.com/en/company/code-of-conduct.html, accessed 01/13/2022.

CEN/TS 16880:2015 (2015). Service excellence: Creating outstanding customer experiences through service excellence, Brussels.

Collis, D.J. and Rukstad, M.G. (2008). Can you say what your strategy is?, Harvard Business Review, 86(4), pp. 82–90.

Crotts, J.C., Dickson, D.R. and Ford, R.C. (2005). Aligning organizational processes with mission: The case of service excellence, Academy of Management Executive, 19(3), pp. 54–68.

Den Hartog, D.N. and Verburg, R.M. (2002). Service excellence from the employees' point of view: The role of first line supervisors, Managing Service Quality, 12(3), pp. 159–164.

DIN SPEC 77224:2011–07 (2011). Achieving customer delight through service excellence, Berlin.

Eisawi, D.A., Sekhon, H. and Tanna, S. (2012). Innovation as a determinant for service excellence in banking, International Journal of e-Education, e-Business, e-Management and e-Learning, 2(4), pp. 336–338.

Fernandez, S. and Moldogaziev, T. (2013). Employee empowerment, employee attitudes, and performance: Testing a causal model, Public Administration Review, 73(3), pp. 490–506.

Gallup (2022). What is employee engagement and how do you improve it?, https://www.gallup.com/workplace/285674/improve-employee-engagement-workplace.aspx, accessed 01/27/2022.

Goran, J., LaBerge, L. and Srinivasan, R. (2017). Culture for a digital age, McKinsey Quarterly, July 2017.

Gouthier, M.H.J. and Rhein, M. (2011). Organizational pride and its positive effects on employee behaviour, Journal of Service Management, 22(5), pp. 633–649.

Heskett, J.L., Sasser, W.E. and Schlesinger, L.A. (2015). What great service leaders know and do, Oakland.

Ho, W. (1999). Organizational transformation for service excellence in a public hospital in Hong Kong, Managing Service Quality, 9(6), pp. 383–388.

Horwitz, F.M. and Neville, M.A. (1996). Organization design for service excellence: A review of the literature, Human Resource Management, 35(4), pp. 471–492.

Hunt, B. and Ivergård, T. (2015). Designing Service Excellence. People and Technology, Boca Raton.

ISO 9001:2015 (2015). Quality management systems — Requirements, Geneva.

ISO 10002:2018 (2018). Quality management — Customer satisfaction — Guidelines for complaints handling in organizations, Geneva.

ISO 23592:2021 (2021). Service excellence — Principles and model, Geneva.

ISO/IEC 20000–1:2018 (2018). Information technology — Service management — Part 1: Service management system requirements, Geneva.

ISO/TS 23686:2022 (2022). Service excellence — Measuring service excellence performance, Geneva.

ISO/TS 24082:2021 (2021). Service excellence — Designing excellent service to achieve outstanding customer experiences, Geneva.

Johnston, R. (2004). Towards a better understanding of service excellence, Managing Service Quality, 14(2/3), pp. 129–133.

Johnston, R. (2007). Insights into service excellence, in: Gouthier, M.H.J., Coenen, C., Schulze, H.S. and Wegmann, C. (eds.). Service excellence as an initiator, Wiesbaden, pp. 17–35.

Kano, N., Seraku, N., Takahashi, F. and Tsuji, S. (1984). Attractive quality and must-be quality, The Journal of the Japanese Society for Quality Control, 14(2), pp. 39–48.

Kraemer, T., Weiger, W.H., Gouthier, M.H.J. and Hammerschmidt, M. (2020). Toward a theory of spirals: the dynamic relationship between organizational pride and customer-oriented behavior, Journal of the Academy of Marketing Science, 48(6), pp. 1095–1115.

Lambert, G. (2016). Service with a smile, thanks to standards, https://www.iso.org/news/2016/05/Ref2077.html, accessed 12/29/2021.

Ludwig, N.L., Heidenreich, S., Kraemer, T. and Gouthier, M. (2017). Customer delight: universal remedy or a double-edged sword?, Journal of Service Theory and Practice, 27(1), pp. 22–45.

Parasuraman, A., Ball, J., Aksoy, L., Keiningham, T.L. and Zaki, M. (2021). More than a feeling? Toward a theory of customer delight, Journal of Service Management, 32(1), pp. 1–26.

Rawson, A., Duncan, E. and Jones, C. (2013). The truth about customer experience, Harvard Business Review, 91(9), pp. 90–98.

Schein, E.H. (2016). Organizational culture and leadership, 5th ed., New Jersey.

Shah, B. and Greene, J. (2015). Liquid expectations. Consumers are setting a different bar for experiences, https://www.fjordnet.com/conversations/liquid-expectations/, accessed 01/01/2022.

Testa, M.R. and Sipe, L. (2012). Service-leadership competencies for hospitality and tourism management, International Journal of Hospitality Management, 31, pp. 648–658.

Ulaga, W. and Reinartz, W.J. (2011). Hybrid offerings: How manufacturing firms combine goods and services successfully, Journal of Marketing, 75(6), pp. 5–23.

Weitzer, M. and Weislaemle, V. (2021). Achieving positive hospitality experiences through technology: Findings from Singapore and Malaysia, in Thirumaran, K., Klimkeit, D. and Tang, C.M. (eds.). Service excellence in tourism and hospitality — Insights from Asia, Cham, Switzerland, pp. 133–147.

Wirtz, J. and Lovelock, C. (2022). Services marketing: People, technology, strategy, 9th ed., New Jersey.

Wong, A., Liu, Y. and Tjosvold, D. (2015). Service leadership for adaptive selling and effective customer service teams, Industrial Marketing Management, 46, pp. 122–131.

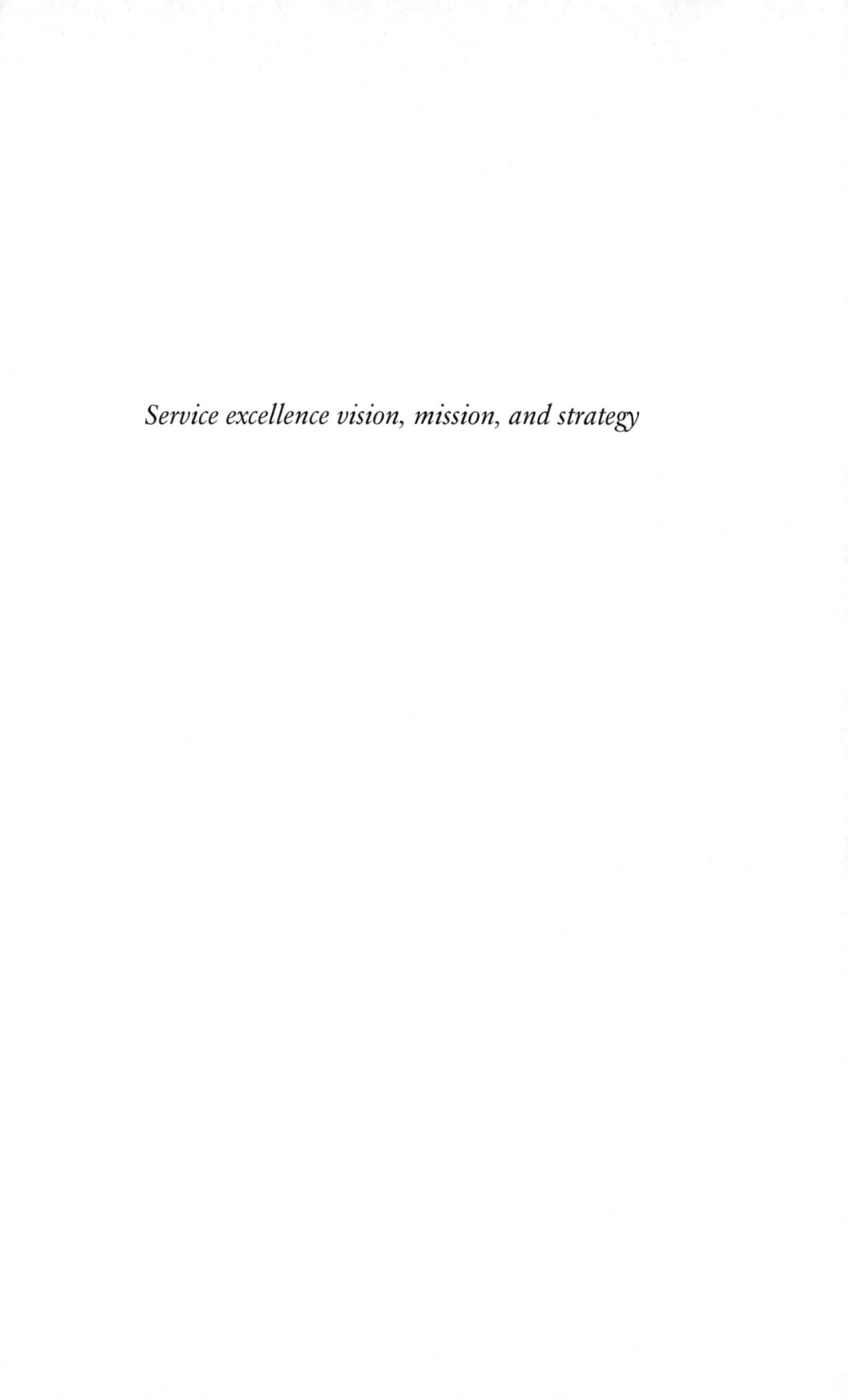

Service excellence vision, mission, and strategy

The strategic anchoring of service excellence at WISAG

Michael Moritz

Management summary

Following a service excellence approach means focusing on the customer. WISAG has decisively expanded this concept: If you run a people-oriented business, you must first cultivate good relationships within your own company – because only then is it possible to transfer the appreciation and delight of the employees to the customer. This article explains which soft and hard factors are essential for the holistic concept of service excellence in the company WISAG, which instruments are used for its operationalization and why this commitment leads to economic success.

1. Service excellence needs emotions

"We want to win the hearts of our customers and our employees." Anyone hearing WISAG's mission for the first time may be fascinated or ask critical questions; fascinated because this particular goal of the company already conveys a high-quality standard and promises customer orientation on an emotional basis, and skeptical because of the justified consideration: How can such a lofty goal be achieved, especially if, in addition to customers, employees are involved? How can quality be achieved that has a lasting effect? However, the experience of the family-owned company WISAG shows that the definition of such goals makes sense and can be implemented successfully. After all, customer satisfaction has become standard and is therefore hardly adequate as a company's "figurehead." In contrast, the emotion-based mission of evoking delight offers the opportunity to distinguish oneself as a company, develop further, and stand out from the competition – depending on the requirement that the mission is meant seriously, is lived, and is anchored strategically.

This approach is particularly interesting when companies are part of an industry such as facility management (FM), in which people-related services are central – and thus people are regarded as social beings – and at a time when a profound transformation process is keeping the economy and society in suspense. Structural change through digital technologies, the transformation of work, changes through new forms of communication, and the enormous pressure caused by the consequences of climate change are triggering multiple uncertainties and therefore require orientation and sustainable rethinking. For the past one to two years, quality and value thinking have been moving into focus on a wide variety of levels. This movement also includes quality in social relationships. "Delight and win hearts"—this strategic service goal requires conviction and courage. In return, it offers future orientation and the opportunity for a company to position itself as a strong employer brand. WISAG also goes one step further by explicitly including employees in the concept – and for good reason.

While a product fulfils the value proposition conveyed via advertising in the consumer goods sector, a service employee must satisfy a customer's expectations in the service sector. The logical conclusion from this shift is that if the relationship between a company and its employees or customers is characterized not only by satisfaction but even by delight, this will trigger a greater sense of well-being and pleasure in dealing with one another. Trust will grow. As a result, the loyalty of employees and customers to the company will be strengthened – even in the long term.

Especially in fast-moving and volatile times, customers are increasingly willing to switch providers. Therefore, counteractive measures must be taken: moving away from a transaction-oriented, primarily short-term customer relationship, which is determined solely by purchasing parameters, and toward an appreciative and learning partnership that cultivates a constructive culture of error, which is consistent and also promises planning reliability. When it comes to creating delight and winning the hearts of employees and customers, the holistic approach of service excellence provides an optimal framework for their implementation.

How can this goal be achieved in concrete terms? What are the possibilities of measurability, evaluation, and promotion? Before we present possible solutions to these exciting questions of operationalization, we would like to say something provocative in advance: Attitude is more important than just a manual in this process. This means that the corporate culture determines the effectiveness of the measures in this context.

2. The founder: A service provider par excellence

The FM industry has an enormous economic significance in Germany that is still underestimated. With around 135 billion euros in gross value added (GVA), FM is one of Germany's top six economic sectors, ranking just behind the automotive industry and even ahead of mechanical engineering (Thomzik, 2018). In addition to almost continuous growth, it demonstrates a high degree of stability and resistance to crises, even under challenging conditions. In the industry ranking "Leading Facility Service Companies in Germany 2021," WISAG Facility Service Holding is in third place with sales of 1,176.9 million euros in 2020. With around 31,300 employees, the company is the largest employer in the German facility services market (Lünendonk, 2021).

The core business of WISAG Facility Service Holding is technical and infrastructural services for commercial, infrastructure and residential properties, and health and social care facilities. Its portfolio is divided into the areas: facility management, building services, cleaning, security and service, catering, gardening and landscape maintenance, and consulting and management.

Since their foundation by Claus Wisser in the mid-1960s, the various Wisser companies all offered infrastructural and technical services for buildings, albeit separately. Increasingly, there was a desire on the part of customers for more integrated and bundled services. In 1993, all the individual companies in the group were brought together under the umbrella of WISAG Service Holding; in 1996, the facility management division was launched. Over the years, WISAG has developed into one of the leading multi-service providers in Germany, divided into three independent business units: Aviation Service, Facility Service, and Industrial Service.

Diversity is a determining factor at WISAG. The company employs people from more than 100 nations. With independent companies in the individual divisions and regions, the entire business is very decentralized. There are different customer structures and customer segments – in the facility service sector, from specialist clinics to shopping centers, each with very individual requirements. The company's service portfolio is correspondingly comprehensive but tailored in each case.

The company is characterized in a unique way by its founder Claus Wisser – a service professional par excellence. His definition of service, always doing more than is actually necessary and being cordially happy to serve the customer, continues to underpin the company's inner values compass. Claus Wisser, the founder and, for many years, Chairman of the Management Board of WISAG, established a corporate culture that promises, "Appreciation leads to value creation." The approach behind this is that employees can exploit their performance potential through a feeling of appreciation and, above all, develop the courage to tread new paths. It is about responding quickly to changes and remaining capable of acting in a complex environment.

3. Operationalization: Relationship, participation, delight

WISAG has been working on its service excellence strategy with scientific support for many years and is building on three strong pillars: firstly, a corporate culture with credible role models that focus on customer centricity and consistent relationship management; secondly, employees who "burn" for their company with a high level of commitment and heart and soul – promoted by effective participation – can delight others; and thirdly, a range of services that follows the principle: what you promise, you have to deliver and always garnish with a voluntary extra step to achieve the service goal of "winning hearts."

3.1 Corporate culture: Values and mission

The market for facility services is highly competitive. Accordingly, a sharp profile makes it easier to sustain one's own position. For this reason, WISAG developed a mission statement around ten years ago in an intensive process. More than 80 managers, 2,000 employees, around 350 existing and over 60 potential customers, as well as industry experts and suppliers were consulted. Numerous employee workshops were also held and market and competitor analyses conducted. The mission statement establishes a central objective: to delight employees and customers and win their hearts. The entire mission statement process and the insights gained now form the basis of the company's strategy on and implementation of service excellence.

In addition to the mission statement, reliable quality management, especially by DIN EN ISO 9001, ensures consistently high product and service quality in the company. This documented proof of quality is an essential building block with which to firmly anchor the awareness of customer orientation and quality among employees. The associated processes and quality management principles are established and well developed at WISAG. However, this certificate is no longer suitable as a competitive advantage. It is now considered standard and therefore no longer represents a future-oriented instrument on its own.

3.2 A company shines from within

It is pretty simple: If you want to delight someone, you have to know how to do it. You have to have a sincere interest in the person in question, in his or her expectations and preferences. It is a matter of finding out how someone thinks and acts. WISAG founder Claus Wisser knew precisely whom he could delight with a morning delivery of bread rolls – and it was not primarily about generating the next deal. Instead, it was about cultivating relationships, about attentive cooperation, about a sense of well-being – on both sides!

Service excellence focuses on the customer's perspective. However, WISAG has decisively expanded this approach. If you run a people-oriented business, the first step is to build and maintain good relationships within your own company with your own employees. Only then is it possible for an attitude of appreciation and delight to be reflected in work with and for the customer. This corporate culture includes a management approach that involves leading by example. Credible role models strengthen the sense of community within the company. What is exemplified on a daily basis shows its positive effect, convinces through authenticity, and is, therefore, easier to understand and adopt as a behavioral norm.

WISAG's corporate culture also includes a unique understanding of cooperation with customers and employees. It pursues the goal of strengthening fundamental identification with the company. A key success factor here is the enormous scope for independent action. Employees thus feel part of a community and develop a sense of pride in their employer. It is also true that customers who participate in the company's development processes feel that they are being listened to, taken seriously, and given a specific scope of action. This prepares the ground for mutual "goodwill," including dealing with complaints, i.e., a respectful error culture. In the best case, a partnership can grow between the service provider and the customer, enabling synergy effects on both sides.

> *"Corporate culture is at least as important to the concept of service excellence as a strategy and a range of tools. Without the right mindset of all employees, the best measures remain ineffective. This means that only good internal relationships shine outward."*

Michael Moritz, Managing Director WISAG Facility Service Holding

3.3 Relationships: For better or worse

It does not matter whether it is soccer, marriage, politics, friends, employees, or customers: good relationships first have to grow and then be nurtured – and not just superficially. If they are to be enduring – in good times and bad – the aim must be to establish deep roots. An investment in intensive relationship building is worthwhile. Once you have won over a customer, no matter how small the order, you can expect to be asked to work with them again and be enabled to expand that cooperation successively. Although the effort required for consistent and individual customer retention measures is high, it is often more effective than the effort required for new customer acquisition. Service excellence has the potential not only to strengthen customer loyalty but also to achieve customer loyalty.

This applies equally to employee retention. The market for building-related services is subject to comparatively high fluctuation. Changes in staff usually also include information and friction losses. Therefore, it is even more critical to delight employees in the company and retain them long-term. WISAG customers enjoy having familiar contact people. Consistency creates a reliable partnership. Low fluctuation offers a further advantage: Anyone who can score points as a facility service provider today with a clear concept for recruiting and retaining employees has a head start in the market, which is suffering from a growing shortage of labor and skilled workers.

3.4 Development system for service excellence

To achieve the service goal of "winning hearts" and always going the extra mile for the customer, WISAG has worked out its own development system. Corporate culture factors like so-called "soft factors" (communicate, convince, delight, and win hearts) play at least as important a role as operational factors. Both are closely interlinked, as will be shown in the following description. It is important to emphasize that "patience is the order of the day." Service excellence is not an absolute state but requires sustained commitment. Every step counts, even the smallest. More can often be achieved with focus than if everything is tackled at once.

3.4.1 Strengthening communication through further training

"It is not what you say, but how you say it," a well-known proverb urges. How, whether, and when people talk to each other significantly influences the result. Is it coherent and does it please? Does it invite you to continue? Communication is crucial at WISAG in terms of service excellence. The topic is covered extensively in the company's comprehensive training program, in which the basics of successful communication techniques are taught in numerous course units. The aim is to operate with a uniform, professional standard throughout Germany (despite all the company's decentralization) and continuously develop communication quality. In addition, there are many training programs for employees that teach them to focus on the customer's perspective consistently.

The overall aim of the training program is to promote a strong sense of self-awareness and self-confidence among employees. Those who work at WISAG are given many opportunities to advance personally and the necessary freedom to make their own decisions. Individual qualification helps to increase employees' motivation and develop leaders from within the company.

3.4.2 How to measure delight

A customer is satisfied when the quality of the services provided is right and when promises are fulfilled. Delight also arises when customer experiences are moments of surprise.

How can the impact and success of different measures be assessed in this context? The customer's needs must be tangible, and it is essential to identify moments of excitement, especially at customer touchpoints (see also Figure 1). After all, customer experiences that can be actively and systematically recorded can be evaluated, changed, and thus improved, always with a focus placed on achieving the service goal of "winning hearts."

Michael Moritz

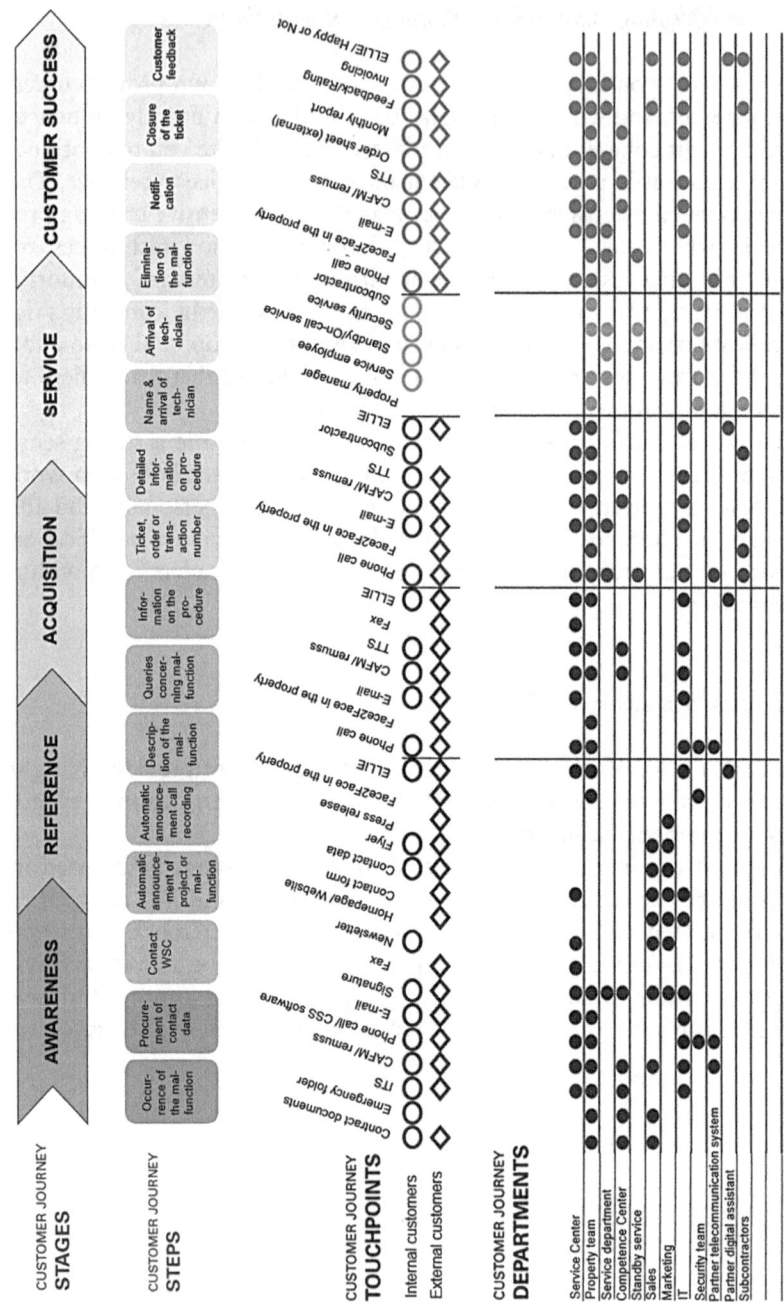

Fig. 1: Touchpoint matrix

The big challenge here is to allow for habituation effects. After all, the principle of perseverance applies: "one-time delight" does not yet shape service excellence, and a bonus service only retains its surprise quality if it does not become the standard.

Systematic feedback

WISAG developed various tools to continuously record and analyze feedback in a comprehensive process involving employees and customers. Since then, the resulting evaluation system has served as a key instrument in continuous feedback collection. The advantages are that the status quo of the various relationships in the company can be evaluated systematically. More importantly, however, changes and thus drivers for development can be identified in time. As a result, recommendations for action can always be derived in order to achieve the desired goals. WISAG's evaluation system is based on two formats: surveys and walk-throughs.

Surveys

For the surveys, target group-oriented questionnaires were created aimed at customers, managers, and employees. All surveys are conducted annually.

The customer survey records how the customers perceive and experience WISAG's values and vision. For example, is the commitment to sustainability well received? Have customers' hearts been won? It also determines which factors have a powerful influence on customer delight (see Figure 2). These so-called "drivers" play a decisive role in aligning fields of action in the next step.

The 360-degree web feedback records how WISAG managers are perceived by their environment and how they fulfil their role model function in line with corporate values. Supervisors, colleagues, and employees are surveyed to create a comprehensive 360-degree picture of their mood.

Finally, once a year, the WISAG Barometer determines the mood of the employees in the individual companies in the form of anonymous surveys. How great is the actual delight? Which factors emerge as drivers of delight in the annual survey? And of course, the results can also be used to conclude whether the measures derived from the 360-degree web feedback have achieved their goals. Respectively, there is a feedback loop between the employee and executive surveys. As standardized processes, the three surveys mentioned above form the foundation of quality assurance and development at WISAG. The holistic approach to service excellence requires all company areas to be geared to generating delight among customers and employees.

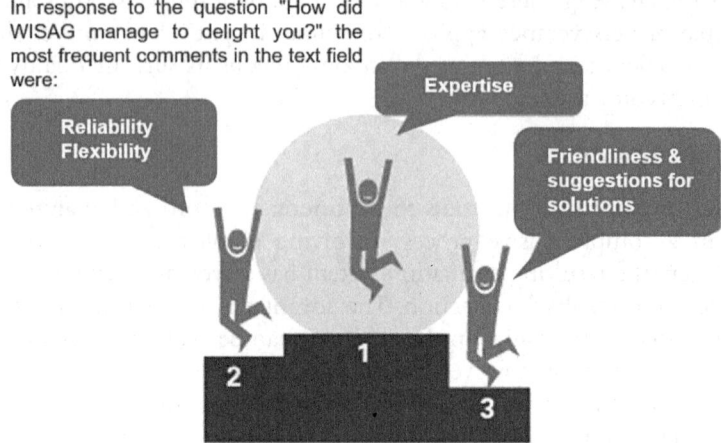

Top 3 statements in the context of delight

Fig. 2: Central drivers of customer delight at WISAG

Walk-throughs

In addition to the surveys, WISAG uses the opportunity to obtain feedback directly on-site and gain realistic impressions. Two different formats are used for this purpose. Both aim to increase customer focus.

The method of spot checks at the customer contact point – unannounced visits as an instrument of quality control – enables WISAG to assess its services directly "through the customer's glasses." During a spontaneous visit, the quality and service offered in a property can be experienced and evaluated "live" at the customer contact point. The aim is to highlight employees' strengths and analyze their weaknesses – without the team having prepared explicitly for a "classic audit" in advance.

The personal presence of supervisors at customer properties: Managers' particular function as role models is an essential element of WISAG's corporate culture. Managers personally visit properties managed by WISAG at regular intervals. On the one hand, these meetings emphasize appreciation and respect for the performance of the property managers and their teams on-site. On the other hand, personal exchanges can be very effective in identifying and jointly discussing opportunities for improvement.

3.4.3 Freedom promotes growth and delight

How can we create delight? What are its drivers? Research in neurobiology, e.g., says that what is learned only remains in the memory if it gets under the skin during the learning process and if the person is not only addressed cognitively but emotionally (Zendesk, 2021; Dunsmoor et al., 2015). This idea works equally well in customer and employee relationships. Here, too, it is possible to define and use drivers of delight. Comprehensive surveys conducted by WISAG have identified various drivers that can increase delight on the part of both employees and customers. The company's annual survey rhythm guarantees regular review and adjustment of its approach in this regard.

Customers respond delightedly to:

- Initiative from the employees
- Transparency in terms of communication
- Continuous improvement of quality as well as employees taking delight in their work

Employees are delighted about:

- Regular communication about customer needs
- Further development opportunities
- Supervisors with a role model function

Brain research confirms that delight helps people to develop their potential. This process works best when people feel connected to communities but at the same time feel the freedom to grow. WISAG has a unique selling point among FM service providers: it offers its employees sufficient creative freedom to make decisions and act on-site, close to the customer. This freedom promotes the development of ideas among employees. For customers, it reinforces the certainty that they basically have a choice in their cooperation with the company and can thus exert a direct influence on it.

3.4.4 Winning hearts: Surprises leave a lasting impression

Humans are creatures of habit. Breaking up entrenched processes, approaches to work, or thought patterns is not easy. However, anyone who wants to generate new ideas to develop good collaboration with customers and employees further and, in particular, to design aha moments needs a creative process.

Service design and design thinking are established concepts that produce exciting and practical results through structured rethinking. Lego figures are sometimes used to illustrate the range of creative processes. WISAG uses these concepts to develop ideas with surprise potential and measures with high added value for its customers.

Generally, the active involvement of employees in the development of ideas leads to positive effects. After all, employees experience customer contact points at first hand in their daily work and are thus best able to anticipate customer needs. The ideas developed can be small and still have a significant impact.

Examples:

A simple sign

Recognizing a malfunction and working quickly to find a suitable solution is an essential criterion for a satisfied customer. A simple sign at the point of contact of the malfunction, signaling that we have detected the problem and are already taking care of it (e.g., "Defect detected, replacement already ordered"), conveys quickly and, above all, visibly that the WISAG team is already in action. It is a straightforward way to increase transparency and give customers a good, safe feeling to delight them.

The sledgehammer

"The sledgehammer" concept was jointly developed for the company's suggestion scheme in WISAG's Facility Management division (see Figure 3). And yes, an original name is of great importance because it promotes an emotional connection. WISAG awards the golden sledgehammer to the region where the best ideas were devised in one year. In addition, the top three ideas – i.e., the "hammer ideas"—are awarded a prize in a year. The ideas submitted come from various areas, such as occupational health and safety, customer satisfaction, processes, employee satisfaction, etc. A jury made up of employees and management evaluates the suggestions, e.g., based on their potential, implementation, and quantitative and qualitative benefits. Non-cash prizes complete this concept.

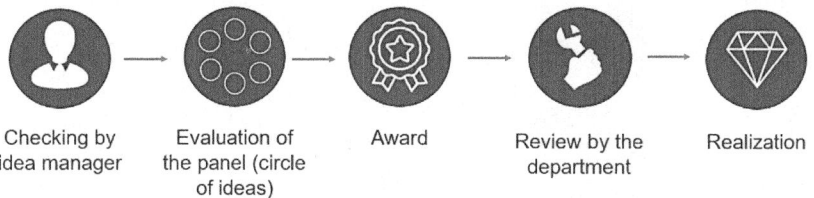

| Checking by idea manager | Evaluation of the panel (circle of ideas) | Award | Review by the department | Realization |

Fig. 3: "The sledgehammer"

The Energy Award

The Energy Award enables WISAG to use the high level of expertise of its specialist employees in energy management even more to the benefit of customers. The Energy Award regularly honors ideas for saving energy and publishes them internally, multiplied as part of the company's "best practice." The broad recognition of new ideas spurs further improvements. In this way, we can work together to offer our customers permanent, top-quality services that provide them with demonstrable added value.

ELLIE – accelerated response time via chatbot

Transparent and solution-oriented communication is a crucial factor, especially at the direct interfaces to the customer. The goal is for customers to have a direct line to the right contact person. This intention ensures that customers feel they are in good hands with their questions, ideas, or criticism.

Digital transformation is changing communication. All-encompassing connectivity, and increased communication and interaction possibilities have led to rising expectations (Zendesk, 2021). Whereas two years ago, a response time of around three hours was considered fast and service-oriented, today, an initial response is sometimes expected in real time. This development means that the bar for achieving service excellence is also very high in FM. Customers increasingly expect to communicate with service providers much as they do in their usual environment: very directly, on the go, and interactively.

WISAG has taken up this expectation and was the first service provider in facility management to actively deploy a chatbot to accelerate response times (see Figure 4). ELLIE can respond directly to customer inquiries via chat. The system is mobile accessible, takes messages or requests for additional services, categorizes concerns, and provides feedback directly to the customer. WISAG customers have reacted very positively to ELLIE, praising the increased transparency and accessibility of the company.

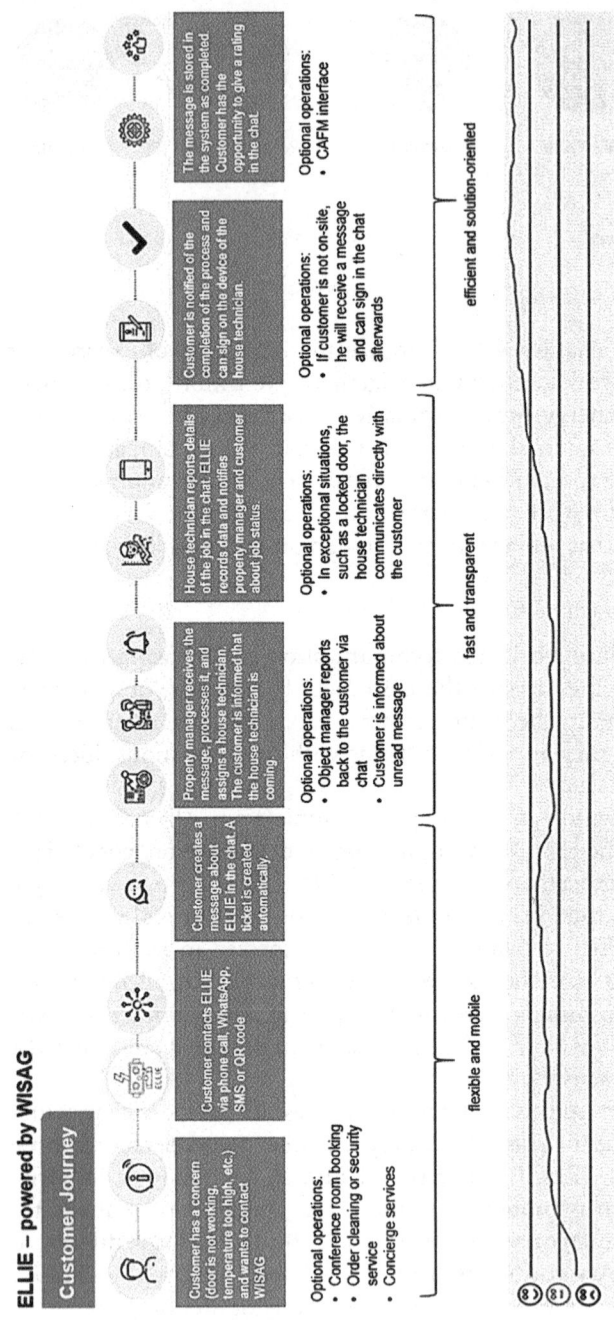

Fig. 4: Customer journey ELLIE

3.4.5 Change is the new normal

Routine means the end of any creativity and, above all, of delight. The concept of service excellence, therefore, thrives on repeated readjustment. This is also because general conditions and customer requirements are constantly changing. Both the company's approaches and the expectations and wishes of customers and employees require constant review, as do the measures used in this respect themselves. This insight also emphasizes that a high degree of willingness to change is a crucial success factor in service excellence.

4. Conclusion

The ambitious service goal of "winning hearts" is firstly achievable and secondly offers excellent advantages to a company – especially in the facility service industry, which is personnel-intensive. The decisive factor here is a corporate culture that focuses on appreciation and cultivating relationships and which centers around the customer's perspective. WISAG goes one step further in this regard and states, "Only employees who feel comfortable in a company through participation and individual qualification and who have the necessary freedom to make self-confident decisions on-site are able and willing to delight customers." Without the right mindset among employees, many measures will remain ineffective. In short: a company shines from within. This unique radiance makes it possible to distinguish oneself as a strong employer brand in a highly competitive market and stand out positively from competitors.

Seen in this light, the holistic concept of service excellence offers the best framework conditions for developing an attitude and suitable instruments for customer and employee delight and sustainable implementation in the company. The result is that the concept can ensure economic success and provide orientation in turbulent times.

At this point, a big thank you to Nadine Speicher, Head of Quality, Service and Process Management at WISAG Building Services Holding. She contributed extensive input to this article with her commitment and expertise.

Michael Moritz

Bibliography

Dunsmoor, J.E., Murty, V.P., Davachi, L. and Phelps, E.A. (2015). Emotional learning selectively and retroactively strengthens memories for related events, Nature, 520, pp. 545–548.

Lünendonk® (2021). Studie zum deutschen Facility-Service-Markt [Study on the German facility service market], Lünendonk & Hossenfelder GmbH, Mindelheim.

Thomzik, M. (2018). Branchenreport Facility Management 2018. Die volkswirtschaftliche Bedeutung der Facility-Management-Branche [Industry report facility management 2018. The economic significance of the facility management industry], Institut für angewandte Innovationsforschung (IAI) e.V. an der Ruhr-Universität Bochum, Deutscher Verband für Facility Management (GEFMA) e.V., Bochum.

Zendesk (2021). Zendesk Trends Report, https://www.zendesk.com/blog/zendesk-sales-trends-report-2021/, accessed 01/11/2022.

Leadership and management requirements

Living service excellence: A secret to success at TeamBank AG

Christian Polenz, Sabine Börnsen

Management summary

Service excellence cannot simply be prescribed to a company. It is like a plant that needs to be nurtured and cared for, that needs time to grow and that only matures with the right tools and proper care. In other words, the idea of service excellence must become part of a company's DNA to have a lasting effect. This article uses the example of TeamBank AG to illuminate such a path. It provides concrete examples of both the theoretical approach and the impact of service excellence.

1. Relevance of service excellence in the financial industry and for TeamBank AG

Digitalization as a driver of industry change – industry boundaries are breaking down

Our world is becoming more digital – in all aspects of life. From the smart control of our refrigerator or shopping lists, our purchasing and travel behavior to the digital vaccination certificate. The COVID-19 pandemic has even reinforced this trend. Many technical devices and possibilities are now considered normal by people who would not have considered them before the pandemic.

This trend has also had a lasting impact on the financial sector, especially on its credit branch. Contactless payment via smartphone, online installment purchases, and digital personal advice at the local bank or via video are just a few examples. However, many of these innovations originated outside the financial industry. Positive experiences and convenience are becoming the general expectation of customers – across all sectors.

"Banking is necessary, banks are not"

"Banking is necessary, banks are not" is a quote from Bill Gates back in 1994. New competitors, such as technology companies or FinTechs, are increasingly putting this into practice and offering individual banking services directly at the customer interface, in particular, companies with an extensive customer reach combined with digital business models, such as Amazon, Google, or Apple. Amazon, for instance, successfully provides its customers with extensive services such as Amazon Prime, Video, Music, Audible and its own Amazon Payment services in addition to its classic marketplace. These offers have created a new competitive situation for traditional banks, which increasingly requires them to establish a similarly intensive relationship with their customers.

However, what is the answer to this systemic upheaval? How can established banks continue to compete successfully in the future? The fact is that change cannot be stopped but should be seen as an opportunity.

Customer delight as a differentiating factor

Trust is the basis for both virtual and non-virtual customer relationships. The possibility of transferring trust-based relationships of recent years to the online world and making it tangible is one of the decisive starting points for banks. If they also manage to set themselves apart by offering permanently outstanding service experiences, especially for customers in challenging situations, they have a real chance of future success.

Particularly with "virtual" goods and services such as loans or electricity, it is essential to have a differentiating feature that is relevant to customers, not only to win them over but also to retain them in the long term. Above all, this can be an excellent service that customers can experience and that offers them tangible added value, which they do not receive from competitors. Customers want their concerns to be taken seriously and want to be treated as equals – not as supplicants. Particularly in the anonymous digital world, established companies have both the opportunity and the challenge of transferring and maintaining personal customer relationships and evoking customer delight. In the case of TeamBank AG, this transfer is paired with the values of the Cooperative Financial Network [Genossenschaftliche FinanzGruppe] (Bundesverband der Deutschen Volksbanken und Raiffeisenbanken, n.d.). Employees of these companies play an elementary role in this type of differentiation. The corporate culture and the attitude of all employees to thinking consistently from the customer's perspective are prerequisites. Overall, this includes a consistent focus on service excellence at all levels – from trainees to the Board of Management.

2. TeamBank AG – the center of competence for modern liquidity management within the Cooperative Financial Network

TeamBank AG is the competence center for modern liquidity management of the cooperative banks with its easyCredit installment loan in Germany, the faire Credit in Austria and the seamless payment procedure ratenkauf by easyCredit. The roots of today's TeamBank AG go back to 1950. Since 2003, the financial institution has been a subsidiary of DZ BANK AG and thus part of the Volksbanken Raiffeisenbanken Cooperative Financial Network. For all product variants, customers can take advantage of the advisory services offered at the local branch or by phone, app, video chat, or online, depending on their individual preferences. This network of innovative products and services offers customers digital solutions and thus access to liquidity anywhere and at any time. TeamBank AG's products are available at more than nine out of ten cooperative banks in Germany and at more than a third of the cooperative banks in Austria (TeamBank AG, 2021a).

3. Service excellence—"standing alone" or an integral part of the overall strategy?

Management philosophy or buzzword – bringing the vision to life

However, a customer-centric attitude that manifests in a company's culture does not emerge overnight. Nor is it sufficient to campaign with customer orientation and merely aim for it in the short and medium-term. A company's sustainable customer-centric performance mainly depends on whether this attitude is reflected throughout the entire company – from its vision and mission to its business strategy and management logic.

At TeamBank AG, the customer is the core of the vision. This vision represents the common image of the company's desired future. Ambitious but also realistic, it provides internal orientation as a clearly formulated goal and acts as a guideline for action—"to contribute to the carefree lives of our customers." Complementing the vision, TeamBank AG's mission shows what the company stands for and answers the question, "What would the world be missing if our company did not exist?" It says, "With future-proof technology and an outstanding team, we delight our customers ..." (TeamBank AG, 2021b).

By simultaneously anchoring it in the bank's strategy through to its operationalization, the service concept is also considered in functions that do not have direct customer contact. This process has been ongoing for many years, consistently integrating a relentless focus on customers – from product development, consulting and sales activities to after-sales services. Moreover, it is a process that must be taken seriously and practiced at all company levels. Consequently, it is an essential part of management philosophy – only in this way does it transfer into the culture of a company and become part of its DNA.

The will to achieve service excellence must be reflected not only in a company's way of thinking but above all in its daily actions. Thus, it becomes a management process that requires targets, measurement, and continuous feedback and improvement. In addition to key figures such as the Net Promoter Score, external audits, such as service excellence certification according to the DIN standard (DIN SPEC 77224:2011) or, in the future, the ISO standard (ISO 23592:2021), are helpful instruments. The neutral evaluation of the current situation provides the company with impetus and enables it to repeatedly challenge its thinking and actions, put processes to the test, and change them in the interests of its customers.

At the end of the day, it is the market and the customers who judge a company's success – and not the company itself – which also applies to TeamBank AG.

4. Mindset and culture – customer delight mirrors the company's DNA

Entrepreneurial activity based on cooperative values

In addition to its vision, mission, and corporate strategy, the company's values are the fourth important component of its consistent customer and service excellence orientation.

TeamBank AG's corporate culture is firmly embedded in the cooperative canon of values. As a member of the Volksbanken Raiffeisenbanken Cooperative Financial Network, TeamBank AG is committed to cooperative values such as solidarity, fairness, partnership, and support for its members and customers (Bundesverband der Deutschen Volksbanken und Raiffeisenbanken, n.d). This mindset, which is focused on the sustainable promotion of its members, shapes the company's idea of service excellence. It creates room for investing in high service quality and customer orientation. The overall basic idea is that lasting customer delight leads to sustainable economic success.

The "honorable merchant"—what cooperative values mean for TeamBank AG

Values create values – for TeamBank AG, the "honorable merchant" is the guiding principle for its sustainable and socially responsible corporate policy. The bank's actions are aligned with this guiding principle – day in, day out. "We are fair, we make it simple, we are personal and appreciative, and we are a team" is the motto at TeamBank AG, symbolizing the corporate culture that has distinguished the bank as an attractive and multiple award-winning employer for many years. In particular, the basic ideas of fairness and partnership form the foundations of its high level of customer orientation – with appreciative interaction and simple solutions in its customers' interests (Bundesverband der Deutschen Volksbanken und Raiffeisenbanken, n.d.).

Learning from the best – learning culture and learning journeys

However, it is still not enough to know what you want to achieve. Rather, the question of "how" must be answered on a daily basis. What better way is there to do this than to learn from the best in terms of "how" and to adapt this knowledge for one's own actions?

For this reason, annual learning journeys for both management and employees have been conducted for several years. Companies outside the financial sector are mainly visited. Companies that are known for their outstanding achievements, such as corporate culture or customer delight, are chosen. One example is the learning journey at Zappos, an American online retailer specializing in fashion with a unique corporate culture based on the principles of holocracy and, above all, with one of the highest Net Promoter Scores in the world. Customers are even helped to purchase goods that the company itself does not carry from other companies – customer delight is the primary goal. This process leads to WOW moments for their customers, who did not expect this support. TeamBank AG, e.g., has translated the experience into so-called "WOW cards." Customer service employees use them to send personalized, handwritten cards as a follow-up to a phone call. Generally, every customer contact has an occasion, such as a name change for a wedding or financial challenges due to illness. Seeing the processing incident and – even more importantly – the person behind it, and showing this through a handwritten personal card in the follow-up to a conversation, surprises many customers and triggers consistently positive reactions.

Employees – the team makes the difference

The essential insight provided by learning journeys is as trivial as it is challenging. The culture, mindset and behavior of employees make good companies outstanding.

What does this look like at TeamBank AG? Team orientation is part of the company's DNA, not just because of the company name "TeamBank." Its employees are offered plenty of scope to act self-reliantly in a modern environment. Colleagues are entrepreneurial co-creators in an outstanding team. Therefore, there are many opportunities to set individual priorities and professionalize oneself in new work areas. Thanks to delayering hierarchies and fast decision-making processes, every employee can take responsibility for projects and drive them forward at any time.

The open and dynamic corporate culture enables professional proximity and easier communication. The focus is on the professional expertise of the employees, and having them address each other by their first names characterizes the interaction between them (a short explanation: In Germany, surnames are usually used, which creates more formal interaction in the work environment). At the TeamBarCamp, which takes place twice a year, employees can bring up topics they are working on or would like to work on. Employees vote together to decide which topics they consider relevant and should be presented. One example here is that an employee from the sales management department gave a presentation on the topic of "happiness." Interactive formats, such as fishbowl sessions, also encourage questions and ideas to be addressed directly to the teams, just as they are to the board and management – not necessarily something you would expect at a bank employee event.

This team orientation also reflects the bank's one common corporate goal. Instead of individual targets, all TeamBankers are measured in the context of the same three equally important components – first choice, portfolio, and profit before tax. The key aspect "first choice" primarily reflects the development of customer satisfaction through the Net Promoter Score, which is measured monthly across the entire customer process and made transparent to everyone. In this way, the actions of an internal auditor, an IT software developer, or a member of the Executive Board are also measured in the context of customer delight, emphasizing the intended sustainable orientation toward service excellence.

5. Now concretely: What does the translation of the values look like?

Internal impact of service excellence orientation – living and exemplifying values

The positive impact of the bank's service excellence orientation toward its employees can also be observed and measured in the long term. Employee satisfaction as well as the engagement index, which is surveyed yearly, reflect the team's internal delight and commitment to what they do every day. In order to constantly integrate new impulses into work, conventional company instruments are explicitly questioned, revised, and changed in addition to the topics already presented, such as the TeamBarCamp or the "first name" culture. For example, there is a "no dress code" at head-quarters, which is untypical for a bank. Additionally, the travel expense guideline has been eliminated and not replaced. Here, acting according to the guiding principle "We travel appropriately" has been passed on to the employees as their responsibility and is entirely in line with the positive image of humanity. The step of giving trust as a company is not something that can be taken for granted. Naturally, there were reservations and uncertainties about making the change. Letting go and relinquishing control is not an easy step to take. It is, therefore, even more pleasing that travel costs have not increased but have even been slightly reduced (before the pandemic). The responsible approach is clearly visible and represents the basis for a further transfer of responsibilities.

It is not just about putting on customer glasses, but seeing through the eyes of the customer

In order to actively adopt the customer perspective, TeamBank AG is also increasingly using design thinking methods and principles to actively involve customers in new developments. In addition to conventional concepts such as customer surveys, there are customer conferences in which real customers are regularly involved in idea development and feedback. There are also formats where employees explicitly develop solutions to topics they have selected themselves, share their experiences at the TeamBarCamp, and integrate them into their everyday work. "Family & Friends" phases, sounding boards with partners and banks, and much more have also become firmly established in the projects. Every piece of feedback and every experience you receive is a gift, especially the critical ones.

Translating the philosophy "carefree" into the thinking and actions of customer and partner dialog services

One concrete example of bringing the customer-centric mindset to life was the customer and partner service center "one contact – the solution" and "100+1." About four years ago, the employees started to make the vision "carefree" an authentic experience for customers. Several learning journeys preceded this project. These, coupled with the employees' own customer experiences, formed the starting point. The core questions were, "What do customers really want when they contact TeamBank AG? And how can the problem be solved directly at the first contact?"

Accordingly, customer service focuses on the "why" of a customer re-quest. In other words, the aim is not, e.g., just to implement the demand for a payment break directly and as quickly as possible, but to understand why the customer wants this. What problem is actually behind the need? Through this customer dialog, colleagues evaluate with the customer whether this is the best way to solve the problem or whether other options could solve the customer's problem even better. Together, the bank and the customer seek and find the most promising solution in genuine consultation. It is essential to find the solution during the initial contact according to the spirit of "one contact – the solution."

How has this claim affected day-to-day work? The basis of such a method is that employees have extensive and holistic knowledge about the products and services and that they also have the skills to exploit it – in other words, they are given a greater degree of freedom and are able to act on this. As a result, specifications for the average length of telephone calls and standardized call guidelines, e.g., have been abolished. The guideline "a call lasts as long as it takes," is not necessarily standard market practice.

Equally important is dealing with the customer at eye level. Because even if the costs in the context of service are often not explicitly discussed or priced, customers do not just pay for the product. The services provided before the contract is signed and, in particular, the services after the agreement are an integral part of an overall customer journey and create lasting customer delight. By offering these holistic solutions, the bank has expanded the scope and intensity of training courses in parallel. Some full-time internal trainers accompany the teams on an ongoing and individual basis and repeatedly provide feedback and impetus for real customer meetings – a daily form of "training on the job."

These two building blocks – how the customers' wishes are handled on the one hand and the empowerment and freedom of action of employees on the other – add up to a more positive customer experience, which customers reward with loyalty. It is an investment in the future and in customer loyalty, which pays off for the company in the medium term. At TeamBank AG, this is measured by the so-called Net Promoter Score or NPS for short.

The Net Promoter Score for the economic evaluation of customer and service orientation

The Net Promoter Score (NPS) is a key figure that reflects a consumer's willingness to recommend a company to others and thus provides information about customer satisfaction and loyalty. Many companies in various industries already use the measurement method worldwide, which makes it easier to compete with new competitors such as Amazon in this critical respect. The NPS is measured by using a short, standardized survey (two questions). Applying an eleven-point scale (from very unlikely to very likely), it first asks customers to rate how likely they are to recommend a company. Generally, the respondents are counted as critics, passively satisfied, or promoters depending on the value given. The ratio resulting from the calculation (percentage of promoters – percentage of critics) of all feedback can range between -100 and +100. The second question asks for the main reason for the evaluation and shows what is already going well and where there is potential for improvement. The NPS is surveyed daily by telephone.

Of course, this focus on service excellence takes time and costs money, but it pays off for both employees and customers. After every contact, the customer is asked, "Was I able to solve your problem?" This first-solution rate has risen significantly in recent years, averaging 90 percent. The positive effects are measurable by the NPS. In addition, they are also noticeable in the back office through a reduced necessity to rework efforts in response to customer inquiries. For example, the NPS for TeamBank AG has increased significantly by 9 points across the entire customer process since 2017, from 39 to 48 (see Figure 1). The goal here is to continue on this path consistently.

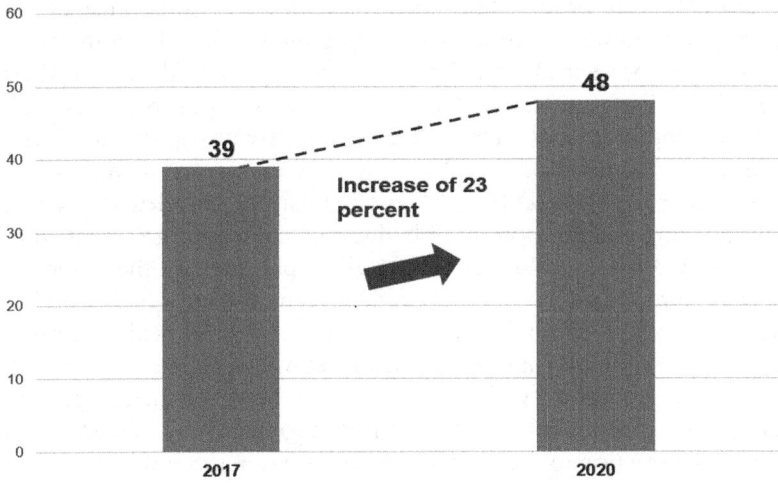

Fig. 1: *Positive development of the Net Promoter Score by 23 percent since 2017 (source: TeamBank AG, 2021b)*

Impact of the COVID-19 pandemic on the Net Promoter Score

The COVID-19 pandemic that hit Germany and the rest of the world in the spring of 2020 did not stop at the credit industry. It even intensified existing trends such as digitalization and its consequences. Generally, at such a time it is conceivable that a company would reduce its provision of excellent services, which would certainly incur expenses – however, this would be the wrong way to go.

Even during the crisis – in which requests for flexible installment plan changes tripled at peak times – the bank's NPS again improved on the previous year. Most feedback from TeamBank AG customers explicitly referring to the service it provided during the pandemic was positive – in this context, the assistance provided in the event of financial bottlenecks was particularly appreciated. However, the most frequently cited reasons, for both positive and negative assessments, did not change due to the COVID-19 crisis. Positive mentions are made in the context of fast payouts and processing, good advice, and straightforwardness.

Service excellence and COVID-19 – seriousness of action shows itself in challenging times

The general culture of trust has shown itself to be a strong pillar of the company, even during the pandemic. During the first lockdown in spring 2020, up to 98 percent of TeamBank AG's colleagues worked from their home offices – from one day to the next. This step was possible because all TeamBank employees had already been equipped with laptops and headsets for years. TeamBank AG had such a good experience with this step that even after the COVID-19 crisis, the regulations on teleworking and mobile working will be more flexible due to a company agreement from June 2020. According to this agreement, all employees have the chance to work from home or on the go for up to 60 percent of their weekly working hours. It is not the hierarchy but the team that decides which scope is appropriate. TeamBank considers hybrid meetings to be the new normal. "Our easyCredit location will always remain a house of interaction and exchange," communicated the Board of Management in mid-2020. This statement is a reaction to the experiences and needs of the employees.

The company's managers also decided and communicated very early on that there would be no layoffs or short-time work. "We are coping with the crisis under our own steam and need the entire team to stand by our customers and partners." This decision was not a matter of course. After all, TeamBank AG's business with its main product, easyCredit, an installment loan for consumers, also declined due to COVID-19. A key reason for this was people's anxiety and the associated general decline in consumption (Statistisches Bundesamt, n.d.).

The same applies for customers – TeamBank AG has maintained its consistent customer orientation. Thus, especially in customer service provision by telephone and chat, the motto, "we lend our customers a personal ear" was acted upon. The average customer conversations lasted longer than before the crisis, especially in the first months of the pandemic. The aim was to understand the customers and their concerns and fears and listen to them before solving their problems. What helped here was a very timely increase in the customer service center with internal staff who had already worked there in the past or were trained and then deployed there.

However, specific measures that go beyond the legal requirements for deferrals were also implemented. One example of this is payment relief: The bank supported customers who were affected by short-time working or unemployment due to the pandemic with additional, flexible, and unbureaucratic payment facilities (TeamBank AG, 2021b).

6. Conclusion – the journey continues

Even though TeamBank AG has already introduced many methods and instruments in recent years and lives them on a daily basis, this can only be an intermediate step. In addition to the NPS, audits for service excellence have also been carried out for years to assess the current situation regularly. The focus here is not on gaining the certificate but on conducting the audit process. After all, service excellence is a continuous journey in which the current service must be scrutinized again and again, be evaluated by external feedback, and be continuously further developed.

At the same time, customers' wishes and requirements change. Even experiences that surprised or exceeded expectations the first time are taken for granted as new standards the next time. Expectations are rising, and it is essential to meet and exceed them repeatedly to be successful with excellent service in the long term. Standing still and resting on past successes is not an option.

Bibliography

Bundesverband der Deutschen Volksbanken und Raiffeisenbanken (n.d.). About us: Cooperative Financial Network, https://www.bvr.de/p.nsf/index.xsp, accessed 01/10/2022.

DIN SPEC 77224:2011–07 (2011). Achieving customer delight through service excellence, Berlin, https://www.din.de/de/wdc-beuth:din21:142853363, accessed 01/10/2022.

ISO 23592:2021 (2021). Service excellence: Principles and model, Geneva, https://www.iso.org/standard/76358.html, accessed 02/15/2022.

Statistisches Bundesamt (n.d.). COVID-19 leads to a decline in private consumption expenditure in 2020, https://www.destatis.de/Europa/EN/Topic/Economy-Finance/PrivateConsumption.html, accessed 01/10/2022.

TeamBank AG (2021a). Management report of TeamBank AG 2020, https://www.teambank.de/wp-content/uploads/2021/06/TeamBank_GB_2020_WEB.pdf, accessed 01/10/2022.

TeamBank AG (2021b). Internal document, accessed 02/15/2022.

Service excellence culture

A highlight in the hotel industry: Creating a vital service excellence culture and anchoring it for the long term

Philippe D. Clarinval

Management summary

Tourism and the hotel industry are particularly facing challenging and uncertain times now. In order to survive in the market, financial resources and a culture that is in harmony with the company's right to exist are needed. It is important to ask oneself the right questions regarding strategic balance and to develop an adapted management style in order to anchor a vital culture for the long term. The latter means that leaders must always closely align their vision, values, and goals with the organization. The prudent application of transactional and transformational leadership can help them inspire their team, implement a relevant organizational culture, depending on the prerequisite that they have a vision, and revise their thought patterns.

1. Why is a service excellence culture needed at all?

The question above may seem rhetorical, but it has to be asked – and it entails further considerations. Do all hotels need such a culture? What does service excellence mean anyway? These are questions I will return to later.

The hotel industry, but equally all other companies in the service industry, has a remarkable impact on the global economy in terms of social and economic development. Services dominate the most innovative economies, and therefore a focus on service quality, "service excellence," is crucial for each company's competitiveness.

The concept of service quality has been around for a long time. A service excellence culture should be recognized within an organizational culture because it sets the tone and serves external and internal consumers. A good and vibrant service culture becomes a way of life within a company by referring to the organizational culture and the manners, behavior, and values of both employees and the company. A service excellence culture is relevant to a hotel because only when there is one do employees develop and flourish, have a positive attitude towards the team, and provide a basis for delivering valued services and creating a unique selling point.

Development of a model for a service excellence culture in the hotel industry

The design of a world-class and inspiring experience for a guest forms the heart of the service excellence model. In order to achieve service excellence in a hotel context, an ideal customer experience has to be designed that is relevant to the guests and will possibly even change their consumer behavior. Following such a practical paradigm, each hotel can create values, manifestos, or service guarantees that illustrate its guests' and employees' experience at it. The paradigm is used to design an excellent guest experience. One of the foundational models is built on all the enmeshed elements in the service chain. The goal is not only to ensure that the internal processes and the customer journey are ideal, but also the attitude and training of the employees, who should experience a similar valuable employee experience as the guests. Employee satisfaction has been overtaken by employee engagement. Trends even predict that employee experience is the new keyword for good foundations on which a relevant service excellence culture can be developed.

2. Service excellence at the Carlton Hotel St. Moritz

The Carlton Hotel in St. Moritz is one of the legendary hotels that have shaped the history of the Grand hotel business and continue to do so today. Guests' expectations of this "Leading Hotel in the World" with its 60 five-star suites are correspondingly high, but the employees also take up their posts with great expectations.

The Carlton Hotel St. Moritz plays in the top league and has top-class competitors in St. Moritz and other famous vacation destinations such as Gstaad, Courchevel, Kitzbühel, or Aspen.

When the prestigious Forbes Travel Guide rewarded the hotel with the maximum number of stars in 2017 for the first time, as one of only a few hotels, we knew we were on the right path. What is this path? It is characterized by the ambition to fulfil as many formal star criteria as possible and to consider the emotional factor. So, what is the point if we meet all the criteria presented in a questionnaire but do not show warm-heartedness? A guest wants to be perceived, to feel his or her needs are understood, and the hotel staff to show appropriate formality or composure. Besides this, the hotel should clearly demonstrate that it is thoroughly proficient in implementing all the background processes that lead to service excellence. In addition to the standards and the emotions, there must also be a willingness to act, to do everything to delight a guest or a colleague. Without presence of mind, anticipation, and action, no sterile standards and no well-intentioned emotions will help.

This line of thought should accompany all service organizations, not just the top hotel industry. However, the complexity of guest service excellence is probably most evident in the hotel industry because the production–consumption continuum, i.e., the time between service provision and consumption, is usually simultaneous. The hospitality industry is still seen too much as a craft rather than a form of interplay between craft and science. In addition, there are often so many people involved that a manager is unable to face this complexity and therefore cannot adapt his or her way of thinking to the realities in the organization.

3. Shaping a culture of service excellence

Hotels can create an excellent service culture by using the quality and volume of service as key differentiators. They can create a culture where all people are encouraged to improve, contribute ideas, and implement appropriate action. The hotel's service culture ensures that all employees are motivated and committed to constantly improving quality. Guests will then become more loyal and satisfied and recommend the hotel to others, boosting profits and growth.

To create an excellent service culture, you can apply three strategic phases. The first step is the right mindset. When all members of an organization have the right mindset, they demonstrate commitment and responsibility. They can behave appropriately in different service scenarios and have a good sense of how to assess situations correctly.

In the second phase, they acquire the necessary skills for delivering excellent services. These are technical skills that both incorporate standards and encourage thinking along the way to deliver a unique service experience, understand the customer's needs, and ultimately create vibrant customer relationships. For example, the guest who complains of a headache at dinner gets a bottle of peppermint oil delivered to the room.

The third phase is about making guest service excellence enduring. For this, we need a structured process that ensures that every touchpoint is followed by an outstanding experience. This process is cross-divisional and thus breaks down the silos of long-established organizational charts.

3.1 Managers' responsibility

The leadership team plays a critical role in creating an excellent service culture but is often the weakest link in the value chain. Top leadership determines the vision and purpose of the hotel or service business and focuses on its organization, removing obstacles and rewarding successes. Leaders must ensure that the value proposition is upheld throughout the organization.

However, maintenance, organization, and management are very static. A general manager is responsible for ensuring that specific standards are respected, but, as a leader, he must also make a vision visible to his employees.

At the Carlton Hotel St. Moritz, we naturally look at all key performance indicators and other metrics, but this focus does not make us shortsighted. We also try to combine standards with emotions and anticipation and act accordingly. There is no point in meeting the standards perfectly but not allowing emotions. Therefore, managers' responsibility is to walk the tightrope within the culture, and create and consolidate the link between *standards* and *emotions*. Both must coexist. Respecting only one or the other unfailingly leads to a devaluation of the service: If we respect only the standards, the service we provide will appear sterile, and if we show only emotions, we will look like lovable but not very competent improvisation artists. Both principles must be harmoniously intertwined. Service excellence is created when standards, emotions, and benevolent anticipation meet and create a common cause. Ultimately, this is also where the difference between service and hospitality is found because "service is black and white; hospitality is colorful."

3.2 The value chain of the hotel

The most important thing for managers is to define their own value chain.

The top premise is to determine the company's *purpose*, the "golden circle" (Sinek, 2011). In other words, every leader must provide answers to the questions "What does my company do?", "How does my company do this?" and, most importantly, "Why does my company do this?" The "why" answers the question of purpose. What is the organization's right to exist? Watch out, by the way: we must not confuse the "*what*" with the "*why.*" The why is always paramount. Profit certainly is not – profit is the positive byproduct.

The Carlton Hotel St. Moritz's purpose is "to give time back its value – through conscious enjoyment and experiences that will be remembered." Broken down to the idea of service, this means in concrete terms that our service should be so excellent and seamless that the guest is not allowed to have any unfulfilled wishes and can concentrate entirely on him- or herself and those closest to him or her. A queue at the concierge's desk or at reception? Unacceptable! Moreover, the guests should find inspiration during their stay and thus experience inner enrichment.

To really live excellence, leaders must take on critical roles. They embody the purpose, set the direction, and live the vision. This proposition sounds easier than it is. First, the vision requires a moral commitment and a shared understanding of what the vision means to everyone. Second, it takes a willingness to adhere to the vision. Third, employees need to take the initiative to implement the vision. Finally, the hotel's staff should focus on never losing sight of the vision and having the tenacity to pursue it.

In addition to *purpose* and *vision*, the second link in the chain is strategy (Trevor, 2019). What is the hotel doing to embody the purpose and how can it promote service excellence through its strategy? What is needed even more, and what should be stopped? To answer these questions, it takes sincerity and honesty, not political phrases that you want to hear or that you have to pass on. It takes hard-hitting and blunt honesty – with oneself and one's environment.

This honesty then also shines through the organization. The saying "get the wrong people off the bus, the right people on the bus, and in the right seats" is true, but you have to know which bus it is, which direction it is going, and who the driver is. Analyzing the organization is as important as asking yourself what competence it takes to guarantee service excellence. The standards and the technical competence should usually already be there. The decisive point is that the *culture* that prevails in the company is the binder between the elements of *purpose, vision, strategy, organization,* and *competence*. Culture includes the unwritten and sometimes yet written laws of how employees treat each other and guests. The company's culture shapes perceivable enthusiasm, ambition, or commitment. It defines how the compelling service vision is lived and how it generally depends on the managers. Indeed, they play a critical role in engaging, onboarding, focusing, and inspiring throughout the organization. Visible and active leadership involvement is crucial to creating an excellent service culture. Managers must emphasize the importance of being visibly engaged and viewing the creation of that culture as a holistic process. However, care must be taken to apply the right kind of leadership.

3.3 Transactional or transformational leadership

Setting rules, monitoring that standards are met, or prescribing structures usually characterize strict management or, to a certain extent, *transactional leadership*, which is based on performance exchange for praise or other gratification, i.e., an exchange between managers and employees. Employees are given a clear target and they have to know the rules to receive praise for their performance and avoid being reprimanded. Transactional leadership is undoubtedly necessary to respect standards and ensure consistency in certain situations. However, transactional leadership rarely inspires employees to strive for excellence.

Managers must be role models in promoting an excellent service culture; they must understand why such service is essential in the organization and act accordingly. So again, the "why" is more important than the "how." Leaders lead in a transformational way by doing the right thing, always motivating, to improve service excellence.

The pillars of transformational leadership (Bass and Avolio, 1994) being practiced at the Carlton St. Moritz are based on how leaders view their employees as individuals and personalities rather than functions. Employees are intellectually stimulated not to remain in the status quo but to question it to a healthy degree and contribute to improving service through these re-evaluations. In addition, they should be inspired and motivated to push their own boundaries and see the hotel as a big picture, rather than just the sum of its individual departments. Leaders can inspire and motivate by developing a positive, altruistic, and charismatic leadership style.

A hotel can use five exemplary leadership practices to improve guest service, which is also illustrated by Kouzes and Posner (2017). One of these is leading by example. Leaders must have a vision, be credible, and believe in themselves. The shared vision must reflect an exciting picture of the future and be admirable. Leaders in hotels are usually department heads or supervisors. They must be able to question processes, and challenge and find new approaches to solutions that align with strategy and, ultimately, purpose. They must be empowered to act in the spirit of purpose and the guest to foster innovative ideas for service excellence. Finally, leaders must have an encouraging heart that provides reassurance to all. Approaches like "Don't give me problems, give me solutions!" can be dangerous because they intimidate employees and steer them away from the purpose and down the path of defensiveness or even cover-ups.

3.4 The importance of work in the context of service excellence

At the Carlton Hotel St. Moritz, we try to elevate leadership to a meta-level that still exists too rarely in the hotel industry. In other words, we ask ourselves what the main reasons for working together are, and what motivates our employees in an economic sector that, for the most part, has a pretty bad reputation as an employer – and not just since the COVID-19 crisis.

The answers we found paint a picture of a mature employee:
First, their *competence* enables them to do their work according to their own quality standards. Then there is the *freedom of choice* to do this work in their own way – they certainly also follow standards, but the bottom line is that they give their work their own personal touch. They are also driven by the *progress* they see and by satisfaction in their (and therefore our) excellent performance. However, the most important reason for them to work in the hotel industry seems to be an awareness of the *importance* of their work. Does leadership play a role in this context? Can leadership make people aware of the importance of their work? One might think that transactional leaders attach little meaning or significance to work and that transformational leaders are the only recipe for success. However, this is not the case. Meaning is a very intrinsic factor that every employee carries within them and sees for themselves, a delicate flower, so to speak, that needs to be nurtured and whose beauty needs to be praised at times. A poor management style destroys the meaning of their work in seconds, and thoughts such as "Why am I doing this anyway?" quickly become predominant. Therefore, in the service industry, managers must be aware of their behavior and their words' negative effects. Employees must be able to take pride in their work; they should be able to see the meaning behind it and be encouraged to do so. Their work influences other people. Therefore, it should always be associated positively, inspire, and perhaps even change less than optimal behavior for the better. A sommelier who shows the guest something unknown or surprising can inspire. The concierge who anticipates wishes lives the company's purpose and can touch guests emotionally.

The role of a leader is to hold up a mirror and encourage the team to self-reflect. Recognizing the meaning of one's own work is not synonymous with completing a task. Often, employees do not even recognize the importance of their work and do not consciously perceive the intended corporate culture around them if no one takes them by the hand and makes them aware of it. The "no-news-are-good-news" manager should therefore have had its day.

3.5 Awareness in the context of a service excellence culture

At the Carlton Hotel St. Moritz, we consequently cultivate a culture of constant feedback and radical honesty. We give permanent feedback and feedforward. We enjoy our work, are there for each other, and try to enrich our guests and colleagues through cordiality – and the best part is that we consciously choose and live this attitude.

Choosing that setting is a cognitive process. It is a process that is consciously activated in the front part of the brain, the prefrontal cortex, which requires trust, creativity, and warmth from everyone involved. In an often highly competitive environment, mindfulness, self-reflection, and alignment of personal and corporate values are essential to creating a sustainable culture. The way staff deal with each other, their voluntary commitment to the highest quality and a certain unwillingness to compromise sometimes require a change in personal habits. That is the reason why neuroscience is essential. Which micro-habits help to *live* – not just *perform* – service excellence? Does the attitude of striving for the highest quality and the greatest hospitality become something you hold in your heart or just an abstract concept in a job description? As long as it is only the latter, you cannot talk about values and even less about culture.

It is the job of leadership to recognize and encourage good behavior. Just as parents always demand "Please!" and "Thank you!" from their children, leaders should encourage and reward habits, ways of thinking, intellectual curiosity, ambition, healthy pride, and the pursuit of improvement. A situation's complexity, volatility, uncertainty, and ambiguity also require employees and leaders to constantly ask themselves what can be learned and what additional steps need to be taken along the way. What are tomorrow's customer needs, trends, and expectations? The conscious thought process of the right to exist and to what extent the strategy, competence, staff, and culture are in line with the company's purpose are indispensable.

4. The impact of COVID-19 on service excellence

The coronavirus crisis has thrown the global hotel industry off track. The markets changed within a short time, and guests' expectations quickly focused on generous space and security measures. Of course, this change has also affected the Carlton Hotel St. Moritz with its international guest structure and exclusive guest niche. Our guests were no longer allowed to travel from one day to the next, although their personal need to do so was unbroken.

What has not changed are the values that a company should live. Our unwillingness to compromise on quality and safety remains. The only thing that needs to change is that the leader has to understand the details even better, recognize the complexity of the task, and continue to embody the hotel's vision. Unfortunately, focus and tenacity often give way to panic and the urge to do something in order to turn everything around. One may – one must – ask whether the old business model is still appropriate, whether lethargy has not set in in recent years, or how to reinvent oneself. However, the right to exist should remain a key feature, and the company has to retain its moral compass. The times after COVID-19 will be very challenging for a long time to come – not because guests are staying away, but because employees are becoming more selective. They are looking more critically at companies' intrinsic values and are willing to try new ways of doing things. When the economy is doing poorly, education does well, and companies must be prepared to offer something new because good workers have evolved in the meantime. The days of employee satisfaction are gone, as is employee engagement—"employee experience" is the new magic word. Employees want enrichment for the time they give to the organization, and it is up to leaders to meet their teams individually, and to stimulate and inspire them.

5. Conclusion

Because of the intrinsic multidimensionality of the hotel industry and its multifaceted nature, it needs a solid cultural foundation to survive. Moreover, the volatile, complex, uncertain, and ambiguous external world does not make this any easier. The answer to the original question of whether service excellence is needed is "it depends." It depends on what kind of hotel industry you are talking about. In the exalted and traditional hotel industry, the clear answer is that it does not tolerate mediocrity. However, when considering new concepts that may be more casual, the question remains. In any case, there needs to be a coherent service that is in line with the company's right to exist. A culture of service excellence is an essential part of corporate culture, and it is definitely needed to avoid just wandering around. Is it easy? No! Does it take time? Absolutely! No manager can change a corporate culture overnight and anchor it for the long term, but it is possible if you have the necessary persistence and vision. In summary, one could argue that leadership is becoming even more complex and that leaders need to be more sophisticated, nuanced, and thoughtful. There is no longer one-size-fits-all leadership (Northouse, 2007). It is up to leaders and their ability to understand this three-dimensionality to secure a company's long-term success. They have a ripple effect on the entire culture of the organization.

Bibliography

Bass, B.M. and Avolio, B.J. (1994). Improving organizational effectiveness through transformational leadership, Thousand Oaks, CA: Sage Publications.

Kouzes, J.M. and Posner, B. (2017). Leadership challenge: How to make extraordinary things happen in organizations, Wiley & Sons, Incorporated, John.

Northouse, P.G. (2007). Leadership: Theory and practice, 6th ed., Thousand Oaks, CA: Sage Publishing.

Sinek, S. (2011). Start with why: How great leaders inspire everyone to take action, East Rutherford: Portfolio/Penguin.

Trevor, J. (2019). Align: A leadership blueprint for aligning enterprise purpose, strategy and organization, London: Bloomsbury Business.

Employee engagement

Employee engagement requires motivation and qualification: The use of blended learning to implement service excellence

Matthias Gouthier, Matthias Raquet

Management summary

"Service business is people business." This statement is particularly true for technical services, where service technicians and their commitment to their work at a customer's site are decisive for a company's long-term success. In order to implement the concept of service excellence at oneservice AG and its subsidiaries in Germany and abroad right from the start, the authors created the Service Excellence Academy. In the onboarding stage, service technicians learn the essentials of service excellence by attending appealing e-learning sessions. Subsequently, the company's use of further training measures as part of a blended learning approach ensures the lasting implementation of service excellence. In the end, the resulting customer delight confirms the success of the concept.

1. Employee engagement as a central element of service excellence

In academia and business, employee engagement has always been regarded as a crucial success factor for service companies (e.g., Markos and Sridevi, 2010). This finding is especially true if a company wants to differentiate itself from its competitors through excellent services, as is the focus of the concept of service excellence (Gouthier et al., 2012). Generally, this insight is explicitly expressed, e.g., in the European standard CEN/TS 16880:2015, in which employee engagement is considered a trigger of outstanding customer experiences and customer delight in the cause–effect chain of service excellence (see Figure 1).

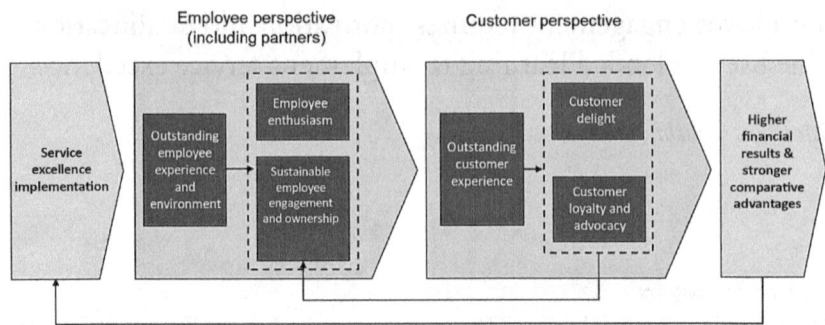

Fig. 1: Employee engagement as a trigger of outstanding customer experience and customer delight (source: based on CEN/TS 16880:2015, p. 8).

Considering the development of previous standards on service excellence, employee engagement is always a key influencing factor in providing excellent services that delight customers. Even in DIN SPEC 77224:2011, the explanations on employees as a company's key resource represent the most comprehensive sub-element of the entire standard. In its further development at the European level, CEN/TS 16880:2015, the employee is also the main guarantor of success. Finally, employee engagement represents one of the nine elements of achieving service excellence in ISO 23592:2021. This element calls for an organization to use human resource processes and tools to promote and sustain shared values, beliefs, and practices to create outstanding customer experiences. The relevance of employee engagement is expressed here simply by the fact that it is a requirement that must be present in an organization ("shall"). If a company wants to be certified according to ISO 23592:2021, it must demonstrate compliance with this requirement. Furthermore, ISO 23592:2021 requires that management "should" ensure that employees are enthusiastic and motivated to deliver outstanding customer experiences and delight their customers.

What is employee engagement? The term is clearly defined in ISO 23592:2021. According to this, employee engagement is the "extent to which employees are committed to the organization, feel enthusiastic about their job and put discretionary effort into their work" (ISO 23592:2021, p. 3). The fact that high employee engagement is associated with higher company, team, and/or employee performance levels has been proven by various studies (e.g., Markos and Sridevi, 2010). One of the best-known approaches to measuring employee engagement is the so-called "Gallup Engagement Index," which shows how each individual is connected to a company and its respective goals (Gallup, 2021). Gallup's

Q12 approach of measuring employee engagement is based on employees' responses to 12 actionable workplace elements that are linked to performance outcomes, including productivity, customer service, quality, retention, safety, and profit. The index provides a comprehensive view of the workplace by outlining the percentage of engaged, disengaged, and actively disengaged employees. Among other things, it reveals that workgroups with a high level of engagement – the upper 25 percent – compared to workgroups with low engagement levels – the bottom 25 percent – have, on average, ten percent higher customer engagement levels or ten percent higher customer loyalty rates (Gallup, 2022).

2. Service excellence in action at oneservice

oneservice AG was launched in July 2017 by the authors of this article and other co-founders. It is a global and vendor-independent service company offering completely managed service solutions and consulting services for life science, diagnostics, and medical devices. It addresses the emerging trend and needs of outsourcing technical services. oneservice's leadership team is comprised of industry experts who have served global enterprises, regional and local companies, and government agencies with consulting, learning, business process, and outsourcing services for more than 25 years.

According to the oneservice business model, it is essential to think outside the box for the individual customer to align service solutions with the fundamental needs of any business – whether the company wants to extend its reach and coverage, complement its service offers, provide dedicated or shared technical support, or serve customers anywhere and on any device. oneservice enables customers to receive cost-efficient service with the highest quality standards. Therefore, oneservice focuses on implementing a cost-efficient service excellence strategy (Wirtz and Zeithaml, 2018). As a strategic and long-term partner, oneservice supports the fundamental employee, customer, and partner relationships that drive customers' business. This process requires the deployment of service technicians who see themselves as problem-solvers rather than mere fitters. With the perfect blend of technical and social and communication skills, oneservice specialists handle the most difficult situations, complicated issues, and hectic days with a smile to ensure their company's reputation for delivering superior quality.

The company's headquarters, oneservice AG, is located in Feusisberg in the canton of Schwyz in Switzerland. In addition, oneservice has offices in

Darmstadt, Dallas, and Manchester, from which the European and North American markets as well as the British and Irish markets are served.

From the very beginning, one of the central focuses of oneservice has been the implementation of service excellence. This dedication is explicitly expressed within oneservice's corporate strategy, in both its vision and mission. Accordingly, the company's mission is to redefine service excellence with best-in-class services. This self-image must be instilled in the employees, which is especially possible during the onboarding phase. At the beginning of the employment relationship, employees are generally more open to new ideas. Consequently, one of the company's principles focuses on its employees. Thus, the basic understanding of oneservice concerning employees is as follows:

- Our employees are the key to success and the driving force behind every process and every partnership.
- Our global teams of experts are dedicated and passionate about understanding each customer's core business issues and tailoring our methodologies to meet the needs of our customers and their customers.
- We design customized solutions with our specialists and represent our customers in front of their customers.

Accordingly, the question that arose even before the company was founded was how the guiding principle of service excellence could be sustainably anchored within the company. As initiators and co-directors of the standardization activities, we integrated the findings from the standardization work directly and immediately into the design of the company's service excellence concept. The ISO 23592:2021 standard describes six sub-elements that are necessary to achieve employee engagement. According to ISO 23592:2021, these are:

1. Recruitment and induction of new employees
2. Continuous learning and development of employees
3. Feedback from customers at an employee or team level
4. Evaluation and assessment of employees
5. A recognition or acknowledgement system
6. An employee feedback mechanism

This article focuses on imparting the relevant knowledge, skills, and abilities on service excellence using a blended learning approach, specifically e-learning sessions.

3. The Service Excellence Academy

Even before the founding of oneservice AG, it was clear to the authors that the sustainable implementation of service excellence often fails due to the following three factors:

1. Lack of knowledge: Both management and employees need profound knowledge of service excellence and how this concept can be implemented.
2. Fear of high costs: Service excellence is a long-term investment and requires the commitment of resources.
3. Tight time: Building service excellence in a company takes time.

Therefore, the question was how to dismantle those three barriers in a company like oneservice. Even after oneservice AG had been founded, it was essential to raise the knowledge of the employees, who typically did not know the concept of service excellence when they were hired, to a qualified level as quickly as possible. For this reason, the Service Excellence Academy was created, initially as an internal company unit.

To overcome the first barrier, the knowledge gap, the authors first developed a simplified service excellence model based on both the CEN/TS 16880:2015 and ISO 23592:2021 standards, which identifies four dimensions (see Figure 2).

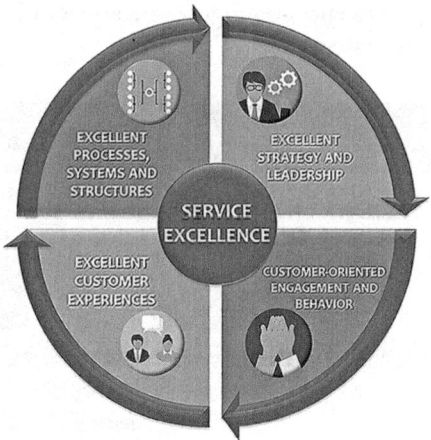

Fig. 2: The simplified service excellence model of the Service Excellence Academy (sources: based on CEN/TS 16880:2015 and ISO 23592:2021)

The two other barriers, i.e., cost and time issues, represent serious obstacles, especially for start-up companies, as was the case with oneservice in 2017 and 2018. The authors promptly realized the potential of e-learning sessions as an efficient and effective solution. E-learning sessions, especially when it comes to basic training, are associated with increases in efficiency and fundamentally with increases in effectiveness compared to classroom training (see Figure 3).

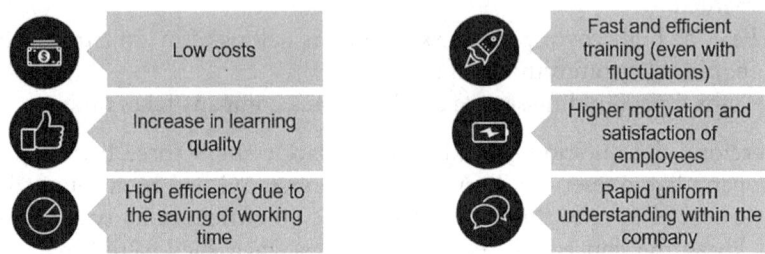

Fig. 3: Benefits of e-learning sessions (source: Service Excellence Academy, 2021)

Therefore, the development and use of e-learning sessions were a central starting point for setting up the Service Excellence Academy. These sessions make it possible to sensitize employees to the topic of service excellence and expand their knowledge in this respect, regardless of time and location. In addition, e-learning sessions, especially when integrated into a blended learning concept (see Figure 4), are ideally compatible with today's digitalization strategy.

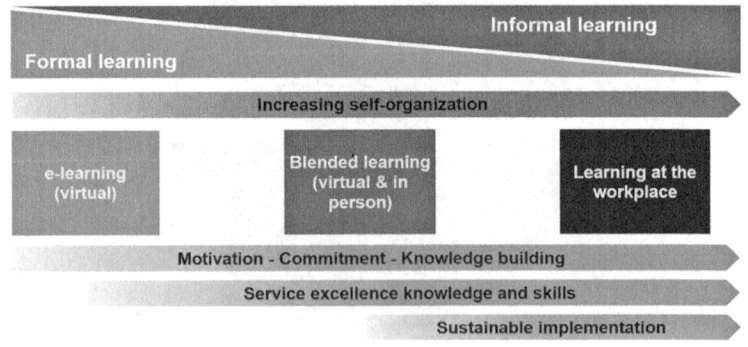

Fig. 4: Blended learning concept for service excellence (source: Service Excellence Academy, 2021)

The proportion of self-organization and informal learning steadily increases from e-learning to workplace learning. While e-learning is primarily about acquiring knowledge, workplace learning focuses on implementing real tasks.

A typical blended learning approach, as used by oneservice, consists of four phases (see Figure 5). First, the company creates a uniform basic understanding of service excellence by using e-learning sessions. In this phase, these sessions must be informative and entertaining. A British agency specializing in the production of e-learning sessions was involved in their development at oneservice. In addition, two professional actors were hired, a US actor for the English e-learning sessions and a German actor for their German counterparts. These initial investments have already paid off, as the satisfaction rates of the service technicians and all other oneservice employees with the e-learning sessions are very high. And the external customers who have booked the sessions so far have also been delighted at their quality.

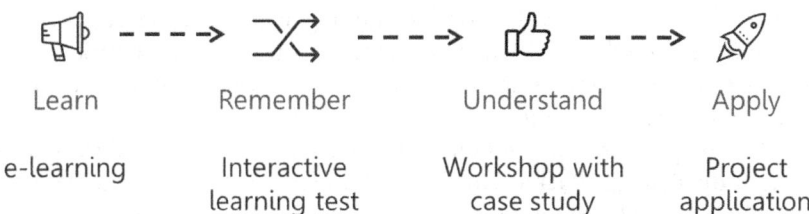

Learn	Remember	Understand	Apply
e-learning	Interactive learning test	Workshop with case study	Project application

Fig. 5: Typical sequence of a blended learning course on service excellence (source: Service Excellence Academy, 2021)

It is vital that the e-learning sessions are fun and that employees acquire relevant knowledge. Accordingly, an interactive learning test is used as a follow-up to the e-learning sessions to retain what has been learned in memory. This procedure represents the second phase of the blended learning concept of the Service Excellence Academy. In the third phase, the knowledge acquired so far is deepened once again. This is done in a workshop in which best practice case studies are used to ensure a better understanding of the content. The workshop can take place as a purely virtual or hybrid event, especially during the coronavirus pandemic, but also as a face-to-face event. Finally, the fourth phase rounds off the blended learning concept by focusing on applying what has been learned in a kind of project training event. Here, it is crucial to train the social and interaction skills of the employees to create moments of customer delight and thus also employee delight. In this way, skills and abilities can be trained that improve the recognition of and inquiry into customer wishes, professional communication, and professional interaction with customers (Barnes et al., 2011). Only if the knowledge gained on service excellence is incorporated into employees' day-to-day actions can such a qualification measure be described as a success. The positive effects on employees' customer orientation skills and the customer centricity of the entire company are proven by customer surveys of oneservice. Accordingly, the company's Net Promoter Score in the last customer survey reached +71 points.

4. Requirements for e-learning sessions on service excellence and its content

In any type of customer service, and thus also in technical service, employees play an essential role in satisfying and delighting customers. To this end, the e-learning sessions developed by the Service Excellence Academy can be used as tutorials to efficiently and effectively train employees to deliver excellent service. The online training is stimulating and easy to use, motivating adult learners and creating a meaningful educational experience. In addition, e-learning sessions can be easily embedded into a learning management system (LMS).

Ultimately, the sessions should enable effective, efficient, and thus satisfying individual goal achievement for the user – while at the same time providing ease of use, good interaction, clarity, good design, and visual appeal for learners (see Figure 6).

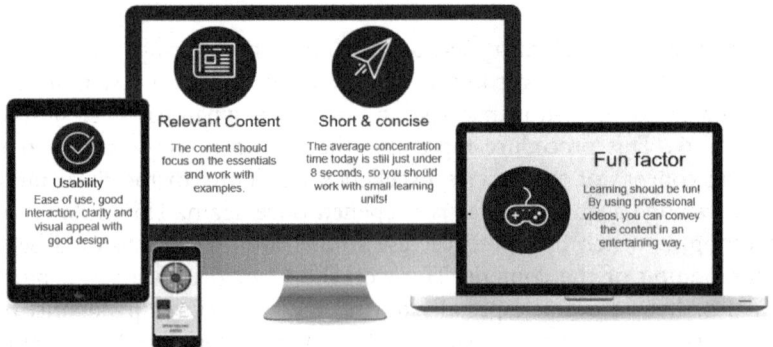

Fig. 6: Requirements for e-learning sessions (source: Service Excellence Academy, 2021)

The e-learning sessions on service excellence were produced in German and English to also allow employees in non-German-speaking countries to address the topic of service excellence. They consist of four modules with a total of 23 lessons. To avoid fatigue, the lessons are kept relatively short, around two to three minutes long. In total, the sessions last about 60 minutes.

The first module deals with general aspects of service excellence (dimension "Excellent strategy and leadership") and answers the following five questions in the individual lessons:

- Why is service excellence relevant?
- What is the difference between customer satisfaction and customer delight?
- What is the connection between service excellence and customer delight?
- What is the service excellence pyramid?
- How can service excellence be integrated into a company's vision, mission, and strategy?

The second module on service excellence focuses on employees and the service excellence culture practiced in the company. Accordingly, the lessons are dedicated to answering the following seven questions:

- How can the focus be consistently on the customer?
- What can an employee do to show the right attitude?
- How can employees interact with the customers authentically?
- What is the key to understanding customers?
- How should critical situations be handled?
- What can be done to provide a personal touch?
- How can a wow-effect be created?

Module 3 deals with the creation of excellent customer experiences. In seven lessons, the following questions are addressed in more detail:

- What is service design?
- What is the added value of generating personas?
- How can the customer journey be mapped?
- What is the Kano model?
- How can actionable ideas be developed?
- What is service prototyping?
- What is service blueprinting?

What to look for when designing excellent processes, systems, and structures is explained in more detail in module 4. The lessons are devoted to the following four questions:

- How can barriers to implementing service excellence be overcome?
- How should customer experiences be managed?
- How can internal service excellence be achieved?
- How can customer delight be measured?

These four modules provide employees with a general overview of and profound insights into the core content of service excellence. They provide a uniform knowledge base on how to anchor the concept of service excellence in a company with a lasting effect.

5. Conclusion

Technical service companies like oneservice AG and its subsidiaries especially benefit from the commitment of their employees. The customer is the focus of the company's efforts. To delight customers, the employees themselves must be passionate about their work. For customers, commitment is particularly evident in problematic situations. Here, the service technicians are able to convince the customer rationally and emotionally, not only through their technical expertise but also, above all, through their commitment and empathy. To continuously promote this employee commitment, oneservice relies on the concept of service excellence, which is communicated to all employees using e-learning sessions integrated into a blended learning concept. As is often the case with successful concepts that are initially used only internally, the next logical step was to offer these tools externally on the market via the Service Excellence Academy. The first customer projects are proof of our success.

Bibliography

Barnes, D.C., Ponder, N., and Dugar, K. (2011). Investigating the key routes to customer delight, Journal of Marketing Theory and Practice, 19(4), pp. 359–375.

CEN/TS 16880:2015 (2015). Service excellence: Creating outstanding customer experiences through service excellence, Brussels.

Gallup (2021). Gallup's employee engagement survey: Ask the right questions with the Q12 survey, https://www.gallup.com/workplace/356063/gallup-q12-employee-engagement-survey.aspx, accessed 09/05/2021.

Gallup (2022). What is employee engagement and how do you improve it?, https://www.gallup.com/workplace/285674/improve-employee-engagement-workplace.aspx, accessed 01/27/2022.

Gouthier, M.H.J., Giese, A. and Bartl, C. (2012). Service excellence models: A critical discussion and comparison, Managing Service Quality, 22(5), pp. 447–464.

ISO 23592:2021 (2021). Service excellence — Principles and model, Geneva.

Markos, S. and Sridevi, M.S. (2010). Employee engagement: The key to improving performance, International Journal of Business and Management, 5(12), pp. 89–96.

Service Excellence Academy (2021). From service management to service excellence: Implementation requires understanding and commitment, internal document, Darmstadt/Feusisberg.

Wirtz, J. and Zeithaml, V. (2018). Cost-effective service excellence, Journal of the Academy of Marketing Science, 46, pp. 59–80.

Understanding customer needs, expectations,
and desires

Customer experience management: Insights and recommendations from CX leaders

Juliane Köninger, Matthias Gouthier

Management summary

Customer experience management (CXM) has experienced a tremendous rise in status in recent years and represents a key success factor for companies nowadays. Nevertheless, comparatively little is known about the characteristics of successful CXM. To close this research gap, the authors conducted a qualitative, explorative study. The essential findings from numerous interviews with national and international CX leaders are described in this article.

1. Insights from an international best practice study

In research, the topic of customer experience (CX) has primarily been analyzed from the customer's perspective. The company's perspective, i.e., customer experience management (CXM), has mostly been neglected (Homburg et al., 2017). Therefore, the authors conducted a qualitative, explorative study to learn more about the implementation of CXM in practice and generate new scientific findings. The design and the key results of this study are presented in the following sections. For the qualitative study, the authors conducted 20 interviews with CX experts from well-known companies. The cross-sector study includes leading companies from financial services, telecommunications, IT, insurance, mobility, retail, tourism, and management consulting. Half of the companies are based in Germany, while the other CX experts come from the U.S., U.K., France, and Asia. The guided interviews were conducted in person, by phone, or via video call. 15 of the 20 experts report from an internal perspective, i.e. they are managers or employees of a company with, e.g., its own CX department and are intensively dedicated to the topic of CX. The other five experts come from consulting companies or service providers specializing in CX and CXM. Consequently, these experts have an external view of CXM. In this way, value-added insights regarding the use of CXM in companies were generated, which are the focus of this article. First, after a brief introduction, the relevance of the topic is depicted. Then, the positive effects of CXM are presented and summarized graphically. This description is followed by a discussion of the study's findings on the implementation of CXM and the creation of a positive CX. Finally, the success factors of CXM obtained in the interviews are illustrated.

1.1 Introduction to and relevance of CX

In today's economic context, which is characterized by intense competition and growing expectations, coupled with an apparent willingness to switch providers, loyal customers are essential for a company's long-term success. In order to maintain not only satisfied but also delighted and thus loyal customers, it is necessary to offer outstanding customer experiences. Positive customer experiences become a decisive differentiator and are highly relevant for customer acquisition and customer loyalty (Becker and Jaakkola, 2020). A study by Gartner (2019) indicates that in 2019, 67 percent of the companies surveyed primarily competed on the basis of CX – with an expected share of 86 percent for 2021. Furthermore, 77 percent of U.S. companies in another study indicate that improving CX will be either critical or very important to the business over the next three years (Qualtrics, 2020).

These statements regarding the relevance of CX were reinforced by our best practice study. One of the experts interviewed confirmed the current trend that, due to increasingly interchangeable products, many companies are no longer able to differentiate themselves from others through their products, but are able to do so very well by offering comprehensive services and outstanding support. Accordingly, companies are pursuing the objective of providing a superior CX to differentiate themselves from the competition. This view is consistent with the statement of another expert, "[...] competitive differentiation now derives from experiences. [...] in most industries, the reality is that people have roughly similar pricing and similar products, so what really differentiates one company from another is how easy it is to do business with them. [...] We need to provide better experiences."

Another expert reasoned the growing relevance of CX with the fact that, nowadays, customers can easily proclaim opinions via social media or online forums and thereby reach a large audience. In principle, every dissatisfied customer has the potential to notify other customers and thus generate negative word-of-mouth.

Generally, all the experts interviewed assign a high priority to the topic of CX both these days and in the near future. For instance, it is described as "one of the strategic priorities" and it is part of the corporate strategy of all companies in the study. A minority does not use the term CX but places the customer at the center of the strategy. Agreeing with this, one of the external experts reinforced this idea as follows, "In many companies, [...] defined as greater than 90 percent, I would say, it is now part of the corporate strategy, thank goodness. [...] in many companies it is already the central topic."

1.2 Positive effects of CXM

The high relevance of CX and CXM is accounted for by their positive effects, which are shown in Figure 1. The structure of the CXM success chain is based on a general success chain of relationship marketing (e.g., by Anderson and Mittal, 2000; Bruhn and Tuzovic, 2002) and an extension of the CXM success chain developed for ISO 23592:2021, which was adapted and supplemented with additional insights gained from the interviews. The starting point of this success chain is the CXM anchored within the company. Systematic CXM, which in larger companies is usually implemented by a CX department, is intended to generate an improved and, above all, positive CX among customers. Within a company, CXM ensures an increase in customer orientation and customer focus in the entire company, which positively influences the CX (Lemon and Verhoef, 2016). As a result, the customer perspective is consistently adapted in developing and optimizing services and products. Between CXM as a starting point and the positive CX perceived by the customer, other internal factors, such as corporate culture, play a decisive role. These success factors of CXM are presented in the further course of this article and are considered mediators of a positive CX. With an increase in a positive CX, the chain of success passes over to the external effects on the customer. As a rule, a positive CX leads to higher customer satisfaction and, ideally, customer delight (Ma et al., 2013; ISO 23592:2021). This effect, in turn, leads to increased customer loyalty, which positively influences the company's economic success (Homburg et al., 2017). In addition, the effects mentioned above are accompanied by further positive results. The upper part of the graph refers to sales increases, while the lower part refers to cost reduction. Both sales increases and cost reductions ultimately have a positive impact on the company's economic success. Satisfied and, especially, delighted customers tend to be less price-sensitive and exhibit a greater willingness to pay. In addition, a positive CX will likely lead to further recommendations via customer satisfaction and delight. Moreover, repurchasing and cross- and up-buying are further potential upsides that positively influence a company's success (Reichheld, 2003; Kranzbuehler et al., 2018). The lower part of the graph shows that fewer complaints are received if a CX is positive or, ideally, outstanding. A decrease in the number of complaints also means a reduction in costs. Furthermore, it costs significantly less to retain a customer than to acquire a new one. Consequently, the acquisition costs saved also positively affect the company's success (Reichheld and Sasser, 1990).

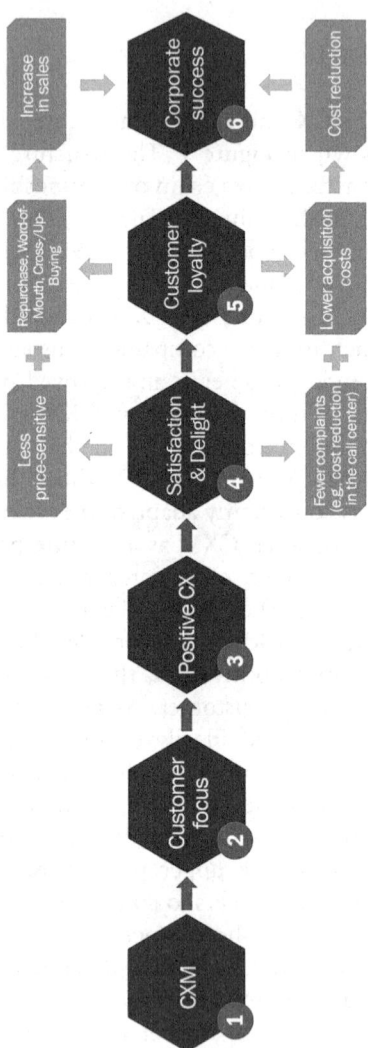

Fig. 1: Positive effects of CXM (sources: adapted from Bruhn and Tuzovic, 2002, p. 487 and ISO 23952:2021 and based on the interview results).

2. Implementation of CXM

In order to operate successful CXM, it must be actively implemented in a company. This chapter presents the main findings of the study on CXM implementation. Figure 2 illustrates the key data on CXM implementation from the best practice companies that were interviewed. The vast majority of these companies have a dedicated team or department responsible for CXM. In most cases, the CX department is either part of the marketing or service department. The reporting structure of the CX department is generally one level or two levels below the executive board and thus relatively high up. In the case of internationally oriented companies, it was noticed that there is usually a central CX team at corporate headquarters. Depending on the company's size, this may be around ten to 15 people. In addition to the CX managers at corporate headquarters, dedicated CX managers work on improving CX in the local markets. On average, these companies established the CX department around 2016 and thus began focusing on the topic of CXM at that time.

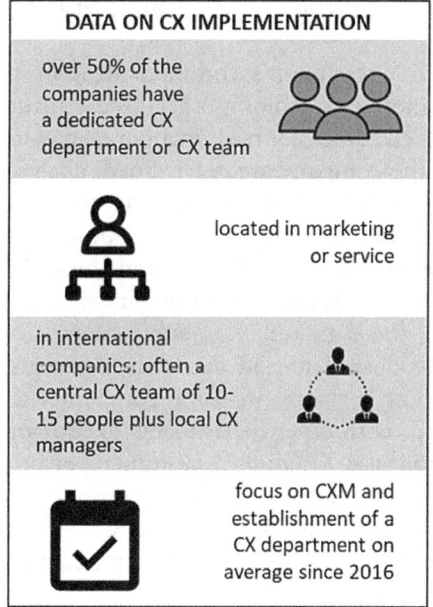

Fig. 2: Data on CXM implementation at best practice companies

In this context, it is interesting to look beyond national borders. The data described above mainly applies to highly developed countries. One of the interviewees explained, "The more developed a market is, the more [...] the customers are already distributed among the companies. [...] binding them to your company has become more and more important. The harder it becomes to win new ones, the more important it is to keep the old ones. Companies see that, too, and are shifting their budgets, so to speak, to serve customers according to their brand promise." Consequently, the key is to retain customers, especially in developed countries. In this regard, the expert emphasized, "The only way to make this truly sustainable is to simply serve the customer well. This automatically makes customer experience management a key strategic issue."

A CX expert from a technical company explained that the focus on CX and its anchoring in the company's strategy have been "a process over the last few years," especially since, in his case, it is an "engineering-focused" company. He highlighted, "I'll say six, seven years ago, something like yesterday, showing our products and our experience to the full supervisory board, would not have happened." This example illustrates that perseverance and continuity are required to establish sustainable and successful CXM.

Moreover, a CX department's common areas of responsibility were identified in the interviews. Among others, these include customer experience design and customer journey mapping, in which the customer's touchpoints with the company are determined, analyzed, and optimized. Usually, personas are defined in advance and are considered in the customer journeys for the respective persona. Another task of CXM is to measure CX, generate customer insights, and thus take the "voice of the customer" into account. In addition to obtaining customer opinions, this includes analyzing the data and, e.g., applying predictive analytics. It is also CXM's task to document and disseminate the insights gained within the company. Furthermore, in some companies the CX department conducts workshops with other departments to promote customer-centric thinking and action and to adopt a customer perspective. Additionally, measures are derived based on customer feedback to improve customer experience. Depending on the company, the CX department additionally comprises the customer contact team and/or product management as well as the social media team.

The findings reflect a typical management approach to CXM, as described by, e.g., Holmlund et al. (2020). Based on the expert interviews, this approach was adapted, expanded, and divided into strategic and operational CXM. Figure 3 shows the strategic and operational levels and process steps of CXM, which are interrelated. The starting point of strategic CXM is the development of the strategy. Here, the goals, guidelines, KPIs, and strategies are defined within the context of CXM. Ideally, this is linked to corporate strategy. The second level, which is dedicated to technologies and processes, involves selecting, and using CX technologies and tools. The aim here is to set up seamless and consistent processes. In particular, the processes must be simple for the customer, even though they are complex internally. The third level of strategic CXM deals with governance. Here, the rules, roles, and responsibilities are defined. In addition, the top management board should ideally be accountable for the topic of CXM. The fourth level deals with culture and organization. Successful CXM requires an expedient corporate culture that is dedicated to customer centricity and allows for agile structures. Besides this, a CX department or a CX team is necessary to drive the topic of CX forward. In this context, the use of cross-divisional CX ambassadors is advantageous in order to embed the topic of CX throughout the company.

Operational CXM is constituted by four management phases. In the first phase, the analysis phase, the identification of relevant customer touchpoints with the company takes place. This is achieved, e.g., by means of qualitative customer interviews. Furthermore, customer personas are determined based on these initial customer interviews, and persona-specific customer journey maps are developed. These customer journey maps provide a good starting point for developing service blueprints, which supplement the customer journey with the mapping of internal processes. This phase is followed by the planning and development phase, which is dedicated to CX design and aims at providing the customer with a seamless customer experience across all channels (Lemon and Verhoef, 2016). For new products or services, the CX is redesigned. For existing products or services, a target–actual comparison is foremost carried out in order to subsequently optimize and adjust the CX design. In the following implementation phase, customer feedback is continuously collected at various touchpoints and channels. Furthermore, this phase includes measuring the experience at the touchpoints through real-time surveys. From these sources important CX-KPIs are determined. The customer feedback is then analyzed, and its insights disseminated to other relevant departments. The aggregated results should be distributed to the top management and all employees who have contact to customers. It is then particularly important to work with customer feedback in order to optimize the services and products, and to initiate appropriate measures to improve the CX. In the subsequent evaluation and adaptation phase, it is necessary to continuously review the CX measures as part of a holistic process of monitoring success. If required, appropriate adjustments should be made in order to achieve the desired effect on the customer. Since the management process is an ongoing procedure, this fourth phase again directly leads into the first phase of the operational cycle (Becker and Jaakkola, 2020).

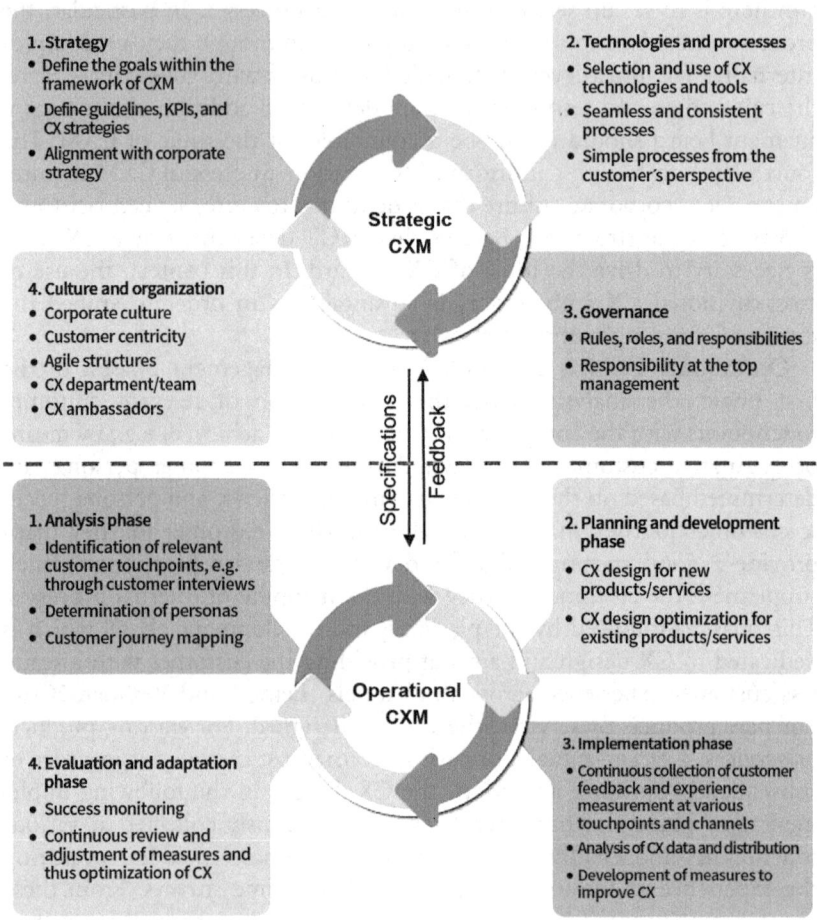

1. Strategy
• Define the goals within the framework of CXM
• Define guidelines, KPIs, and CX strategies
• Alignment with corporate strategy

2. Technologies and processes
• Selection and use of CX technologies and tools
• Seamless and consistent processes
• Simple processes from the customer's perspective

Strategic CXM

4. Culture and organization
• Corporate culture
• Customer centricity
• Agile structures
• CX department/team
• CX ambassadors

3. Governance
• Rules, roles, and responsibilities
• Responsibility at the top management

Specifications ↓ Feedback ↑

1. Analysis phase
• Identification of relevant customer touchpoints, e.g. through customer interviews
• Determination of personas
• Customer journey mapping

2. Planning and development phase
• CX design for new products/services
• CX design optimization for existing products/services

Operational CXM

4. Evaluation and adaptation phase
• Success monitoring
• Continuous review and adjustment of measures and thus optimization of CX

3. Implementation phase
• Continuous collection of customer feedback and experience measurement at various touchpoints and channels
• Analysis of CX data and distribution
• Development of measures to improve CX

Fig. 3: Levels and process steps in CXM

3. Creating a positive CX

A widely used definition of CX comes from Lemon and Verhoef (2016, p. 71), who describe CX as "[...] a multidimensional construct focusing on a customer's cognitive, emotional, behavioral, sensorial, and social responses to a firm's offerings during the customer's entire purchase journey." This definition emphasizes the subjective and individual character of CX (De Keyser et al., 2015). CXM is mainly concerned with creating positive to outstanding CX. The latter are defined in ISO 23592 as "significantly better than usual customer experience" (ISO 23592:2021, p. 2). In this context, it should be emphasized that companies can only generate the basis for a positive CX (Becker and Jaakkola, 2020). Ultimately, each customer decides to what extent interaction between him/her and a company is classified as positive, neutral, or negative. Furthermore, previous experiences affect the current and future CX (Lemon and Verhoef, 2016).

As part of the expert interviews, the CX leaders were asked about their individual definition or description of an outstanding CX. Accordingly, central basic determinants should first and foremost be fulfilled so that CX is perceived as positive and, based on that, can be judged as outstanding. Basic determinants include competence, friendliness, price–performance ratio, speed, simplicity, and quality. One expert summarized it as follows, "[...] if my counterpart, the company that delivers this experience for me, so to speak, if they are competent, if they are friendly, [...] if they also have a fair price–performance ratio, if they don't keep me waiting forever [...], if the processes are simple and the quality is good." Furthermore, for some experts, "remaining in the loop" is relevant for a positive CX, whereby the current status in the customer process is known and presented transparently. In this context, an expert explains it as follows, "[...] when it is clear to me what the next steps are."

In order for CX to be perceived as outstanding, specific determinants for an outstanding CX were identified in the interviews. For instance, proactivity and anticipation are to be mentioned here. As one expert described, "Well, the best customer experience for me is when I don't actually have to explicitly worry about what's happening anymore, but it somehow comes to me." For another interviewee, an outstanding CX is characterized by the fact that the company "anticipates my customer process to a certain extent. That I am offered services, so to speak, or that the company already thinks ahead and supports me, e.g., in a purchase, in my purchasing decision accordingly." Another CX expert emphasizes flexibility and responsiveness to customer needs, "If perhaps the person with whom you interacted [...] simply deviated from scripts and didn't follow the standard during the interaction."

Furthermore, the buzzword "human brilliance" is mentioned and elucidated by an expert as follows, "[...] if you have an employee, a service employee, that you meet and he does everything intuitively, that he reads your wish from your lips, [...] or even thinks one step further. And not because it's in some textbook, not because it's scripted, but because he just understands exactly what you want and even goes a step further and thereby delights you." Another CX expert puts it in a similar way, "I think what is really central to customer experience is the human in the middle. [...] ultimately, customer experience is relative to whomever you deliver it. So, great customer experience to me is understanding who the human is and tailoring that to their preferences, expectations, and emotional state and everything else around the person." A further CX expert shares the same view, "to me it's being familiar without being overfamiliar. It's like, you know who I am, and you know what I need as a customer, and you make it easy for me to get those things. But it never feels invasive. [...] It's like you find just the right line of making sure I have everything I need as a customer, but you never step over that line." In addition, the experts highlighted the issue of appreciation for creating an outstanding CX. For instance, one of the CX leaders spoke of positive effects by contacting both satisfied and dissatisfied customers after their feedback, "I show appreciation to the customer by calling and saying, thank you for your feedback, what else can we do for you? And so on." A further interviewee confirms appreciation as being relevant in experiencing an outstanding CX, "I always felt valued in the process."

Repeatedly the terms a "moment of surprise," a "wow experience," and "exceeding expectations" were mentioned or as an expert stated: "Outstanding is when things happen [...] that the customer did not expect at all." Another expert similarly reported as follows, "If people are friendly and go the extra mile and totally exceed my expectations." Consequently, these wow experiences shape the CX, which usually leaves the customer emotionally touched. Being an emotional experience, it will usually be remembered by the customer for longer, and these are exactly the experiences which will be recalled and be decisive in an upcoming situation where the customer needs to decide to stay with the company or not.

Figure 4 summarizes the above-mentioned determinants of a positive CX. The light gray determinants are a necessary basis for a positive CX, while the dark gray determinants promote an outstanding CX.

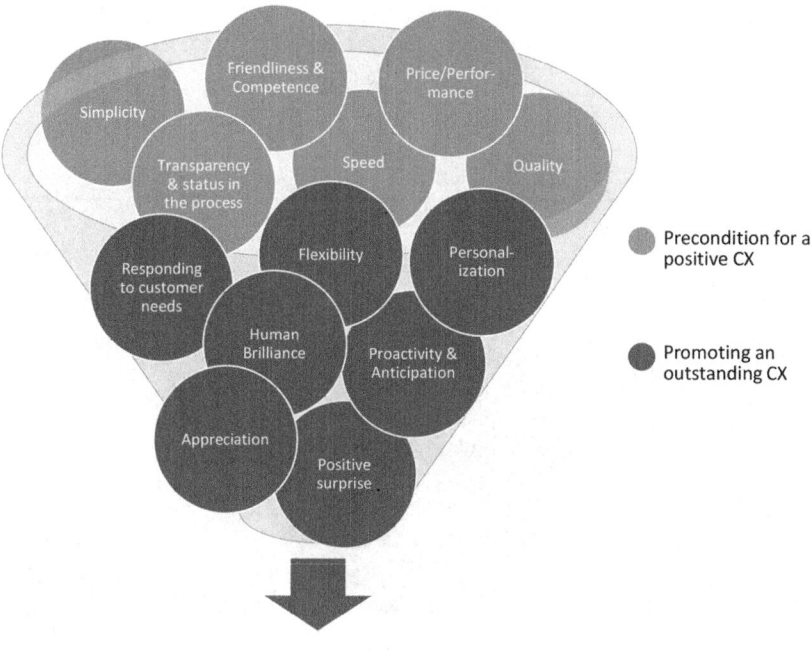

Outstanding CX

Fig. 4: Determinants of a positive to outstanding CX

4. Success factors of CXM

Finally, six key success factors of CXM were identified in the expert interviews. This section presents these findings regarding the success factors which are summarized in Figure 5.

Fig. 5: Success factors of CXM

4.1 Top management support

A decisive success factor of CXM is the support of top management. The following statements from CX leaders substantiate this, "It must always be the will of top management that a company focuses on the customer." In addition, "From the company's point of view, absolute management buy-in. The entire top management and also middle management have to be behind it so that it works." Another very sincere quote from a CX expert is worth mentioning at this point, "I'm usually not the person who says that the board has to do it first, but that's also part of it at this point, that it's exemplified." An expert who advises companies on CX mentioned in this context, "The best ones I've seen are the ones in which the C-suite are involved, you know, there's a program sponsor, there's a clear road map [...]. And once you have the right stakeholder on the top, then everything else like resourcing, budget, and everything tends to be unlocked." A further interviewee explains the relevance of top management as follows, "I can tell the individual employees as much as I want that they should change their behavior, as long as it doesn't come from the board [...]. As long as the board is not fully behind it and leads by example, [...] it will not work." Moreover, continuity and a long-term strategy, pushed by top management, are essential for sustainable implementation success.

4.2 *Corporate culture*

In order to implement a successful CX program, a suitable corporate culture is required. This requirement has already been emphasized by Homburg et al. (2017) and is confirmed by this study. In the interviews, it was repeatedly of importance that the topic of CX must be rooted in the company and lived in the company to be successful. One of the experts, for instance, accentuated, "If the entire organization is not interested in it and does not live it and does not implement it in its daily activities, then a dedicated department at that point is of no use to me. That just paints a nice PowerPoint, but it's just not lived in the operational sense." The following statement correspondingly highlights the same necessity, "And the employees in the organization have to be taken along, and they have to live it. Otherwise, the whole tool and the great technology won't be of any use. And I always see [...] as a problem [...] that many [people] always think that just because they have now introduced some 'fancy' customer measurement tools, everything will be fine now, and the rest will do itself. Exactly the rest is actually the exhausting part."

According to a CX consultant, a transformation is often necessary to successfully establish CXM in a company. He explained and justified this as follows, "[...] it often goes hand in hand with a transformation. Because thinking from the customer's point of view and overcoming departmental boundaries, so to speak, is not directly part of companies' nature. [...] But for these customer experiences, for these improvements, they have to. And that's [...] why we often speak of transformation projects in this context." Finally, clear words on the need to link CX with corporate culture are found in the following quote, "If I try to pack customer experience only into measurement methods, data, and facts, and consider that as a KPI that I want to manage, without that being part of the corporate culture and without me believing that it works, that it is of value and important to have a good relationship with customers, then I will probably lose at that point."

4.3 Dedicated employees

The employee has a unique role in the emergence of a positive or negative CX. Thus, a CX leader who was interviewed aptly named it as follows, "The biggest challenge is people, and the biggest success factor is people. Especially in service because they make the difference, positively and negatively." Complementing this, another expert emphasized, "Happy employee – happy customer, [...] that you also take care of the well-being of your employees, because that has an impact." Similarly, one of the experts put the connection as follows, "Following the hypothesis that the customer experience can never be better than the experience of the employees who take care of the customers. Because if the employee is insecure and in chaos, then the customer perceives that, and then the customer experience can no longer be flawless." Consequently, the employee is a decisive success factor in a positive CX.

4.4 CX measurement

In order to find out more about the customer's perception of CX, it is essential to ask the customer for his or her perception and opinion. This way, as a company, you get the real customer's view. The importance of CX measurement has been highlighted in research by, e.g., Lemon and Verhoef (2016) and was supported by the qualitative study. In this context, one of the experts clarified, "In the past, we [...] thought the way we think would be good for the customer, but yeah, they didn't want it that way." Similarly, another interviewee affirmed, "It's often very difficult to see what the customer likes without asking the customer what they like." One of the experts explained, "You have to make it tangible and measurable, too." Consequently, CX leaders use both qualitative and quantitative methods to measure CX. The most commonly used method is the customer survey. Recently, surveys tend toward live feedback to get the customer's opinion without a time lag. It is of most value to collect CX data in one place, such as in a dashboard. From this, CX metrics such as Net Promoter Score (NPS), Customer Satisfaction Score (CSAT), Customer Satisfaction Index (CSI) or Customer Effort Score (CES) are extracted and compared over time. In addition, the use of social media analytics and semantics allows one to learn more about CX without directly asking the customer. Moreover, a company's employees with direct customer contact are a fruitful source of information that is not to be neglected. It is beneficial to link and analyze CX data with operational data to obtain a comprehensive picture of CX. The data can also be connected to a CRM system to gain a 360-degree view of the customer. In this context, one of the experts emphasized, "Measurement is all well and good, but measurement for me is only [...] about 20 percent of customer experience management. The other thing is actually working with it and improving something." This statement leads us to the next success factor in CXM, the use of CX data.

4.5 Use of CX data

The CX measurement just described is essential to be able to manage CX. However, no progress can be made in improving CX without the active use of data. At this point, two quotes from the interviews are worth mentioning, "[...] from my point of view, it is always important that you do not measure in order to measure, but in order to derive measures." Furthermore, "[...] measuring is not the end of something, but the start of something." Consequently, a company should work intensively with its insights into CX and derive measures in order to ultimately optimize it. For this purpose, it is important that the insights gained are actively disseminated within the company and made available to the relevant departments. In addition, as described by Becker and Jaakkola (2020) and confirmed in this study, the measures taken and their successes should be reviewed continuously and adjusted if necessary.

4.6 Cross-functional working

Another success factor is cross-functional working to create a positive customer experience. The necessity of a multidisciplinary approach was already underpinned by Lemon and Verhoef (2016) and is confirmed by the experts interviewed. In this regard, one expert emphasized, "[...] don't put your departmental interests first; after all, everyone works on behalf of the customer, and only if the customer is happy can salaries be paid." Here, it is crucial that the individual departments do not follow "silo thinking" but together enable a seamless and carefree customer experience. Therefore, teams can be brought together temporarily, for instance, or a regular exchange between different departments can be established. As one of the experts clarified, "[...] for example, you have to bring the product people together with the people who do the related service. So you develop products that are easier served by the service team." For the customer, it is irrelevant how many different departments are involved in providing the product or service. For him or her, the overall experience with the respective company should be seamless. Cross-departmental exchange, usually initiated by the CX department, is therefore needed. In line with this, one expert underpinned the existence of a central CX team as follows, "[...] you need a central team that steers and drives the whole thing and approaches it with the right mindset."

5. Conclusion

With interchangeable products and increasing competition, generating positive to outstanding CX plays a critical role in differentiating a company from others and in it retaining its customers. With the help of CXM, the creation of a positive CX is influenced. The explorative, qualitative study conducted by the authors provides beneficial insights regarding the implementation of CXM and the success factors of CXM. Since a company needs satisfied, delighted, and, in particular, loyal customers to survive successfully in the market, the topic of CXM will continue to play a decisive role in the future.

Bibliography

Anderson, E.W. and Mittal, V. (2000). Strengthening the satisfaction–profit chain, Journal of Service Research, 3(2), pp. 107–120.

Becker, L. and Jaakkola, E. (2020). Customer experience: Fundamental premises and implications for research, Journal of the Academy of Marketing Science, 48, pp. 630–648.

Bruhn, M. and Tuzovic, S. (2002). The management process of relationship marketing, Proceedings of the 10th International Colloquium in Relationship Marketing, Kaiserslautern, pp. 483–497.

De Keyser, A., Lemon, K.N., Klaus, P. and Keiningham, T.L. (2015). A framework for understanding and managing the customer experience, Marketing Science Institute Working Paper Series, 2015, Report No. 15–121.

Gartner (2019). Gartner for marketers: 2019 Customer experience management study: Marketers take more control as CX expectations and budgets rise, https://emtemp.gcom.cloud/ngw/globalassets/en/marketing/documents/2019-cx-management-study-research.pdf, accessed 01/12/2022.

Holmlund, M., Van Vaerenbergh, Y., Ciuchita, R., Ravald, A., Sarantopoulos, P., Villarroel Ordenes, F. and Zaki, M. (2020). Customer experience management in the age of big data analytics: A strategic framework, Journal of Business Research, 116, pp. 356–365.

Homburg, C., Jozić, D. and Kuehnl, C. (2017). Customer experience management: Toward implementing an evolving marketing concept, Journal of the Academy of Marketing Science, 45(3), pp. 377–401.

ISO 23592:2021 (2021). Service excellence — Principles and model, Geneva.

Kranzbuehler, A.-M., Kleijnen, M.H.P., Morgan, R.E. and Teerling, M. (2018). The multilevel nature of customer experience research: An integrative review and research agenda, International Journal of Management Reviews, 20, pp. 433–456.

Lemon, K.N. and Verhoef, P.C. (2016). Understanding customer experience throughout the customer journey, Journal of Marketing, 80(6), pp. 69–96.

Ma, J., Gao, J., Scott, N. and Ding, P. (2013). Customer delight from theme park experiences: The antecedents of delight based on cognitive appraisal theory, Annals of Tourism Research, 42, pp. 359–81.

Qualtrics (2020). Insight report, The global state of XM, 2020: Survey of 1,292 executives from Australia, Canada, France, Germany, Japan, Singapore, U.K., and U.S., April 2020, https://www.qualtrics.com/xm-institute/global-state-of-xm-2020/, accessed 01/12/2022.

Reichheld, F.F. (2003). The one number you need to grow, Harvard Business Review, December 2003, Reprint R0312C, pp. 1–11.

Reichheld, F.F. and Sasser, W.E. (1990). Zero defects: Quality comes to services, Harvard Business Review, 68(5), pp. 105–111.

Designing and renewing outstanding customer experiences

Hospitality 4.0: How digital services improve the travel experience

Björn Becker

Management summary

Despite the above-average emotional involvement of its customers, the travel industry is widely standardized and characterized by intense price competition. In addition to networks and connectivity, excellent services, information, and offers that accompany and support travelers on their journeys in a situation-specific manner and thus improve the experience are levers for differentiation in this market. This is especially true considering 2020 and 2021, when the COVID-19 pandemic dramatically intensified the competitive environment and made a good and well taken care of travel experience even more important. In the context of a unit cost-driven industry, implementation requires the efficient and integrated use of different service channels to realize the opportunities offered by digitization in the information and service sector. Lufthansa Group Airlines is pursuing a service strategy to differentiate itself from the competition.

1. Presentation of the Lufthansa Group

With a revenue of 36 billion euros and more than 138,000 employees, the Lufthansa Group was one of the largest aviation groups in the world in 2019. In that year, the Group generated EBIT of 2 billion euros and, with an EBIT margin of 5.6 percent, was once again one of the most profitable aviation groups in the market. The Group invested over 3.5 billion euros in new products, services, aircraft, and production facilities (Lufthansa, 2020). In 2020, revenue fell by 63 percent to 13.5 billion euros due to the coronavirus pandemic (Lufthansa, 2021).

The core of the Group, which comprises more than 500 companies, are the airlines, including the largest ones: Lufthansa, Swissair, Austrian Airlines, Eurowings and Brussels Airlines.

In recent years, the Lufthansa Group has undergone an intensive modernization process to prepare itself for the challenges in the aviation market, which is characterized by overcapacity and price wars. It is not least thanks to this intensive, sometimes painful process that excellent economic results had been achieved by 2019. The Lufthansa Group was able to play an active and shaping role in the ongoing market consolidation process.

One aspect of this modernization is its consistent use of digital possibilities in sales and service. While the rationalization projects in the 1990s were primarily intended to achieve unit cost optimization, usually at the cost of reduced service volumes (e.g., by shifting processes 1:1 to the guest), the opportunity offered by digitization lies in a combination of improved customer service with simultaneously optimized unit costs. The Lufthansa Group Hub Airlines (brands Lufthansa, Swissair and Austrian Airlines) have worked intensively on improving and digitally supporting their services in recent years, which is also reflected by the corresponding awards they have received (e.g., Future Travel Experience Most Innovative Airline Europe 2017, IATA Fast Travel Platinum Status, Skytrax 5* Airline).

The COVID-19 pandemic also led to existential challenges in the Lufthansa Group. But even during this time, when nearly all projects had to be stopped, the company pushed ahead with digitization and structural change to restart with efficient structures and differentiating services when traffic resumed. In addition, digital and thus contactless services gained further importance during the pandemic against the backdrop of infection protection and the massively increased complexity of immigration document requirements, which can only be covered with a smart service channel mixture of efficiency and personal support.

2. Service strategies as differentiation in the airline market

For many years, the air travel market has been characterized by overcapacity, falling average ticket prices, and standardization of services. Beyond the basic needs of safety (including infection control), reliability, and network quality, many airlines are interchangeable from the perspective of their customers. Excellence in customer service is thus one of the few ways to differentiate oneself from other companies and represents an essential part of a strategy against pure price competition. At the same time, the often emotionally charged travel experience (positive, e.g., in the case of a successful vacation, and negative, for instance, in the case of irregularities) offers many opportunities to practice service excellence, from personalized surprise moments to fast, professional and accommodating service recovery.

In terms of the production of air travel services, airlines are dependent on system partners in many respects (e.g., airports, air traffic control, ground transportation to and from airports), which play an essential role but cannot be directly influenced by most airlines. Infrastructures, in particular, are often unable to keep up with the steady passenger growth of circa five percent per year (IATA, 2017) that has been seen for years. This development, which was slowed down by the setback in 2020 and 2021 but probably not fundamentally stopped, and the permanent unit cost pressure due to falling ticket prices have led to an increasing need for innovation. This has the goal of constantly offering better and individual services, independently of local infrastructures, at lower unit costs, while at the same time making more targeted use of personal human service as a genuine differentiation factor.

Used correctly, digitization can significantly alleviate the tension between service excellence, cost pressure, infection control, and infrastructure shortages.

3. Digital transformation and opportunities for service excellence

The term "digital transformation" defines itself as a significant change in everyday life, the economy, and society through the use of digital technologies and techniques as well as their effects (Pousttchi et al., 2019).

Accordingly, digital transformation does not just refer to development in IT projects. Instead, it is a holistic approach to adapting organizations to agile working methods and faster action and reaction speeds to meet society's fast-moving demands and thus those organizations' customers. This starts with often lengthy planning and budgeting processes, continues with decision-making and release regulations, and extends to the know-how and attitude of the people involved, especially concerning governance, planning, market launches, and decision-making under uncertainty.

At the same time, few topics are so strongly characterized by superficial treatises such as digitization and digital transformation. The abstract level with buzzwords such as "disruption," "agility," "innovation," etc., is too seldom left behind to talk specifically about the opportunities offered by these developments for business processes and services. The background to this situation is multifaceted: On the one hand, there is still a great deal of ignorance and uncertainty due to the relatively rapid developments of recent years. According to a study, 92 percent of DAX executive boards had no demonstrable experience of the challenges posed and opportunities offered by digitization (Die Zeit, 2017), and the situation was and is often not much better at the management levels below. On the other hand, actual and supposedly threatening disruptions create intense pressure to react and change. Many companies are trying to find their way in this situation – but a holistic and, at the same time, operationalizable strategy on how digitization can be used for a company's goals is found too rarely (McKinsey, 2018).

Pousttchi et al. (2019) define the three dimensions of value creation, value proposition, and customer interaction on which digital transformation in a company acts. Value creation refers to the internal optimization of processes and structures necessary to realize the benefits of digitization. The effect of digital transformation on value proposition relates to products, services, and revenue models, i.e., the improvement of existing services and the optimization of the associated revenue models. Finally, the customer interaction dimension refers to the potential of direct customer communication and interaction. All three dimensions are highly relevant for a service company such as an airline.

Lufthansa has systematized its digital transformation by dividing it into horizons (see Figure 1): the digitization of operational processes, service improvements for customers, and new business models.

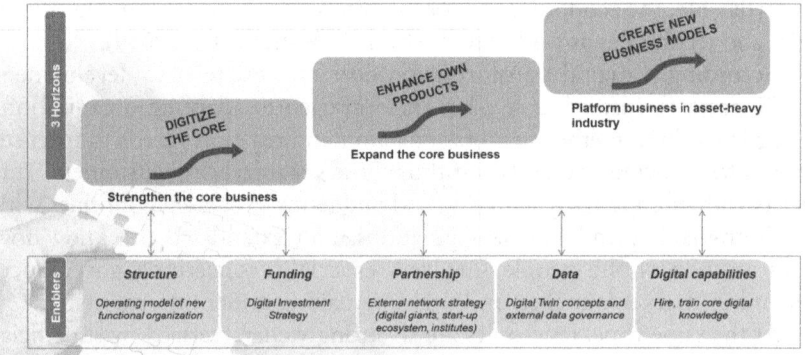

Fig. 1: The three horizons of digitization

While the first and second horizons aim to improve the existing core business, the third horizon deals with the opportunities and risks of new business models with disruptive potential. Examples of such business models are the online (book) trade shaped by Amazon, innovative transportation concepts (e.g., Uber), or music streaming services (e.g., Spotify). They all have in common that they have attacked and changed the existing market with its business models in its fundamental mode of operation (e.g., the stationary book trade). This does not necessarily mean that this market is dissolving entirely. After 2005, the stationary book trade market share in Germany fell from 54.8 percent to 46.2 percent in 2019, so it has by no means collapsed (Börsenverein, 2016; 2020). However, it has increased the pressure on existing market participants to work out their unique selling proposition for customers and differentiate themselves from the competition. Market players who do not react quickly and adapt their business model and customer relationships will disappear. The developments due to the pandemic since the beginning of 2020 are additionally accelerating many of these changes. For example, the need for change in retail is increasing due to the shift to e-commerce, as is the pressure on airlines due to people becoming accustomed to video conferencing or vacationing in their home country. Customer loyalty, e.g., via a high Net Promoter Score (NPS) and a meaningful customer relationship, at least with the most important customers, becomes all the more important in phases of weaker growth.

The first and second horizons open up significant potential for service improvements, operational process improvements, simultaneous cost reductions, and thus competitive advantages that help in the battle for market share. The first horizon focuses on digitizing core operational processes, e.g., in production in the industrial sector or the performance of services in the service sector. For instance, in the case of airlines, this includes operational processes at departure gates, check-in by staff, contact centers, or aircraft handling. The second horizon is primarily concerned with products and services that directly impact the customer. In the case of airlines, these services are typically provided via digital channels such as apps or messengers and vending machines at airports.

Digital transformation is not an end in itself but a means to an end – in this case, service excellence. To achieve this, it is necessary to digitally support both internal operational processes and customer touchpoints and connect them. Only then will the full potential of digitization be leveraged. This approach can be compared with the Industry 4.0 concept, which links all participants in a production chain digitally and in real time, thus materializing efficiency gains in logistics and production control (BMWi, 2022).

Applied to the travel chain, Hospitality 4.0 thus describes a service concept based on networking between the airline and its passengers using their digital devices, the employees on board and on the ground, and the infrastructure at the airport, such as check-in or baggage drop-off machines. In this case, the services are both reactive, i.e., problem-solving, and predictive, i.e., problem-avoiding. This intelligent and forward-looking combination of digital and personal services and contacts is a key success factor in developing a holistic service concept from the customer's point of view, as described in the next section.

4. Service design of Lufthansa Group Airlines

4.1 Service strategy

The methods of service development have changed with the opportunities presented by digitization: While automation and streamlining (and thus primarily the goal of cost reduction) were at the forefront of many new self-services until a few years ago, digitization offers companies the opportunity to develop services that combine lower unit costs with better customer experience.

Figure 2 shows that airlines provide services along the travel chain via several channels. In addition to traditional personal service, e.g., at the counter, personal services are offered by telephone, e-mail, social media, online contact forms, and still letter and fax. Behind these analog and digital channels is a human service employee who receives the inquiries, researches the background, and develops and offers solutions by contacting the guest again via the same or an alternative channel.

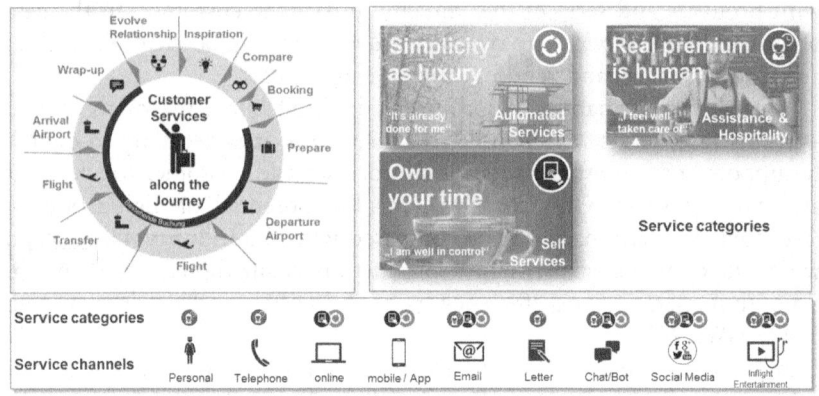

Fig. 2: Service categories and channels in the travel chain

Other channels include self-services on websites (e.g., www.swiss.com), apps (e.g., Lufthansa app), or machines (check-in or self-bag-drop machines at airports). The essence of these services is that they guide the guest semi-automatically through a user flow and, depending on the channel, offer more or less independence from infrastructures and opening hours.

More and more fully automated services have been added in the last one to two years, primarily supported by chatbots that work on social media channels, on websites or in apps. Initially, it is no longer a human being who answers questions or carries out transactions for the guest, but a computer that acts and communicates like a human being (Mulfati, 2020).

For an airline to implement the Hospitality 4.0 concept across these different channels during a journey, fundamental aspects in its service design must be considered. Services should be targeted, integrated, intuitive, and predictive:

- The various touchpoints must be used in a targeted manner. Simple, standardized transactions can be performed via digital channels in self-service or even completely automated terms and only their results displayed. One example is a simple check-in, which can be performed by the guest in a self-service or even completely automated form (the guest then automatically receives his/her boarding pass 24 hours before departure via in-app message, e-mail, SMS, or a social media messenger).

- In both cases, the guest is independent of the airport's infrastructure and predefined times and thus gains more freedom in travel planning. At the same time, the airline can focus the scarce infrastructure and the offer of personal services at the airport on more complex cases, necessary assistance, and hospitality, and thus use them in a more targeted manner.

- Channels must be integrated from the customer's perspective. When switching between channels, e.g., from the chatbot to a human contact center agent (e.g., because the case cannot be solved by the chatbot), an integrated experience must be created, e.g., through automated information handovers. The guest should not have to restate their request at each touchpoint. All touchpoints must have the same information regarding the customer's previous journey and their experiences relevant to the service in order for the airline to respond to the guest in an empathetic and informed manner.

- Communication and transactions must be intuitive. Travel – especially since the pandemic – is a complex service in which many different requirements must be met. In addition to the security requirements of the airlines themselves, there are the information and security requirements of the countries involved (e.g., visa, health, and entry procedures), integrated baggage logistics, group travel, fare systems, etc. This results in a complex system with many participants and, in some cases, interdependent process steps. Services must "hide" this complexity from guests, guide them, and thus create a positive, safe experience.

- Services should be forward-looking in two ways: On the one hand, the guest is given a suggestion as to the next step that makes sense for him/her individually and, if necessary, the required information or suitable offers are also provided directly. It is essential that this service is personalized and situation-related because the same guest may have different needs in different situations (e.g., customers known as business travelers who are flying on vacation with their families).

- The second approach is predictive problem prevention, i.e., the anticipatory avoidance of problems in the next steps of the travel chain. This approach is comparable, e.g., with the predictive maintenance approach from the Industry 4.0 concept. Based on data analyses of their previous travel experiences and the current operational situation (e.g., delays), problems in the travel chain of each individual passenger are predicted and solutions are developed or offered. Lufthansa Group Airlines already provides such a service for its top customer segment by scanning guests' travel histories and solving foreseeable problems preventively (e.g., the plane with which a passenger is supposed to fly from New York to Munich tomorrow is delayed from another rotation, cannot make up for it, and will accordingly have a delayed arrival in Munich, which in turn would lead to the passenger missing a connecting flight. Based on this, solutions are sought and the guest is contacted with an appropriate suggestion, even though they did not know they would have a problem until now). Other possibilities are predictable long waiting times at checkpoints, which can be made aware of early enough. The possibilities of digitization and data analytics offer airlines the opportunity to scale such services to larger customer segments and thus more passengers.

Lufthansa Group Airlines has operationalized these principles via the three service categories of automated, self, and assistance & hospitality services, which can be seen in Figure 2.

Automated services

Services are provided automatically to make the traveler's journey as comfortable and easy as possible. This is always possible if all the necessary information is available and the guest does not have to make a selection or has already made one. In the above-mentioned example of automated check-in, the passenger must have provided all the necessary travel information and, if necessary, a seat preference when booking. The guiding principle of this service category is "It's already done for me"—as a guest, I no longer have to worry about anything; the next step in my travel chain or the solution to a problem is delivered to me automatically. Another example of this category is automatic rebooking or hotel reservations in case of irregularities. In this already unpleasant situation, the guest is thus at least not only presented with a problem but also directly with a proposed solution, which he/she can accept or adapt again (via self or assistance services, see below).

This service category also includes the travel-related notifications that keep the traveler informed about their trip and the next steps (e.g., gate changes, boarding, baggage status, etc.). One recent example is the storage of vaccination information in the Lufthansa app or the customer profile that is used automatically during check-in to process the necessary document checks.

An intuitive service design is vital for the guest to understand that an action has been carried out for him/her. Otherwise, it can quickly lead to uncertainty, especially among inexperienced travelers. The principle of anticipatory services is implemented in this context by providing targeted information and recommended actions for the next step as well as tips on potential problem areas (e.g., waiting times at security checks at the time of departure) when the service result (e.g., the boarding pass) is played out.

Self-services

If information or choices are still available or interactions are necessary, self-service is the first choice for low to medium complexity services. These services are usually based on notifications (e.g., an invitation to check in or a baggage status message). The guest responds with an action, e.g., on their mobile device. The guiding principle for this category is "I'm well in control." This means that the services provide the guest the freedom to decide where and when to use them. Check-in and baggage preparation are no longer necessarily done at the airport. Travelers can choose to prepare them at home or at the hotel by using self-check-in and self-baggage tagging to the point where they no longer have to wait before going through the security check. Particularly in times of a pandemic with complex entry regulations, the additional benefit for travelers is that they can be assured, in a kind of checklist procedure, that all the necessary preparations have been made and their documents are sufficient before they start their journey.

Assistance & Hospitality services

In times of advancing digitization, personal services form a strategic cornerstone for differentiation and achieving service excellence. Other airlines have also recognized the importance of employees as hosts and problem-solvers and placed them in the foreground (see, e.g., Wirtz et al., 2015).

It is essential here that the limited personal service, which is not very scalable in the short term and comparatively cost-intensive, is used in a targeted manner – on host services, especially in the premium segment, and on assistance in complex or emotional situations (e.g., connecting flight missed in a foreign country), in which human and personal contact relieve travelers of uncertainty and give them the feeling that someone cares about them.

Such an assignment confronts employees with changes, some of which are considerable: Whereas traditional areas of assignment for employees were characterized by limited but deep expert knowledge (e.g., as a check-in agent), generalists are needed who can understand the process, sometimes across several flight segments, and devise solutions. They do not have to be experts in all subject areas themselves but need appropriate back-office contacts to help as needed. More important here are process thinking, a strong focus on service excellence, and solution orientation because the requirement in personal service is that the customer receives help from their first contact, regardless of whom they contact.

This focus on touchpoints will only succeed if all service channels and categories are used in a targeted manner, as Figure 3 shows.

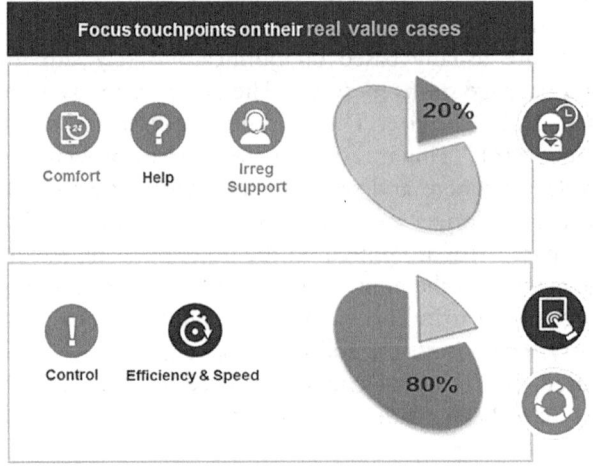

Fig. 3: Targeted use of service channels and touchpoints

Only if the majority of standardized transactions can be handled via automated services and self-services, is it possible to use personal service for the necessary differentiation. It is not true, e.g., that only personal service can help in irregular situations. It is precisely here that, due to the limited scalability of personal care, support is needed from the other service categories to be able to offer passengers information and solutions quickly and efficiently. A good example to illustrate this is the wave of calls during the COVID-19 crisis: during the crisis, flights had to be cancelled months in advance. This long-term cancellation scenario is very unusual for airlines so there was no digital self-service available for the customers to rebook or refund their flights and everybody had to call. The call centers were overwhelmed by calls up to ten times as high in number as normal – which led to long waiting times and lost calls.

One development worth mentioning in this context is the new possibilities offered by in-flight connectivity. Particularly in Europe and the USA, the technical possibilities are developing rapidly on long-haul routes across the oceans. They make it possible to offer all the service categories mentioned above in addition to infotainment during a flight. From the customer's point of view, this opens up new possibilities, especially in the case of service recovery, but also social services. It is foreseeable that with this development, the service concept on board will also have to evolve beyond the current security, hospitality, and food and beverage provisions.

4.2 Service design methods

Services are developed at Lufthansa Group Airlines according to the customer journey management method and design thinking approaches. In this process, journeys are depicted in (partial) journeys at different levels of abstraction and with varying levels of detail to capture the situations, information needs, experiences, and emotional states of travelers in different situations along the journey and to determine weak points.

A prototypical model is used in which so-called Discover and Describe circles are first run through with the help of the customer journey management method to then address the weak points found in ideation and prototyping workshops. According to Kolko (2015), the primary focus of design thinking is empathy with the guest experience. With this in mind, the customer journey management workshops are conducted using three very intuitive guiding questions:

1. What is our guest experiencing right now?
2. What questions and information needs does our guest have right now?
3. How is our guest feeling right now?

Keeping the three core questions mentioned above in mind helps to focus on the guest's perspective and empathize with their experiences. In particular, this consistent adoption of the customer's perspective in the service experience is a challenge, as project teams often run the risk of becoming too absorbed in the process – and in production-oriented ways of thinking – and of losing sight of the guest's perspective along the entire travel chain in favor of particular forms of optimization in the context of their own project. One more element are customer co-creation sessions where services or user interfaces are developed together in customer labs, applying prototyping methods and using direct customer feedback.

In the context of introducing this working method at Lufthansa Group Airlines, roles were created that are technically responsible for the sub-journeys of our passengers and roles that monitor compliance with the working method in workshops. This has resulted in an efficient organization that focuses on technical expertise and new working methods, thus identifying new insights and service improvements.

5. Summary and outlook

Service development has made significant progress in recent years due to digitization and the introduction of new working methods such as design thinking and customer journey management and is standard in all customer-centric companies. Digitization will continue to offer great opportunities for the service industry to support internal and customer-centric processes to improve services while reducing costs. Regardless of the specific industry, the successful providers will be those that succeed in exploiting and integrating the opportunities and strengths of the different service categories to differentiate themselves from the competition.

Lufthansa Group Airlines has set out to use these methods and exploit these opportunities to achieve significant improvements in customer service. Even if this claim cannot yet be met everywhere and in every case, a clear goal has been set, the path has been taken, and many improvements are evident – both in industry feedback and market position and, most importantly, in the daily feedback from our guests.

Bibliography

BMWi (2022). Industrie 4.0, Federal Ministry for Economic Affairs and Climate Action, www.bmwi.de/Redaktion/EN/Dossier/industrie-40.html, accessed 01/11/2022.

Börsenverein (2016). Buch und Buchhandel in Zahlen 2016 [Book and book trade in figures 2016], Börsenverein des Deutschen Buchhandels e.V.

Börsenverein (2020). Das Buch in Zeiten von Corona – Perspektiven für den Markt [The book in the coronavirus crisis — Prospects for the market], Börsenverein des Deutschen Buchhandels e.v., https://www.boersenverein.de/tx_file_down load?tx_theme_pi1%5BfileUid%5D=5485&tx_theme_pi1%5Breferer%5D=htt ps%3A%2F%2Fwww.boersenverein.de%2Fmarkt-daten%2Fmarktforschung% 2Fwirtschaftszahlen%2F&cHash=fbcae2ddefcbf1a8897e3e6c4a9c3c4, accessed 08/05/2021.

Die Zeit (2017). Aus der alten Welt [From the old world], Die Zeit, No. 40, 09/28/2017.

IATA (2017). Economic performance of the airline industry — end 2017 update, www.iata.org/economics, accessed 01/11/2022.

Kolko, J. (2015). Design thinking comes of age, Harvard Business Review, September 2015, pp. 66–71.

Lufthansa (2020). Lufthansa Group — Annual report 2019, https://investor-relation s.lufthansagroup.com/fileadmin/downloads/en/financial-reports/annual-reports/ LH-AR-2019-e.pdf.

Lufthansa (2021). Lufthansa Group — Annual report 2020, https://investor-relation s.lufthansagroup.com/fileadmin/downloads/en/financial-reports/annual-reports/ LH-AR-2020-e.pdf

McKinsey (2018). Why digital strategies fail, https://www.mckinsey.com/busines s-functions/mckinsey-digital/our-insights/why-digital-strategies-fail, accessed 01/10/2022.

Mulfati, J. (2020). Airlines use chatbots to automate customer service as requests soar, https://apex.aero/articles/airlines-chatbots-automate-customer-service-reque sts-soar/, accessed 01/11/2022.

Pousttchi, K., Bouzzi, B., Gleiß, A. and Kohlhagen, M. (2019). Technology impact types for digital transformation, 2019 IEEE 21st Conference on Business Informatics (CBI), https://www.researchgate.net/publication/335362246_Technology _Impact_Types_for_Digital_Transformation, accessed 01/11/2022.

Wirtz, L., Heracleous, N. and Pangarkar, N. (2015). Managing human resources for service excellence and cost-effectiveness at Singapore Airlines, Managing Service Quality, 18(1), pp. 4–19.

A healthy future that tastes good!
Culinary excellence as an innovative customer experience at Helios Hospitals

Carsten K. Rath, Enrico Jensch

Management summary

People's health has been the leading discussion topic in politics and society worldwide since COVID-19 at the latest. In an increasingly regulated healthcare industry, the re-municipalization of private hospitals as a COVID-19 remedy is currently being controversially discussed without merit. However, the future cannot belong to re-municipalization and further regulation. Instead, new holistic, cross-sector, digitally complemented forms of care and service seem more promising. Carsten K. Rath, an entrepreneur and "Germany's No. 1 service expert" (n-tv), and Enrico Jensch, the COO of Helios Hospitals, are convinced of this. With the pilot project "6 chefs, 12 stars," the two experts have taken a bold first step. Medical quality is expected today, but service and culinary excellence are not yet. Their success in pursuing this approach and many satisfied patients provide an incentive for further refinement of the project, which is unique in Germany and, above all, tasty.

1. Service excellence as an opportunity for the increasingly regulated healthcare industry

1.1 The healthcare industry in Germany is stagnating

2020 and 2021 were challenging years that put the global healthcare industry to the test. Do its traditional structures and procedures work even in stressful situations such as the COVID-19 pandemic? At this stage, previously concealed deficiencies are coming to light. In addition, the pandemic clearly shows who is geared up for future medical care when compared internationally and who is lagging behind the (digital) trends.

Compared to the German economy as a whole, the healthcare industry has experienced continuous growth. At the same time, it was considered a crisis-proof industry – at least until recently. The Berlin-based Wifor Institute reveals that this formerly constant development is declining. Even before the pandemic, the total value of goods and services in the healthcare industry dropped by 400 million euros. Similarly, the employment figures had already started to decline slightly before the pandemic from 2018 to 2019. At the same time, around 12,500 medical technology companies and

360 pharmaceutical and biotechnology companies created almost as many jobs as the German automotive industry (Hempel, 2020).

At first sight, these figures sound promising. However, an international comparison is rather sobering: the reputation of Germany as the pharmacy of the world is losing ground in direct comparison with other countries, such as the U.S. and Asian countries. Innovations in healthcare in such essential areas as clinical research, digitalization, or biotech start-ups are increasingly taking place outside Germany. A trend that has so far only been quietly emerging, but is an important step towards a modern healthcare future, is the focus on healthcare specialty centers based on the American model (Klöckner, 2021; Olk, 2020).

Particularly in this pandemic period, which has been going on for over two years, everyday hospital operations are determined by the efficient deployment of doctors and nursing staff and political decisions. Efficiency is like a sword of Damocles hanging over the heads of those who really only have one thing in mind: to ensure the best possible health and rapid recovery of their patients.

New concepts in the hospital environment need one thing above all now: courage, a clear vision, and an assertive voice that establishes a new, forward-looking attitude in the industry.

Helios Hospitals have been responding to this call for many years and are setting completely new and, above all, enjoyable standards with their new pilot project "6 chefs, 12 stars." It is just one of many projects at Helios Hospitals, which are pursuing the goal of "service excellence" in all areas.

1.2 Helios Hospitals – economic growth meets quality management

"We give people value for life – throughout their entire lives."

This vision of Europe's leading private hospital operator, Helios Hospitals, focuses on people, the patients, and adapts to them. Seeing things from a patient's perspective and anticipating processes, procedures, and expectations from their point of view is the great challenge that has to be met. At the same time, the experts at the clinics are constantly looking ahead and are thinking about new care models across sectors.

Around 73,000 employees implement the mission of offering the highest quality outcomes through professionalism and close cooperation every day. Every year, about 5.2 million patients receive treatment at 89 clinics, 123 medical care centers, and six prevention centers at Helios. Helios has access to a competent and medically extensive network as a part of the Fresenius healthcare group. In addition, Helios is a partner in the "We for Health" clinic network and is developing new skills and expertise in the fields of fertility and occupational medicine.

A strong drive for innovation and far more than a dose of courage to break new ground are literally in Helios' blood. In 1994, Dr. Lutz Helmig, M.D., founded Helios Hospitals with its four clinics in Germany (Bad Schwartau, Bochum, Volkach, and Bleicherode). Within the next few years, Helios Hospitals developed from a small innovative hospital operator to the largest hospital company in Europe (a. u., 2022). Steady growth, transparency, and innovation are their core corporate values alongside patient health. In 2005, e.g., Fresenius expanded the company with the Wittgensteiner Kliniken Group. In 2014, Helios took over 41 hospitals from RHOEN-Klinikum AG and also established itself on a broader base nationwide.

With the patient constantly in focus, Helios was a pioneer in quality management back in 1998. The system of "Measure – Improve – Publish" is applied in a similar form today in more than 410 hospitals in Germany and Switzerland. In addition, the "Initiative Qualitaetsmedizin [Quality Medicine Initiative]" (IQM) was launched in 2008. Since then, the 500 members of the IQM have been continuously reviewing and improving medical quality in the hospitals in a peer-review process.

"Helios stands for the best medical outcome quality – we demonstrate this transparently and visibly for our patients via our quality indicators," emphasizes Enrico Jensch. However, developments in society show that the hospital market in Germany is undergoing structural change. Most patients now take medical quality in Germany for granted and are developing new needs beyond medical treatment. Jensch states further, "A change in thinking needs to take place in the healthcare sector: We have to think of our patients much more as customers. Our services are comparable with other hospitals. Today, well-informed customers are much more independent in their decisions and are looking for more performance and service – they expect lower-threshold service and healthcare. Our efforts must be directed increasingly toward creating a customer journey and ensuring that people enjoy Helios healthcare services and remain loyal to the brand for a long time. We are convinced that service plays a decisive role in this process and is the new quality of tomorrow."

This shift in thinking is taking place, on the one hand, through new service concepts that perceive the patients as customers and, on the other hand, through rethinking long-established structures. For example, the new business areas at Helios have been dedicated to expanding the services offered by Helios Hospitals since 2018. These include the medical care centers, Helios Occupational Medicine, the Helios Prevention Center, and digital offers. All these areas use the Germany-wide network and existing expertise to break new ground easily and quickly. One important aspect here is overcoming the often rigid sector boundaries, which divide the hospital sector, e.g., into "outpatient" and "inpatient."

Enrico Jensch emphasizes, "We want to make it possible for our patients to receive services from a single source – not to have to choose one or the other. Whether it is a preventive health check-up, occupational health advice, an inpatient admission, or follow-up treatment with a family doctor or in a rehab clinic – the decisive factor should be what patients need, not which door they walk through first. Care must be able to be provided on an as-needed basis in the interests of the patient." This approach is supported by digital platforms such as the Helios patient portal, which offers patients numerous digital services.

"Our actions are focused on providing people the best possible medicine – helping them to get and stay healthy," sums up Enrico Jensch.

1.3 Healthcare – but with excellent service, please

If you follow the media reports on the healthcare industry these days, you will mainly read: figures, data, and facts. Economic stagnation on the one hand, rising patient numbers (and most recently, a declining number of patients as a result of suspended treatment due to the pandemic) and a shortage of skilled workers on the other. Quality management as the nucleus of the healthcare business receives no or too little attention in the public media.

A change has been underway for a long time to the effect that satisfaction after treatment no longer depends solely on the quality of medical treatment, but also on the recovery process. This includes numerous factors from accommodation to catering, personal interactions, and communication. These interpersonal relations are based on a special attitude: service orientation. After all, service is an attitude that applies across all sectors and achieves positive results across all industries.

As a service expert, Carsten K. Rath knows what is missing from the public discourse: customer orientation or, in this case more correctly, patient orientation. Only those who put the patient at the center, and ahead of the most established processes, will achieve a satisfactory result: rapid recovery and health prevention. "The process serves the person and not vice versa," comments Carsten K. Rath.

The services offered are only as good as they are perceived emotionally by the recipient, i.e., the patient. And emotions are known to be an essential aspect when it comes to satisfaction. The patient immediately senses the attitude with which the nursing staff and doctors treat him or her. The moment he or she has to seek medical care, he or she takes advantage of an expected service that he or she could obtain from many different places. He or she rarely makes the decision based on financial figures, but rather on emotions. He or she wants to get well as quickly as possible while being recognized as a customer with many needs. A patient also wants to be treated with an attitude of service excellence.

You probably associate service excellence more with a service you receive on a vacation at a nice resort, for example. Or you may think of completely different services that you use more frequently in your everyday life, such as a visit to a hairdresser or getting your car repaired. A visit to the doctor or even to the hospital probably do not come to mind at first.

"In this regard, service excellence works across industries and is quite independent of the level of experience or professional ranks and Americanized titles of the performers. Empathy, attentiveness, and a customer-oriented demeanor are the keys to an excellent attitude. The decisive factor is not so much the 'what,' but rather the 'how,' the attitude," explains Rath.

"Do you feel that your life is a little bit more beautiful and joyful after a service you have used? Then you have probably encountered it – service excellence." (Rath 2018a; 2018b)

2. Service with taste: The Helios Hospitals pilot project "6 chefs, 12 stars"

2.1 Hospital and culinary arts – a contradiction in itself?

In Germany, the term "hospital food" is used as a metaphor for "bad food." Helios recognized this very early and has always given food an essential role. The employees of the company's own catering service are constantly working on the quality and selection of the meals they provide. They had already created modern processes at an early stage with so-called cook and chill procedures to provide the numerous patients throughout Germany with the best possible food – while the quality of the food offered is increasing.

"When we launched the '6 chefs, 12 stars' project, our food supply was already at a very good level. However, other hospital operators had followed in our footsteps and, from our point of view, a new and fresh approach was needed for the future direction of our catering. This required an external perspective – and ultimately an excellent external and internal team to bring the new challenge internally to the patients with the usual quality and quantity," says Enrico Jensch about the start of the project.

2.1.1 *Visions at first glance: Carsten K. Rath and Enrico Jensch lay a culinary foundation*

Enrico Jensch and Carsten K. Rath shared a love of high-quality food that delights the palate and is also healthy long before they met in 2018. Enrico Jensch finally witnessed service expert Carsten K. Rath on stage at a Helios annual conference in 2018, as he enthusiastically introduced his heartfelt topic of service excellence.

The spark between them was thus ignited and the basis for their exciting collaboration was established.

Although entrepreneur Carsten K. Rath did not focus on culinary arts in his keynote speech, this quickly became the focus of the subsequent discussions. Service excellence takes on different faces across industries and wants to live itself out in a variety of facets.

Patients expect safety and service at Helios Hospitals, always against the background that they leave the hospital in a better condition than when they entered it. Tasty and healthy cuisine makes their stay in hospital much more enjoyable and the recovery process much more pleasant – the two experts agree on this.

2.1.2 *The basic ingredient that creates something new out of seemingly irreconcilable opposites*

Until 2019, many people still considered a hospital stay and good catering with the highest culinary standards to be a contradiction in terms. But from the idea of "we've always done it that way" something new may also emerge – something innovative, maybe even something bold, crazy. When a new idea is brought to the table and the first critics shake their heads, you can be sure that you are on the trail of new potential.

Progress wants to set colorful new standards and delight tastefully.

2.2 From the stage to the plate: Project milestones in the culinary concept

2.2.1 From the idea to the concept

After the Helios annual conference, Enrico Jensch decided to establish culinary excellence at the Helios hospitals. Therewith, he took a courageous step into terrain that had not yet been ventured into in hospital operations. But he knew from previous Helios history that it was precisely these unconventional approaches that had ultimately shaped the Helios corporate brand and spurred on new growth opportunities.

Six chefs of the highest caliber were to be involved – each one a passionate professional in his or her discipline, charming, humorous, and ready to drive an innovative concept forward in an extraordinary environment. The team was quickly identified: six top chefs, who could not be more different, have created a tasty milestone in the culinary arts of the healthcare industry with their dishes.

Among others, top chefs Thomas Bühner, Christoph Rüffer, Nils Henkel, Hendrik Otto and, in the future, Sophia Rudolph and Paul Ivic will be part of the team. Enrico Jensch and Carsten K. Rath are accompanying the project as strategists, also adopting the perspective of critical consumers.

In this top-class team, you will find everything but off-the-shelf ideas. Thus, specially tested and favored dishes are designed and selected by the star chefs: A total of twelve tasty and healthy lunch dishes are created. For the first time, the experts are combining the pleasurable world of top-class gastronomy with the often painful experience of a stay in hospital. At the same time, the experts are setting a new milestone in healthcare.

2.2.2 From the show plate to the hospital

So how is a gourmet plate transformed for hospital operations? The answer to the biggest challenge in this project is provided by Hofmann Menü-Manufaktur, which has already been working with Helios for many years. Every day, Hofmann Menü-Manufaktur delivers up to 22,000 meals to Helios Hospitals, ready to be frozen. The range of meals is vast – the portfolio includes traditional as well as vegan and vegetarian food and special diets tailored to the needs of the patients.

Quality is also the top priority in the Menü-Manufaktur: Each dish is subject to strict purity requirements and undergoes various internal quality controls. Together with the star chefs, the star dishes are devised directly on-site in Boxberg and repeatedly tasted and refined until everyone is delighted with the result.

2.2.3 The coronavirus crisis as a source of inspiration – from the kitchens at home to the hospital

An unplanned milestone in the project was the coronavirus crisis. It also banished professional chefs to their home offices or stoves at home. Was this global crisis now to herald the end of the project even before it had really taken off?

Innovative ideas are based on a clear vision. If unforeseen incidents occur, it becomes apparent how sustainable this vision is, even in everyday life or stressful situations. Sometimes unexpected events even broaden the current perspective, as in this project.

The star chefs put on their cooking aprons and took advantage of the upcoming home office time to cook their favorite dishes at home. When a professional chef cooks in his or her own kitchen, this is certainly not yet particularly surprising or inspiring; unless, of course, you get to enjoy the prepared meal yourself. Or you install cameras in the kitchen so that outsiders can also enjoy the entire cooking show.

All six professional chefs were looking forward to this unique opportunity to record their skills and passion in a completely unconventional way in a home setting. Using cell phone cameras, a professional tripod and, above all, a great deal of enthusiasm, the professionals cooked their favorite dishes in their private kitchens. This very spontaneously initiated video documentation preserved the experiment and became a public favorite, even before the "6 Chefs, 12 Stars" project had started its lifetime test on-site in the hospitals. For viewers, this created the basis for a perfect week of nutrition, as the dishes were released on a weekly basis.

The recordings are as diverse as the chefs and the respective dishes themselves: Christoph Rüffer combines his love of his homeland with young herring tartar on potato pancakes in one dish and shares a classic fish recipe: plaice "Finkenwerder Art" with cucumber salad. Creativity and traditional cooking are the cornerstones for him at the stove.

Michelin-starred chef Hendrik Otto combines the tastes from his early childhood days with the flavors of the world and always takes his guests on a journey. "Cooking tasty dishes is something emotional, and should be fun and uncomplicated," Otto explains. His recipe for "Poor Knights" [Arme Ritter] will delight all dessert lovers. But of course, the chef also puts hearty dishes on his plates: With his "Krautfleckerln," he combines Croatian, Austrian, and Bohemian cuisine.

Star chef Nils Henkel pursues his very own approach with his creations, whether at home or in his restaurant. He became known for his "Pure Nature" cuisine – a new German cuisine that surprises its guests with unusual textures and flavors. His asparagus with mascarpone and garden herbs is surprising because of its additional ingredient: coffee. His grain salad becomes fruity and summery light with the addition of juicy peaches, kefir, and spruce shoots.

For top chef Thomas Bühner, the food on the plate is a symphony composed in a culinary way – great feelings are awakened by the interplay of the entire orchestra, the ingredients and the flavors used. The beet gazpacho with smoked salmon he created is conjured up on the plate in ten minutes and is a real source of energy. His whole-grain pasta with parmesan and pine nut oil is also very energy-rich.

The results of this unplanned home cooking are approachable and very personal home stories – in the form of a YouTube video series. Viewers are inspired to cook a delicious and healthy meal for perfect nutrition on their own stove with just a few ingredients. The dishes are explained step by step and are therefore very easy to cook. With the selected ingredients and the right combination of flavors, they are nevertheless refined in taste and different from the usual type of homemade lunches and dinners. All the ingredients are available in the supermarket around the corner and are even gentle on the household budget. After all, health that tastes good should find a permanent place in every kitchen without hurdles.

2.2.4 *Successful launch of lunch and a cookbook to go*

After the various testing and tastings in the chefs' kitchens and on-site at Hofmann Menü-Manufaktur, the ready-to-serve dishes were served for the first time at the Helios hospital Bad Saarow in early 2020. Here and in five other hospitals, 70 patients gave them an average grade of 1.8 during the trial run. No one expected a patient satisfaction rate of 95 percent.

Flavorful culinary experiences that promote health and are especially well received by patients: this overwhelming result spurred us on to continue.

Patients at Helios Hospitals can now decide for themselves whether they want to enjoy the classic menu or the menu inspired by the star chefs during their stay. Have you ever had lemon potato gnocchi with artichokes in a spicy vegetable broth at a hospital? For every palate, a suitable and healthy dish is prepared.

But that is not all. The Helios team and the project team are keen to ensure that the dishes they develop continue to have an effect beyond the patients' stay in hospital. Recuperating patients and their relatives can continue to eat according to the cooking professionals' ideas, by watching the tutorials in the cooking videos or taking home one of the limited-edition cookbooks, in which interested parties will find a summary of the chefs' expertise: the books present both detailed recipes developed for the hospital stay as well as the favorite dishes of the chefs from their home-office stories (Rath, 2020).

The photo shoot for the colorful cookbook introduced the tasty dessert of the project: At the invitation of Hendrik Otto, all of the top chefs met to prepare the cookbook together at the Hotel Adlon Kempinski in Berlin, Germany. The top chefs once again cooked their favorite recipes while being professionally recorded. Background interviews with the individual chefs round off the experience of reading the cookbook.

The result is a comprehensive cookbook with healthy dishes that can be recreated and with tips from health experts. Valuable background knowledge for each recipe is provided by Helios' health expert Prof. Dr. med. Michael Ritter, Chief Physician for Angiology, Diabetology and Endocrinology at Helios Hospital Berlin, together with Helios' dietician Jana Wolf. They comment on the recipes and explain why the ingredients used are so healthy.

3. Culinary excellence as a growing USP at Helios Hospitals

3.1 Reheated dishes do not taste good. Advanced creations do

If the "6 Chefs, 12 Stars" project has shown one thing, it is that bold steps pay off and formerly contradictory concepts like hospitals and cuisine can merge into a fascinating and tasty experience. Actually, the project could now be considered complete. The dishes conceived could easily be offered each year again. Very few patients will have longer-than-average hospital stays, so the extensive selection of dishes will not become monotonous too quickly.

But patients and now also catering are the focus at Helios. Especially in still challenging times, service quality is completely focused on the patient. Thus, dishes are not reheated every year, which would clearly contradict the service quality strived for. Instead, the culinary concept has been developed further, improved and, of course, varied every year.

Because even the culinary arts are subject to the Helios principle: measure, evaluate, improve or, in this case, taste and flavor again. In the new edition of the project, six top chefs meet once again and, together with Hofmann Menü-Manufaktur, bring new, healthy dishes onto the patients' plates and into the exclusively produced cookbooks in the form of recipes that can be cooked at home.

This time, home stories and background interviews do not arise due to an external crisis but are deliberately included in the concept.

With the new edition of "6 chefs, 12 stars," the bitter aftertaste of a sometimes longer-than-planned recovery process will also be replaced by tasty hospital cuisine in the next season. The road to health is through the stomach, and the three pillars of service excellence can significantly improve this.

3.2 Outlook

The future of Helios is more digital, more international, and even more focused on service quality in its individual medical facilities and business units – we want to offer people a healthcare platform 24/7, 365 days a year and be their companion on a long journey.

Following the success of the pilot project, culinary excellence as a part of service excellence will become a permanent feature in all 89 Helios hospitals in Germany and will become an integral part of all healthcare at Helios. The pandemic did not harm the implementation of the project or even force the initiators to abandon it.

The opposite was the case. Changed external circumstances – elective restrictions in hospitals enforced by politics – made it possible to raise the dimension of the health issue to an even more personal level. The chefs' home stories inspired Enrico Jensch and Carsten K. Rath to take a next step and bring the idea of healthy, tasty cuisine to every interested household. So, if patients and employees cannot come to us, we go to them. The project's target groups have thus even expanded many times.

Innovations always arise from preceding problems that need to be solved. A crisis is always an opportunity for the courageous. The only question is how this opportunity is used for the benefit of the customer and patient. With its new culinary delights, Helios Hospitals target patients who seek clinical care.

At the same time, interested parties can now also participate in the development of taste outside of a hospital stay or visit: A specially initiated merchandise web store offers customers numerous other articles that focus on physical and mental well-being. Everyone knows that a healthy diet is essential for cell regeneration. Nevertheless, sometimes we need a gentle reminder in the hustle and bustle of everyday life. This reminder may bring pleasure and reach us long before the body sends warning signals.

According to the motto "Instructions for staying healthy," customers can find all the background information on the "6 chefs, 12 stars" project, including recipe videos, interviews, and information about the professional cooks, on the website www.helios-kochbuch.de. An additional calendar, a seed plant set, or herb tin serve as a reminder for one's health and can also be given to relatives and friends as a gift.

Culinary excellence and, in general, service orientation in everyday hospital life are comparable to the service concept in the hospitality industry (Jensch, 2020). It is the task of every employee to live the company's mission statement in his or her daily work processes and to make people feel good (Rath, 2017). When does the attitude of service excellence start? In hospitality, even before the restaurant is visited or the hotel room is occupied. A friendly first contact via e-mail or telephone leaves the famous first impression and paves the way for further service experiences (Rath, 2018a; 2018b).

This is similar to a stay in hospital. Healthcare services begin well before a patient is admitted to hospital and are experienced by the patient throughout their stay. The Helios team offers additional services to anyone who wants to take advantage of them. Its focus is also on preventive care, and its ultimate goal is for patients to stay healthy or to become healthy again quickly. If a subject is to have a lasting effect, it must grow and needs constant professional support. Steady steps lead to a profound result.

"Our promise of 'Best Service' applies to our patients as well as to our employees," comments Corinna Glenz, Managing Director of Human Resources. Service excellence, like health management, is complex and multidimensional. Service can only reach patients if it is internalized in the attitudes and thoughts of employees and lived on a daily basis. Excellent leadership is an important prerequisite. Employees are like patients, individuals with different potential and desires. Whoever ignores these in the company, reaps just as much ignorance in the long run and, at best, a 9-to-5 attitude. Motivated specialist staff, who can devote sufficient time to the patient and also to their own training, distinguish a standard hospital from an outstanding hospital like Helios.

The figures show that Helios' employees are just as passionate about the guidelines: On average, Helios' employees have been with the company for about 10.6 years. In our fast-moving, digitalized age, that is a real success in terms of service. The team is the driving force when it comes to improving patients' health. Human resources also face major challenges in the healthcare sector. Helios, therefore, relies on a future-proof HR strategy and does not oppose the changes in the world of work, but grows with them.

Everything is in transition. Companies with a promising future, such as the Helios Group, use it to surpass themselves again and again on all levels: entrepreneurial, personnel, medical and also tasteful.

That is what sets innovations apart. This is the perfect breeding ground for practical service excellence.

Bibliography

a. u. (2022). Helios healthcare, https://helios-international.com/about-helios, accessed 01/12/2022.

Hempel, M. (2020). The health industry in Germany and Europe, Federation of German Industries, https://english.bdi.eu/publication/news/the-health-industry-in-germany-and-europe/, accessed 01/11/2022.

Jensch, E. (2020). Service ist die Qualität von morgen [Service is tomorrow's quality], in: Rath, C. K. and Westermann, R. (eds.). Die 101 besten Hotels Deutschlands 2020/2021 [The 101 best hotels in Germany 2020/2021], Cologne.

Klöckner, J. (2021). Gesundheitsindustrie sieht Standort Deutschland in Gefahr [Healthcare industry sees Germany as a business location in danger], Handelsblatt, https://www.handelsblatt.com/inside/digital_health/bdi-strategiepapier-gesundheitsindustrie-sieht-standort-deutschland-in-gefahr-/27002054.html?ticket=ST-1230957-qBe1mWuqijiLBfNAXZks-ap5, accessed 04/14/2021.

Olk, J. (2020). Gesundheitsindustrie warnt: Attraktivität Deutschlands als Forschungsstandort sinkt [Healthcare industry warns: Germany's attractiveness as a research location declines], Handelsblatt, https://www.handelsblatt.com/politik/deutschland/studie-gesundheitsindustrie-warnt-attraktivitaet-deutschlands-als-forschungsstandort-sinkt/26617394.html, accessed 04/14/2021.

Rath, C.K. (2017). Ohne Freiheit ist Führung nur ein F-Wort. Mitarbeiter entfesseln. Kunden begeistern. Erfolge feiern [Without freedom, leadership is just an F-word. Unleash employees. Inspire customers. Celebrate success], Gabal Verlag.

Rath, C.K. (2018a). 30 Minuten Service Excellence [30 minutes of service excellence], Gabal Verlag.

Rath, C.K. (2018b). Für Herzlichkeit gibt's keine App. Service-Excellence in digitalen Zeiten [There's no app for cordiality. Service excellence in digital times], 3rd Ed., Gabal Verlag.

Rath, C.K. (2020). 6 Köche, 12 Sterne. Unsere Lieblingsgerichte für Ihr Zuhause [6 chefs, 12 stars. Our favorite dishes for your home], Cologne.

Service innovation management

Best practice Deutsche Telekom - Reinventing service: How we turn customers into fans

Ferri Abolhassan

Management summary

Significant changes usually require a radical approach – whether in sports or business. To raise Deutsche Telekom's customer service to an excellent level, we are currently fundamentally reinventing it in some areas – with more customer proximity, more professionalism and more services that are consistently designed with the customer in mind. With our "Re-Invent" policy, we want to turn our customers in Germany into real fans. A day-one mentality, ambidexterity and a radical customer focus are our keys to success.

1. Introduction

Richard Fosbury was born in Portland, Oregon, in 1947. His friends just call him Dick. At 1.93 meters, he is an extremely lanky guy and seemingly made for the high jump. In fact, however, he was an "uncoordinated wannabe athlete," as he says of himself. He could not get to grips with the usual jumping technique at all: in the straddle, the jumper crosses the bar face down, with legs straddling it. For Dick, 1.60 meters was the end of the line – he never jumped higher than that using the straddle technique. So, he started experimenting.

While everyone else was jumping off forward, the Oregon State University student simply tried it backward. No one had ever done that before. His home coach Bernie Wagner was not delighted at all: "You're not going to do anything like that! You'd be better off joining the circus." But Dick was undeterred and quickly jumped ten centimeters higher than using the straddle technique. That is why he continued to refine his own technique: He took a curved run-up, turned his torso on take-off, flew head first backward over the bar and landed on his back.

"If kids try to imitate it, it will wipe out a whole generation of high jumpers because they'll all break their necks," warned Payton Jordan, head coach of the U.S. Olympic team. Furthermore, people at sports science conferences discussed why this jumping technique could not work. But despite all the prophecies of doom, Dick competed with his unconventional technique at the 1968 Olympics in Mexico City. At first, the competitors laughed at him, but then everyone was amazed: Dick did not fail a single attempt up to 2.22 meters. In the final, he was the only jumper to clear 2.24 meters and won the gold medal – setting a new Olympic record.

"He jumps like someone falling out of a thirty-story window," wrote one reporter. "His style is spectacular, but also very individual. I don't think he will have much influence on the future of high jumping," said Soviet coach Yuri Dyachkov – but he was very much mistaken because Dick's extraordinary jumping technique is easy to learn: four years later in Munich, the 16-year-old Ulrike Meyfarth jumped to an astonishing world record and Olympic victory – with Fosbury's technique. In the following years, the "Fosbury Flop" became the new standard in the high jump and the world record was raised to 2.45 meters. Such heights would never have been possible with the straddle.

I am a big fan of Dick Fosbury and his story. Why? Because it shows us that it is worth being courageous, questioning the status quo, finding your own path, and then following it consistently – regardless of what others think or say about it. I always have to think of the following saying from a calendar: "Everyone said it couldn't be done! Then someone came along who didn't know that and just did it." Dick Fosbury was just that kind of guy. He went about it without any preconceived notions, experimented without blinkers, without restrictions to his thinking, and did not allow himself to be discouraged by critical companions. He simply did things differently and believed in himself and his cause. Only in this way did he succeed in fundamentally reinventing the high jump.

2. The Dick Fosburys of business

In business, too, there are always Dick Fosburys who do not care about existing standards and conventions. They take an unconventional approach, think "out of the box," and thus drive innovations that sometimes cause disruptive shocks in the entire industry: Does a smartphone need buttons to be able to write on it? Until 2007, everyone would have thought of devices like the Nokia Communicator and said, "Yeah, sure. How would that work without buttons?" But then Steve Jobs came along and completely turned the market upside down with the iPhone. Since then, touchscreens have become the new standard and smartphones without buttons are the new normal. But the intuitive operating concept of the iPhone and the high level of user-friendliness associated with it are still considered unrivaled today. For this reason, Apple's iPhone was the best-selling smartphone worldwide in the fourth quarter of 2021 – 14 years after its launch

– and gave Apple a market share of 22 percent. In second and third place were Samsung (20 percent) and Xiaomi (12 percent) (Canalys, 2022).

Let us jump back to 1985, when the first Blockbuster video store was founded in Dallas. The chain grew rapidly, peaking at around 9,000 stores and 60,000 employees. One of its customers was Reed Hastings. One day, he was annoyed that he had to pay a $40 fine for returning "Apollo 13" too late. So, in 1997, he set up an online movie shipping company himself and deliberately did not charge his customers for returning DVDs late. He quickly added a subscription model by which his customers could rent as many DVDs as they wanted. And DVD shipping was a success, but Hastings was already thinking one step ahead and, from 2007, focused on streaming content that his customers could access directly via the Internet. With his innovative video-on-demand concept and radical customer orientation, Hastings turned the entire entertainment industry upside down. Today, Netflix is the leading streaming entertainment provider. In 2020, the company's stock market value surpassed the Walt Disney Company for the first time, at $195 billion. And Blockbuster? They filed for bankruptcy back in 2010.

My final example of an unflinching difference-maker is Jeff Bezos: In 1995, he founded Amazon as an online mail-order company for books. He subsequently focused on competing with major booksellers like Barnes & Noble and Waldenbooks. But that approach was only moderately successful. So, Bezos positioned Amazon more broadly and launched Amazon Marketplace in 2000. This allowed third parties to offer their items online through Amazon, dramatically increasing Amazon's selection and sales. The third-party marketplace, combined with Amazon's own direct sales of more than just books, eventually made Amazon the Western world's preferred online shopping destination. In 2006, it added cloud computing services (Amazon Web Services), which lead the industry today. Thus, Bezos, who stepped down as CEO in July 2021, shaped Amazon into one of the most valuable companies in the world. In 2020 alone, it generated $386 billion in revenue.

3. Jeff Bezos' recipe for success

There is no question that Amazon's dominant market position and sometimes rigorous working conditions are debatable. Still, apart from that, I think Amazon is an awe-inspiring success story and a prime example of a company that keeps reinventing itself. That is why it is worth taking a closer look at Jeff Bezos' convictions and management methods.

As early as 1997, e.g., he wrote in his first letter to shareholders that he planned risky investments, some of which would certainly go wrong, while others would go through the roof. For him, the flops were not failures but lessons for the future. And he was right in his prediction: the Amazon Fire Phone, Amazon Destinations, and Amazon WebPay may have been flops, but Amazon Marketplace, Amazon Web Services (AWS), and the Amazon Echo have turned into real sales rockets. The underlying message is to be bold, take risks, and be prepared that not everything will work out the way you want it to. But if you use these setbacks to get better, something really great can come out of them.

The second important lesson: For Jeff Bezos, it was always "Day One." He always managed Amazon as if the company was still on its first day because, in his eyes, "Day Two" was already stagnation. "Followed by irrelevance. Followed by excruciating, painful decline. Followed by death. And that is why it is always Day One." According to his logic, even after 26 years on the market, Amazon is only at the beginning of a great success story, with the best yet to come. That means you should avoid stagnation as a company, instead always stay hungry, question yourself, never rest complacently on your laurels. You should make every effort to remain a "Day One Company" permanently. "No matter how old or big your company gets, keep the spirit and drive of a start-up," is the advice of Jeff Bezos (Bezos and Isaacson, 2020).

He also demanded that his employees think efficiently and logically and make fact-based decisions, e.g., when setting up new logistics centers. At the same time, however, he always gave them the freedom to develop their own ideas that did not fit in with core business approaches—"invent and wander" he called it. In plain English: "Think of something and let your mind wander." That is the opposite of efficient and logical, but in this out-of-the-box thinking, intuition, curiosity, and experimentation guide the thoughts, and that is often how the most remarkable innovations emerge. The best example is Amazon Web Services: What does renting data storage in the cloud have to do with selling books? At first, nothing! Nevertheless, this has become an extremely lucrative business and a second pillar for Amazon.

The trick is to find the right balance between rational decisions and creative whimsy. This ambidexterity is often described as an enormously important management skill, and, in my view, it is. On the one hand, managers must be able to successfully develop the bread-and-butter business through continuous improvement and efficiency gains (exploitation); on the other hand, they must also be able to uncover new opportunities and enable true innovation through experimentation and flexible action (exploration). Reconciling both is no easy task, but it is worthwhile (Christensen, 2016).

Last but not least, perhaps the most important secret to Bezos' and Amazon's success is a radical customer focus. While other companies are thinking about how they can sell even more books, Amazon is thinking about how it can make the experience of reading books even better for its customers. It was through this that Kindle was born. The first version of it sold out within hours, and over 25 percent of Kindle reviews reportedly have the word "love" in them. So, customers love this product, which gives them an even more enthusiastic reading experience. But with Kindle, Amazon has not only improved the experience for its customers, it has also tapped into new revenue streams at the same time. An actual win-win situation! Customers and companies benefit equally. Hence, Bezos' tip: Always think radically from your customer's point of view! Only do things that are good for your customers. And never settle for the second-best solution. Better is always possible!

4. The "Re-Invent" policy of Telekom Service

I see many parallels here with Telekom Service: We, too, have to manage a balancing act between simply doing things right and radically reinventing ourselves. It is about successfully combining efficiency and creativity, achieving ambidexterity, safeguarding day-to-day business and at the same time breaking new ground, driving innovation. We, too, must approach each day as if it was day one because the competition never sleeps, and our customers' expectations are constantly evolving – keyword "Liquid Expectations:" What is special today will be expected of all other providers tomorrow. That is why we, too, have to keep reinventing ourselves, even if we have already changed a lot in recent years.

In 2017, we began to redefine our service and put people back at the center of our business – customers with their individual wishes and expectations, and employees with their very personal skills and experience. And this rediscovery of the "superpower of people" has paid off (Abolhassan, 2020): We have increased our first-solution rate, which is very important for us, to 55 percent. This means that we resolve more than one in two customer concerns at the first contact. We have reduced the number of canceled technician appointments to less than one percent – with 30,000 calls a day. And we have reduced the number of customer complaints by an impressive 85 percent – with 60 million contacts per year.

These key figures alone show that we are on the right track. But external awards also underline that we are making progress with our service transformation: In 2021, e.g., we once again won the "Grand Slam" of the telecommunications industry, i.e., all four major hotline tests conducted by connect and CHIP. And we also won the connect shop test. In addition, Focus Money named us "Service King" in our industry. This means that we offer the best customer service in 50 out of 56 major German cities.

Should we now sit back, relax, and celebrate ourselves? No, we should not! We are sticking with Jeff Bezos: we are not resting on our laurels. We are still a long way from reaching our goal because the best service is not a sprint, but a marathon. You need a lot of staying power. And for us, every customer contact is a test that we want to win at the end of the day. That is why we launched a new strategy program called "Re-Invent" at the beginning of 2021. We want to reinvent our customer service in many places, heralding the next step in our transformation process. For us, it is still Day One.

Three topics are the focus of our "Re-Invent" program (Abolhassan, 2021):

1. We want to get even closer to our customers with hybrid and, in the future, fully convergent regiocenters.
2. We would like to further increase the professionalism of our employees to solve customers' concerns even more often right from the first contact.
3. With our "Einfach.RICHTIG.Machen." [Simply.Do it.RIGHT.] initiative, we want to improve the quality of our processes and workflows wherever necessary.

4.1 Regionalization: New customer proximity

That sounds easier than it is. But we have not only clearly defined our goals, but also the way to get to them: For example, we want to meet our customers wherever they are – in their environment, in their language, with a permanent team that knows its way around the place, feels responsible throughout, and forms a genuine customer relationship. To this end, we have already established nine regiocenters across Germany, some of which are hybrid, to serve our customers from particular areas. Five more regiocenters will follow by the end of 2022.

At each of these locations, hundreds of colleagues are working together across disciplines and – where necessary – also virtually: the customer service representatives for our fixed-line and internet customers, our technical customer service, our field service, the dispatchers, and at some locations we have even closely integrated our business clients account managers, our technicians, and our Telekom shops. In short, the regiocenters are where we pool all our expertise to find even faster solutions for our customers.

We no longer have the silo view that is common in many service centers. The entire Regio team works for our customers. The regiocenter can usually fully solve their concerns no matter what the customers want. To do this, employees from all teams sit in one area or work very closely together virtually. This direct exchange helps solve problems more quickly and creates a new commitment to our customers. We are responsible as a cross-functional team, we take care of a customer's concern holistically and do not pass on the customer unnecessarily; that is the basic idea.

Our ultimate goal is to have fully convergent regiocenters that deal with the mobile and fixed-line issues of private customers and business clients alike. In this way, we want to offer our 70 million customers in Germany a personal solution to their concerns, if possible right from the first contact – from person to person, in a familiar language, with the necessary local flavor. In our view, this is a very important lever for achieving a high level of customer satisfaction in service.

4.2 Expertise: New knowledge

The second lever is new professionalism. Here, too, we are focusing on the "Re-Invent" idea because despite all the necessary digitalization, people still make the difference in service – the customer service representatives, the field service, and the store employees, with their years of experience, their great empathy and expertise. There are still enough moments in everyday service when a smile easily beats a hundred computers. In such cases, however, it is not just a matter of wanting to help; our people must then also be able to help (Abolhassan, 2020; 2021). Nothing is more frustrating for the customer than someone who wants to help but cannot do so. Surely everyone has already had their own painful experiences of this – whether at the doctor's, in a department store, or in a restaurant.

So, we are investing even more in the professional competence of our customer service representatives, service technicians, store employees, and other specialists (Abolhassan, 2021). With HR tools such as our Competence Guide, with the help of special training rooms or terminal walls, with virtual training and face-to-face coaching, every employee can work on their individual development areas, get to know our products even better, build up or refresh their technical understanding, and thus expand their professional horizons step by step. As management, we create the necessary framework conditions for this. We ensure the required degree of freedom and provide our employees with the best digital tools – such as MagentaView, which creates a holistic view of our customer relationships. Knowledge is power – the power to provide customers with the best possible advice. At the same time, we are trying to make learning even more fun. After all, knowledge is also fun, and professionalism is always a question of inner attitude: Only those who show initiative and learn out of intrinsic motivation will develop further. And only service staff who do this will be able to help customers in a targeted manner in the future (Abolhassan, 2021).

Globalization and digitalization have made our service world extremely fast-paced. Product life cycles are becoming shorter and shorter. And everything that can be connected is being connected. As a result, our homes are becoming control centers and home networking is becoming increasingly complex. That is another reason why I am arguing for new professionalism in service. Far too often, I experience a lack of the necessary technical understanding. Learning something only once no longer does justice to the increasing complexity of our products and services. Only if we keep at it, work on our technical expertise, and keep up with the pace of digitalization and technical change, can we continue to help our customers in the future.

It used to be said, "You can't teach an old dog new tricks." It may be that this admonition to school beginners still works today. However, the possible deduction that an "old dog" is finished with a subject when he is older is problematic. The opposite is the case. I am firmly convinced: "Learned" was yesterday! Today, we need a different basic understanding of what is essential in life: the willingness to learn something new every day. This also includes the insight that learning is not a punishment but a gift that brings every one of us forward throughout our lives – and makes impeccable service possible in the first place.

4.3 Radicality: New services

The third major lever of our "Re-Invent" program is that we look at our processes and ways of working and examine where we can become even more straightforward, even more user-friendly, and even better for our customers. To do this, we radically put things to the test as if it were our first day as a company – just like Amazon's day-one philosophy. We turn things inside out and completely reinvent ourselves in several areas – consistently and without blinkers. This is how we create innovative services with tangible added value for our customers (Bezos and Isaacson, 2020).

We have already achieved the first quick wins: These include our new concierge service for changing a fixed-line provider. What is it all about and what is so special about it? We want to offer customers who come to us from competitors a delightful first customer experience. We want their switch to go flawlessly. We have had a provider changing service since 2016, and around 420,000 customers used it in 2020, but with "Re-Invent" we are reinventing this service and systematically thinking about it from the customer's perspective. Our goal is to provide an all-around carefree service like the concierge in a five-star hotel.

The central question for us was: What do new customers want when they switch from another provider to Telekom? We know from our customers' feedback that they want a contact person who will give them the best possible advice throughout the change, who knows the job in every detail, who they can rely on 100 percent, and who they can reach at any time, if possible, just like a hotel concierge.

We, therefore, started the "Re-Invent" process of our provider changing service by describing customer expectations. As early as the design phase, we involved our customers via our "Telekom-Ideenschmiede" (a think tank) and asked them whether our service struck a chord with them. They expressly confirmed their desire for personal support during the switching process. In addition to telephone contact, they also wanted the option of communicating with their concierge via e-mail and Messenger. And around 65 percent of our customers expressed a desire for a permanent support team.

With these findings in mind, our project team set about implementing them: We brought together concierge teams of four specialists each as contacts for the switching process in round-table groups. This means that our customers do not only have a contact person via SMS, as was previously the case, but a fixed team that can also be reached by phone and e-mail. In the future, these teams will serve customers from their respective regions – just as is customary in our regiocenters. This creates more customer proximity, ensures clear responsibilities, and simplifies communication.

How does the provider changing service work in practice? Our concierge service starts with the first customer contact: The consultants take plenty of time for a detailed initial discussion. They ask about the customer's initial situation and individual wishes and needs. We document the conversation results digitally and then accompany the switching process throughout – from the confirmation of the order to connection by our service technicians.

The concierge informs the customer about all the important steps and answers any of his or her questions during this period. In this way, no information, such as a subsequent change request from the customer, is lost. Our desk groups are familiar with all the orders from their regional customer base and can always provide information on their current status in the event of queries – until the change is complete and the customer has confirmed that their connection is working, and even beyond that, namely, until the first telephone bill is issued. In the past, there have often been queries about bills. Now we proactively ask whether everything is suitable for the customer.

At the end of their provider change, we survey all customers in detail. Using this feedback, we can develop our concierge service quickly and agilely during ongoing operations. We are gradually rolling out all the elements that have proved successful in the field test. We are also continuing to support the concierge service with our "Telekom-Ideenschmiede" to drive it forward in close cooperation with our customers.

For example, we have planned a feedback lounge and a virtual workshop. Feedback from our employees also flows into the design of the service. And at the end of the day, the concierge service for the provider changing process serves as a blueprint for other concierge services – e.g., for customers who move or build a house and need a fixed-line and internet connection at their new address. In this way, we consistently put our customers first and offer them innovative and impeccable service. This is what we understand by "Einfach.RICHTIG.Machen." [Simply.Do it.RIGHT.].

Our Digital Home Service, which we launched in April 2021, also falls under this heading. For this, we have subjected our popular computer assistance to reinvention and rethought it from the customer's perspective. With the Digital Home Service, we support people with all applications in their networked home, which has become increasingly important as the central hub of our digital lives, and not just during the coronavirus pandemic; keywords "home office and homeschooling." With our new service, we provide expert assistance in optimizing WLAN, as well as in setting up smart home devices, laptops, tablets, and smartphones or installing the corresponding software.

This offer is aimed at everyone – regardless of whether they are a Telekom customer or a customer of another provider. We help all users quickly and competently, on request even up to four times a year directly on-site. To this end, we have put together three different service packages for all interested parties, which are billed monthly. With this full-service package, we are able to meet a growing customer need and at the same time close a gap in the market. There has never been a service of this kind on the German market. Here, too, we are talking about a genuine "Re-Invention."

5. Have the courage to continue on the path

"You can never solve problems with the same way of thinking that created them," Albert Einstein once said. And I can only agree with that. When I set out in 2017 to revamp Telekom's customer service, it quickly became apparent that I would not succeed with existing means and methods. If you want to create something new, you need the courage to question everything and break new ground. I admit that this is not easy, and it takes a great deal of energy. Even culturally, it is an enormous challenge that cannot be overcome overnight.

And then you have to have the courage to actually change something and perhaps fail or not be successful fast enough. Many managers shy away from this, too, and prefer to play the stockholder. For me, however, adopting the attitude and thinking of Dick Fosbury, Steve Jobs, Reed Hastings, and Jess Bezos is essential when it comes to fundamental change. For real innovation, you simply need this courage, this conviction, and this radicalism – also in customer service (Christensen et al., 2011).

That is why I am pleased with and proud of my team of over 30,000 people, who see our policy the same way and actively support it. Without their conviction and passion, we would not be able to reinvent ourselves as an organization. Together, we have already achieved a great deal in recent years and turned good service into the best service in our industry. But that is not enough for us! We have not yet met our own standards. We have not yet reached our goal.

With our "Re-Invent" program, we want to turn our customers into true fans: the best service always and for everyone! A day-one mentality, ambidexterity, and a radical customer focus are our keys to success here. We can only achieve our goal of impeccable service and service excellence if we completely reinvent ourselves in many areas while not neglecting our core business and while consistently focusing on every customer. We are aware that this is a marathon, not a sprint. We still have a long way to go. But we have staying power and will not stop until we have reached this goal. Because for us, every customer counts! And the best is yet to come!

Bibliography

Abolhassan, F. (ed.) (2020). Superkraft Mensch: Warum der Mensch im Service den Unterschied macht [Superpower people: Why people make the difference in service], Frankfurter Allgemeine Buch.

Abolhassan, F. (ed.) (2021). Wissen. Macht. Spaß. – Die neue Fachlichkeit im Service [Knowledge. Power. Fun. — The new professionalism in service], Frankfurter Allgemeine Buch.

Bezos, J. and Isaacson, W. (2020). Invent and wander — The recipe for success: The collected writings of Jeff Bezos, Redline Publishing.

Canalys (2022). Apple retakes top spot in global smartphone market in Q4 2021, https://www.canalys.com/newsroom/canalys-global-smartphone-market-Q4-2021, accessed 02/11/2022.

Christensen, C.M. (2016). The innovator's dilemma: When new technologies cause great firms to fail, Harvard Business Review Press.

Christensen, C.M., Matzler, K. and von den Eichen, S.F. (2011). The Innovators Dilemma: Warum etablierte Unternehmen den Wettbewerb um bahnbrechende Innovationen verlieren [The Innovators Dilemma: Why Incumbents Lose the Competition for Breakthrough Innovations], Vahlen.

Managing customer-experience-related efficient and effective processes and organizational structure

B2B, B2C, or rather H2H? Service excellence in the B2B environment using Brenntag as a success example

Svenja Daniel

Management summary

Brenntag SE is the global market leader in distributing chemicals and ingredients, playing a key role as a link between customers and suppliers in the chemical industry. To differentiate itself from other companies in this highly fragmented environment, service excellence has become much more important in recent years. Managing customer expectations and continuously improving the customer journey are of utmost importance, especially for interchangeable goods. Understanding what customers need, expect, and want is taking on an increasingly important place in today's world.

1. Chemical distribution – a relatively unknown market with great potential

Chemical distributors are companies that play a critical role primarily in the manufacturing industry, supplying them with the materials needed to produce their own goods. Distributors buy, store, sell, and supply chemicals and ingredients and offer a wide range of services, such as blending, packaging, technical assistance, formulations, supply chain optimization, laboratory services, and advice on regulations, safety, waste treatment, and environmental aspects.

In view of all these aspects, chemical distribution links chemical producers and the processing industry.

Consequently, chemical producers usually do not sell their products directly to the smaller and geographically challenging end customers. Outsourcing, which is the replacement of the producer's services with an external distribution company, is essential in today's chemical and ingredient industry. The goal of outsourcing is to work with another company to achieve mutual and sustainable growth (Sellig et al., 2010).

The chemical distribution industry has evolved tremendously in recent decades due to the increased demand for chemicals and adopting processes along the value chain. Chemical producers have focused on their core skills of production, product innovation, and selling chemicals to their larger direct customers. Therefore, today's trend is to outsource smaller to medium-sized customers, whose businesses are usually more challenging for producers, to distributors (Budde et al., 2006).

Nowadays, the chemical industry consists of three parts: production, distribution, and consumption. About 80 to 90 percent of all chemicals are sold directly to customers by the manufacturing company, and distribution companies sell only 10 to 20 percent of chemicals. This market share is expected to increase due to the continuing trend toward outsourcing (Sellig et al., 2010). This includes, among other things, a more complex business strategy, smaller orders, and customers buying multiple products from the distributor acting as a wholesaler. All of these attributes play a significant role, in part because of the following factors:

- lower complexity – especially in markets with smaller volumes or a fragmented customer base
- access to new markets – improving geographic reach and market access
- value-added services – fades and inventory management gain importance
- savings in total cost of ownership – cost reduction through downsizing one's own production operations
- rising standards – distributors are very well positioned to meet increasing quality and safety standards

Especially for smaller volumes, smaller countries, and smaller customers, chemical distributors can offer more efficient logistical solutions, value-added services, and reduced complexity for both consumers and producers. Producers may have difficulty meeting these requirements due to limited operations and the need to focus on their core attributes.

But even today, the chemical distribution industry is highly fragmented. There are more than 10,000 distributors worldwide, which can be divided into commodity and specialty distributors. Therefore, chemical distribution is a highly promising and dynamic market that differs not only in terms of prices. Customers have increasingly high demands, which are fueled by the private as well as the professional environment. To serve these demands and expectations, the importance of service excellence is also increasing, which in turn can directly influence customer experience (Globalnewswire, n.d.).

2. Brenntag SE

An essential part of the chemical distribution industry's history is comprised by the company Brenntag. Brenntag is the world's leading chemical and ingredient distribution company, making it a significant actor in the industry. In 2020, Brenntag had more than 17,000 employees, operated in

77 countries at more than 670 locations, and supplied more than 10,000 different products to approximately 185,000 customers. In 1874, Brenntag was founded as an egg wholesaler. After nearly four decades, the company entered the chemical business and renamed itself "Brenntag." The name is a shortened form of "Brennstoff-, Chemikalien- und Transport AG" (fuel, chemicals, and transport plc). As mentioned earlier, the chemical distribution industry was already highly fragmented at the time. Brenntag recognized the need for a supra-regional distribution company that could deliver across borders. Therefore, Brenntag expanded its warehouse network and product range in 1950 and became an international company in 1966 with its first acquisition outside Germany. From then on, Brenntag expanded its business worldwide, acquiring various chemical distribution companies. The company also invested in new technologies for warehouses to offer value-added services along the supply chain. This strategy helped the company to become the market leader in the full-line distribution of chemicals and ingredients and to simplify the processes between chemical producers and distributors (Brenntag, n.d. a–d).

3. Brenntag and service excellence: A journey worth taking

3.1 The first step is the most important but also the most difficult

At the beginning of our journey, we had to choose a place to start from. Our pilot countries, the UK & Ireland, were quickly found due to their strong interest in the topic, and it did not take long for interested colleagues to volunteer to participate. During an initial internal assessment, it emerged that the consensus was that as a global market leader in chemical distribution, we offer very good customer experiences. To verify this, we decided to work with an independent market research institute. This collaboration consisted of developing a comprehensive questionnaire explicitly targeting customer experience. We then sent this survey to all customers, regardless of their size or business potential. We also conducted telephone interviews. After about four weeks, the data and information were collected to start the analysis. The results were then presented to the managers in our pilot countries.

Based on the results, we had to admit that the services delivered were not as excellent as we had previously assumed. Many of our customers were not fully satisfied. There were several aspects on which we scored very well, but there was also much room for improvement. Thanks to this insight, and thanks to our customers who shared their experiences and assessments with us, we were able to start at exactly the right point, and we received concrete suggestions as to what should be given the highest priority.

We relied on internal support to address these problem areas and looked for a training program. Brenntag managers in our pilot countries quickly found what they were looking for and sent 25 colleagues on a twelve-day training course on service excellence. Following the training, these Brenntag employees took their delight and newfound knowledge back to the company and led the improvement projects addressed at their sites.

To get an overview of whether the initiatives launched had made a lasting difference, in the following months, we introduced monthly tracking as a further step. This was much shorter than the 360° analysis but targeted the key issues and thus showed a Net Promoter Score (NPS) every month.

At this point, our pilot countries had been our focus for more than two years and were already showing some significant successes in the area of service excellence. These successes included not only an increased NPS, but also a decreased customer churn rate, and increased revenue and profit. This prompted us to say: the topic needs to be rolled out more widely, as it positively impacts our entire business.

3.2 An all-encompassing framework

The first step had been completed; we had proven how service excellence has a positive impact on Brenntag's business model. Now it was a matter of developing a concept for all other countries that, on the one hand, suited the culture and set-up in each individual country, but on the other hand, still left the countries freedom for their creativity and local differences as well as specialties.

The first step was to gain a uniform understanding of our customer journey. In several one-day workshops, the "Brenntag Customer Journey" was developed and subsequently designed (see Figure 1). This journey can now be used to show customers and employees what influence they have on customer experience and that every employee is part of this customer experience.

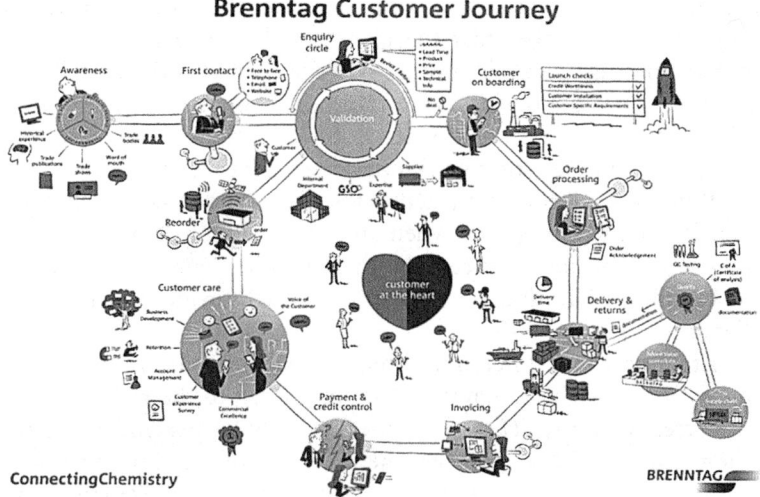

Fig. 1: Brenntag's customer journey

Then, the framework was created based on the experience of our pilot countries. It included the most essential topics to guarantee successful implementation of the model. First of all, it was a matter of explaining what exactly service excellence is. For this purpose, a pyramid was selected and backed up with a practical example (see Figure 2).

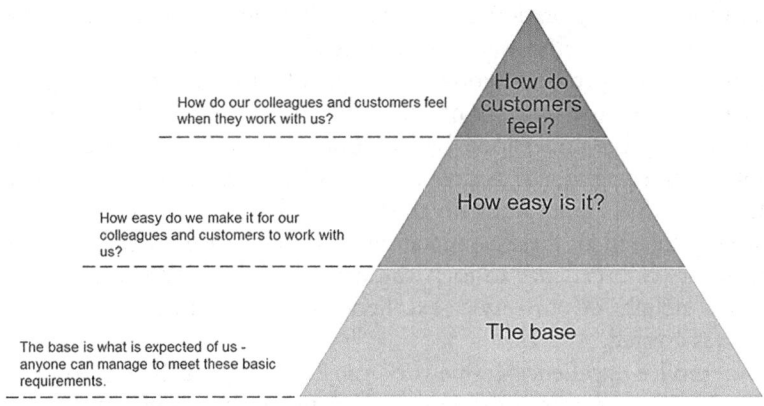

Fig. 2: Service excellence pyramid

Ask yourself the question: What do you remember about your last flight? The answer is usually that the drinks were expensive or there was no food.

Maybe you had little legroom, or you remember the movie you watched. You also often remember that the plane was late or experienced turbulence. But now, ask yourself another question: What is the core business of an airline? The core business is to transport passengers safely from A to B at the right time. The core business is not to offer delicate food, lots of legroom, or a wide selection of entertainment. Yet few people remember if their flight was on time and whether the plane landed safely. This aspect is taken for granted. It is only when an airline cannot deliver on its core business that it no longer meets the basic requirements in our pyramid, and it becomes more difficult or impossible to provide passengers with excellent service still.

The situation is not different at Brenntag. Its core business is to deliver chemicals and ingredients safely, at the right time, to the right place, and in the correct quantity. This can work flawlessly 98 percent of the time, but the customer will never forget the 2 percent of the time that did not go optimally. However, the 98 percent of the time when everything went optimally does not guarantee that the customer will automatically become more loyal. Customers expect to receive their order according to the terms that have been agreed upon.

To implement service excellence, a proper basis must first exist. After that, it comes down to the two most important points: How easy is it to do business with us, and how does our customer feel about it? Is it complicated to place an order? Do invoices or quotations arrive at the customer's door with errors, if any? Does the customer have to ask more often to get their quotation or a sample? These are all questions we need to ask ourselves to find out how easy it is to do business with us. For the emotional aspect, questions to ask include: In this day and age, does a driver observe the hygiene measures that need to be adhered to? Does the customer feel understood by his contact person? Are the customer's problems taken seriously? Is the customer's business model understood in order for us to respond optimally to their needs?

We considered all these aspects in order to introduce the successful concept of service excellence to each country and region. When this worked well and delight at our service excellence continued to grow, the framework was created.

Our service excellence framework can be imagined like a house (see Figure 3). The first step is that someone wants to move into this house. In our case, that someone per country or region takes responsibility for the topic of service excellence.

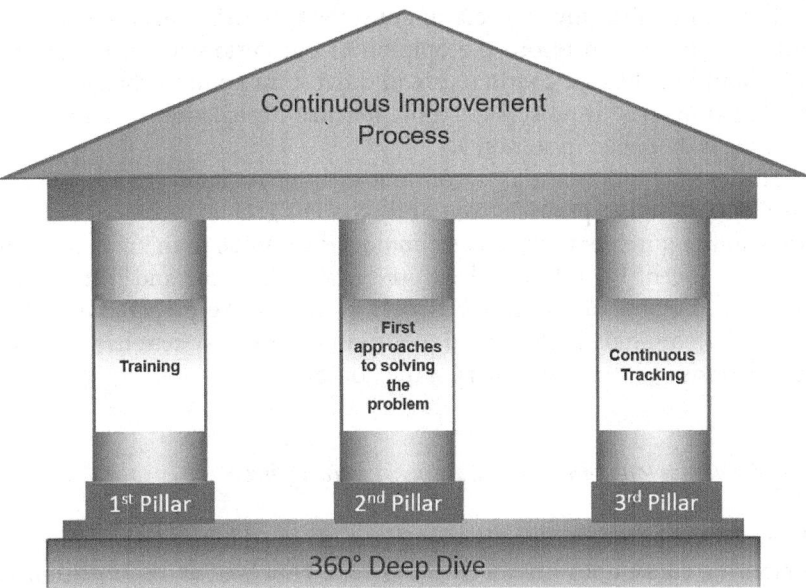

Fig. 3: Service excellence framework

After that, the foundation of the house has to be built. To do this, we worked with an external market research institute to initiate a 360° deep dive. This deep dive is an all-encompassing survey of our customers that was conducted both online and offline via telephone interviews. The deep dive was also conducted on a country-specific level to address local differences. Based on this, the pillars of the house were then built. The person responsible for service excellence in a country will not manage to introduce service excellence into all company areas without support. For this reason, the first pillar is the training pillar. In cooperation with a train-the-trainer program for service excellence, we have trained over 300 colleagues in Europe, the Middle East, and Africa (EMEA) to provide support and drive service excellence further into the organization. Section 3.3 explains the training in more detail.

The second pillar is based on the initial problem-solving approaches. Following the deep dive, it has already been possible to identify which problem areas we need to address, where our customers are not being served optimally and, of course, what are the areas in which we already offer service excellence and how we should expand or maintain these areas. These initial problem areas will be addressed with the second pillar.

The third pillar involves continuous tracking. This means that it is essential not only to record the opinion of our customers once, but that this should be the case continuously in order to respond to changes in the market as quickly as possible. A more detailed explanation of continuous tracking is described in section 3.4.

The roof of the house is a continuous improvement process. Service excellence is a concept that is constantly changing. Our customers' expectations and requirements change, technologies continue to mature, and new ones are added. In addition, there are always calculable and incalculable crises. In the field of service excellence, we have to be prepared for all of this and accordingly build a continuous improvement system based on the foundations and the three pillars of the house.

3.3 We need a forest fire – or at least many blazing fires

As explained in the previous section, we need to address all situations and establish a continuous improvement system. However, as also mentioned, this cannot be done by a single person. Chemical and ingredient distribution is still a very local business, so we need colleagues locally and in many different positions and areas who are eager to achieve service excellence and take this desire into the company.

The most important point here is to reach as many people as possible because every bit of support helps to make the company more customer-centric. For this reason, one of our approaches is to be present: to be present when colleagues start working at Brenntag, and also to be present during the journey that colleagues experience with Brenntag and to always be open to suggestions and advice as well as criticism.

The next important aspect is to have trained as many people as possible. However, why is training so necessary? Often, companies measure key figures and measure them again without translating the lessons learned into action or knowing how to deal with these key figures. However, service excellence is not just about measuring metrics. Service excellence is also about optimizing customer satisfaction – both internal and external – and retaining our customers in the long term. We have to demonstrate that it is easy to do business with us, and we have to be or become their supplier of choice – their favorite, so to speak. The service excellence training course explains how it is now possible to bring together key figures, measurements, processes, and personal impressions. It gives colleagues tools and techniques that can be used to map customer journeys – to analyze the experience at each customer touchpoint, and to put in place processes and procedures that can turn around negative experiences and define a standard of excellence in internal and external service.

On this basis, Brenntag decided to offer three days of classroom training on service excellence in each country. Depending on the size of the country and the number of employees, between twelve and 80 people were trained in this topic. In addition, we relied on the "train-the-trainer" principle and added a two-day train-the-trainer course after the three-day service excellence training. In this way, we were able to guarantee that colleagues from a wide range of areas could pass on their knowledge to their colleagues.

However, when the coronavirus pandemic broke out in March 2020, we had to make some changes. After some trial and error, we set up a very effective service excellence program that runs purely virtually. Twice a week, over a period of five weeks, there were two hours of face-to-face training via video conferences, and the participants were able to work on the topics they had learned about in group sessions thanks to virtual group rooms. In addition, there was homework that could be observed and practiced during the most ordinary everyday situations, such as shopping or online shopping. This purely virtual presence also saved travel and accommodation costs. We also managed to train even more colleagues than had initially been planned. By the end of the first quarter of 2021, Brenntag had trained more than 320 people in the EMEA region on the topic of service excellence.

This best practice subsequently spread to the other global regions and was also used there in the course of 2021 to train colleagues in all areas and, as described in the heading, to start a forest fire or many blazing fires.

The task of the trained service excellence ambassadors is to work in collaboration with the person responsible for service excellence on problem issues identified in this area in a country or region and to contribute their expertise.

3.4 Feedback is the key

Feedback is the key to many aspects of service excellence, be it feedback from employees or feedback from customers.

Internal feedback

Part of our training, as already mentioned, is to involve colleagues and collect ideas and feedback along the customer journey from an internal perspective. The employees of a company bring with them a distinctive knowledge and can name many points in advance with which our internal and external customers are not fully satisfied. In addition, they often have possible solutions or ideas for improvement. For this reason, it always makes sense to obtain internal feedback in addition to external feedback.

External feedback

Customer feedback, or external feedback in general, is essential to bring the outside view inside. Brenntag has decided to establish a global feedback system that is consistent across the Brenntag world. The feedback system is based on the real-time approach, i.e., sending surveys in real time to be as close as possible to the actual experience of a customer. To realize this, in compliance with the GDPR, the survey software was connected to our CRM systems to get information about each transaction and send valuable customer data along with it. Currently, surveys are sent to customers for the following transactions:

- invoice
- quotation
- sales call
- visit from the account manager
- complaint

The customer receives a survey on the above-mentioned topics within a few minutes. Only the invoice survey is sent a week later or on the requested delivery date to ensure that the customer can also answer the delivery questions. Customers can be contacted four times a year and receive at least two different surveys. An example of this is as follows: Customer A received an invoice in January and the survey was sent with it. Customer A is then blocked for three months and cannot receive another survey until April. In April, however, customer A can only receive surveys on topics other than the invoice topic. The survey on the subject of invoices is not activated again for customer A until July. Accordingly, surveys have a break of six months and customers three months.

When a customer takes the time to answer the survey, their response is not only fed back into our survey tool for analysis purposes, but also into our CRM systems. Within our CRM systems, our salespeople can thus see precisely how a customer has rated Brenntag and whether there has been any improvement or deterioration. This is also an excellent basis for communication.

Furthermore, feedback is used to initiate so-called close-the-loop processes to contact customers and discuss their evaluation or simply to thank them for their feedback. Monthly and quarterly analyses and reports are created to determine the problem areas and create improvement projects based on them.

For this reason, feedback is vital, as it gives us internal insights into our company and allows us to keep the external perspective in mind and focus on our customers' perceptions, experiences, and personal impressions.

4. Outlook

Service excellence within Brenntag has shown us, especially in the pandemic years 2020 and 2021, how valuable it is and how efficiently crises can be responded to. In addition, the increasingly relevant global focus has brought us a huge step closer to harmonization and standardization and promoted a lot of best practice sharing and cross-regional cooperation. Accordingly, the years 2022 and 2023 will be entirely dedicated to "harmonization" and "exceeding" to further drive service excellence at the global level as well and to strengthen and expand the already existing cross-regional mergers and to launch global unification projects. In this way, the strengths of all countries can be brought together to achieve the common goal of shaping a customer-centric enterprise. It should make no difference whether we function in a B2B or B2C company. We are working with people, so the name should be Human-to-Human (H2H). To achieve this, we will set global priorities to start from, and improve upon and develop a standard of service that is comparable across the Brenntag world. Customers will not notice any significant differences. Achieving this standardization and harmonization will take some time. Still, with our top management's and our colleagues' support, we will also succeed in this endeavor to bring Brenntag closer to a future H2H business.

Some concrete steps include:

- the further rollout of our standard survey tool
- working with commercial sectors to demonstrate the monetary impact of service excellence
- launching global improvement projects
- raising further awareness through communication tools
- implementing a detailed close-the-loop system that can be used worldwide

Brenntag is far from the end of this exciting journey, and service excellence is a journey that will probably never end and will constantly reveal new opportunities. This should not be seen as a burden, but as an opportunity: Customers are changing, Brenntag is changing, we are all changing, and we need to respond to these changes as a company and close the gap to our customers' requirements. It will be exciting to see what the future years will bring and where the journey will take us based on all these developments. One thing is certain, though: we may be a B2B company, but at heart, we have always been H2H.

Bibliography

Brenntag (n.d. a). History of Brenntag, https://www.brenntag.com/en-at/about/history/, accessed 01/11/2022.

Brenntag (n.d. b): Annual report 2020, https://annualreport2020.brenntag.com/annual-report-2020, aufgerufen am 24.06.2021.

Brenntag (n.d. c). Our history, https://www.brenntag.com/en-at/about/history/, accessed 5/15/2022.

Brenntag (n.d. d). Welcome to Brenntag in Germany, https://www.brenntag.com/en-de/, accessed 01/12/2022.

Budde, F., Felcht, U.-H. and Frankenmoelle, H. (2006). Value creation strategies for the chemical industry, Weinheim.

Globalnewswire (n.d.). Chemical distribution market size to reach US$ 412.4 Bn by 2030, https://www.globenewswire.com/news-release/2021/10/28/2323297/0/en/Chemical-Distribution-Market-Size-to-Reach-US-412-4-Bn-by-2030.html, accessed 01/26/2022.

Sellig, G. J., LeFave, R. and Bullen, C.V. (2010). Implementing strategic sourcing, van Haren Publishing.

Monitoring service excellence activities and results

Service excellence in customer experience at E.ON SE: The role and use of the Net Promoter Score

Kristina Rodig, Christopher J. Rastin

Management summary

This article lays the foundations for a Customer Experience Service Excellence program at E.ON SE. Given the recent history of energy market liberalization in Europe, it has been a new challenge for utilities to put customers first, understand their needs, address their concerns, and delight customers beyond their expectations.

The research findings of the Global Research and Insights team forms the basis for planning and implementing initiatives by the Global Insights and Customer Experience and Marketing teams. Together, they form the foundation for creating sustainable differentiation in customer service and energy branding in an increasingly intense competitive environment and form the foundation of Customer Experience Service Excellence at E.ON.

1. What is E.ON's Customer Experience Service Excellence Program?

A Customer Experience Service Excellence Program (CSEP) can be complicated, difficult to understand, and costly to implement. However, when done with proper planning and coordination, a CSEP can be designed and implemented pragmatically and without "over-engineering."

There are many models of service excellence, ranging from Johnston's framework for service excellence (Johnston, 2004) to the work of the ISO/TC 312 Technical Committee on Excellence in Service, which is currently in development by the global standards for service excellence at ISO. Informed by these models, E.ON has taken a pragmatic approach to the design and implementation of its CSEP, incorporating the fundamentals of a logic model for performance measurement in conjunction with multiple service excellence models.

The development and management of the E.ON CSEP was not easy or quickly accomplished and required a return to basics: the questions of whether such a program was necessary for a low-interest market and whether E.ON and its customers would benefit from it.

At E.ON, the CSEP assumes that the level of customer loyalty and delight can be derived from a customer's willingness to recommend E.ON to a friend or colleague – the Net Promoter Score (NPS®)[1]. In short, NPS is a score ranging from -100 to +100 based on the question "On a 0-to-10 scale, how likely is it that you would recommend E.ON to a friend or colleague?" This 11-point scale divides respondents into those who give E.ON a score of nine or ten (promoters), while those who give a score of six or less are considered "detractors." Those giving a score of seven or eight are known as "passives." The percentage of detractors is then subtracted from the percentage of promoters (based on the entire sample) (Reichheld, 2003).

Aware of the limitations of the Net Promoter Score (Hayes, 2010; Morgan and Rego, 2006; Keiningham et al., 2008), NPS was determined as the metric from which to develop the Customer Experience Service Excellence program for E.ON. The limitations of NPS are briefly discussed later in this chapter.

1.1 Why a Customer Experience Service Excellence Program for E.ON?

European energy markets have undergone various forms of liberalization since the 1990s. In June 1996, European Union economics and energy ministers agreed on the first directive to liberalize the internal electricity market. Unlike the United Kingdom, e.g., Germany has never had a single national energy supplier. However, despite the coexistence of several electricity suppliers, there was little competition in the electricity market (Delia, 2013). Table 1 on European market liberalization outlines the core differences before and after liberalization.

Before Liberalization	After Liberalization
Vertically Integrated Market	Privatization of state-owned electricity monopolies
	Separation of competitive segments
	Restructuring of generation and transmission
	Creation of a public wholesale energy market

Tab. 1: European market liberalization (source: Delia, 2013)

---

1 Net Promoter®, NPS®, NPS Prism®, and the NPS-related Emoticons are brands of Bain & Company, Inc., Satmetrix Systems, Inc. and Fred Reichheld. Net Promoter Score[SM] and Net Promoter System[SM] are service brands of Bain & Company, Inc., Satmetrix Systems, Inc. and Fred Reichheld.

The impact of energy market liberalization in terms of service excellence is clear – competition. With the introduction of a competitive market, customers suddenly had the option of switching suppliers, and it was up to energy companies to create and communicate competitive advantages. With completely identical commodity products and limited opportunities for price differentiation, the issue of service and service excellence plays a prominent role in companies differentiating themselves from the competition. This answers the question of "why" there is a need for E.ON's CSEP.

As the program evolved, it became increasingly clear that such a program would give E.ON a competitive advantage over the growing number of even new market entrants. Previously, E.ON did not have a consistent method of measuring and understanding customer experience and service perception across all markets and no uniform measurement with defined benchmarks for performance. This lack of consistency led to disorganized teams with no consensus on what was good or bad customer service excellence, which led to disagreements about the best ways to address customer service challenges and the definition of success.

In developing the CSEP profile, these challenges were addressed through a series of questions (see Table 2): whether there is a general need for this type of program; the extent to which this program aligns with E.ON's corporate strategy and priorities; who would be the beneficiary of this program; the extent to which E.ON has the necessary financial resources to implement such a comprehensive program in our key markets; and whether there is or would be buy-in from internal, external, and regional stakeholders.

Question	Reply
Was there a need for a CSEP?	Yes, with the introduction of competition, there was a need to understand customers and their needs better. There was confusion about definitions and measures.
Was the overall program consistent with E.ON's strategy and priorities?	Yes and no – in the wake of market liberalization, E.ON has updated its strategy and policies to reflect the need for customer centricity.
Who would be the beneficiaries of this program?	E.ON customers were identified as the direct beneficiaries of this program.

Question	Reply
Were the necessary resources available to implement this program?	The different forms of liberalization within European countries required the establishment of individual programs. A central center of excellence was established to guarantee the transfer of know-how and to be able to influence regional budgeting and priority setting.
Would stakeholders accept such a program?	The program was introduced as a "top-down" program. Clear targets were implemented from 2010 onwards, initially to enable sufficient resource and competence development and later (from 2014) to link bonus payments to managers with target achievement.

Tab. 2: NPS program profile

1.2 Development of a performance measurement strategy

Even defining the construct of service excellence is complex, not to mention developing performance metrics. At E.ON, e.g., NPS was chosen as the metric for assessing performance to nuance the distinction between meeting and exceeding customer expectations – is the customer only satisfied or is he/she delighted?

Based on the need for a CSEP, NPS was selected as the metric that would most efficiently help E.ON understand customer experience, enabling a company-wide focus on appropriate customer interaction measurements and intervention strategies.

In core processes, regular customer surveys are conducted at relevant touchpoints and measure the willingness of customers to recommend us. The cumulation of these measurements after multiple touchpoints is known as Journey NPS (jNPS), which enables E.ON to better understand and improve specific customer interactions. However, the limitations of this approach were quickly recognized, primarily because this form of measurement only allowed NPS to be monitored over time and provide a self-reference/benchmark but did not allow for comparison with competition.

Since energy utilities are a low engagement product category, with about 30 to 60 percent of customers having little or no contact with their supplier for six months or longer, a strategic NPS measurement system (sNPS) was developed that allows direct comparisons with competitors in our markets, regardless of contact frequency.

sNPS are collective and used according to the following criteria:

- They are collected by an independent agency via an online panel;
- are based on a nationally representative sample;
- the reference group of competitors follows the same sampling logic;
- the mapping of the respective market structure is derived from natural fallout, with market share fluctuations for a single competitor being no more than three percent.

From these measurements, a performance measurement strategy was developed to provide the basis for evaluating customer experience in achieving pre-defined targets for jNPS and sNPS.

In addition to NPS, brand performance and consideration by non-customers are measured to round off the target picture.

Figure 1 shows the logic of a possible target structure that integrates perceptions of both existing customers and non-customers.

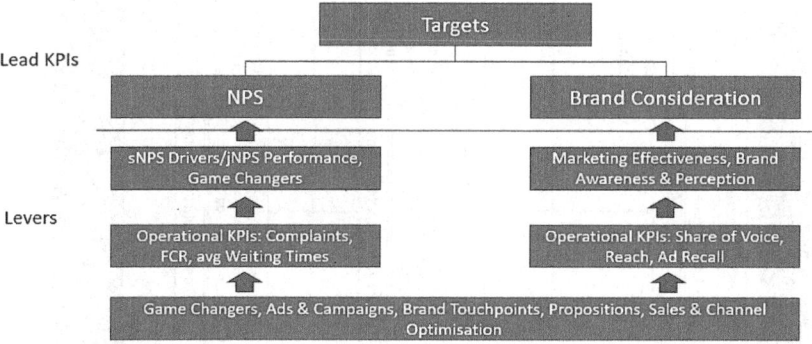

Fig. 1: Target hierarchy

1.2.1 The CSEP Logic Model

Any excellence program initially requires an investment in staff, IT support, management resources, etc. To better justify this investment, a logic model was developed for the CSEP that provides an understanding of the complex operations of the program and how performance is monitored (see Figure 2). The model creates a common understanding of the inner workings of the CSEP and its dependence on operational and management performance to achieve the desired program outcomes, which, in turn, improves communication among these interdependent groups (McLaughlin and Jordan, 1999).

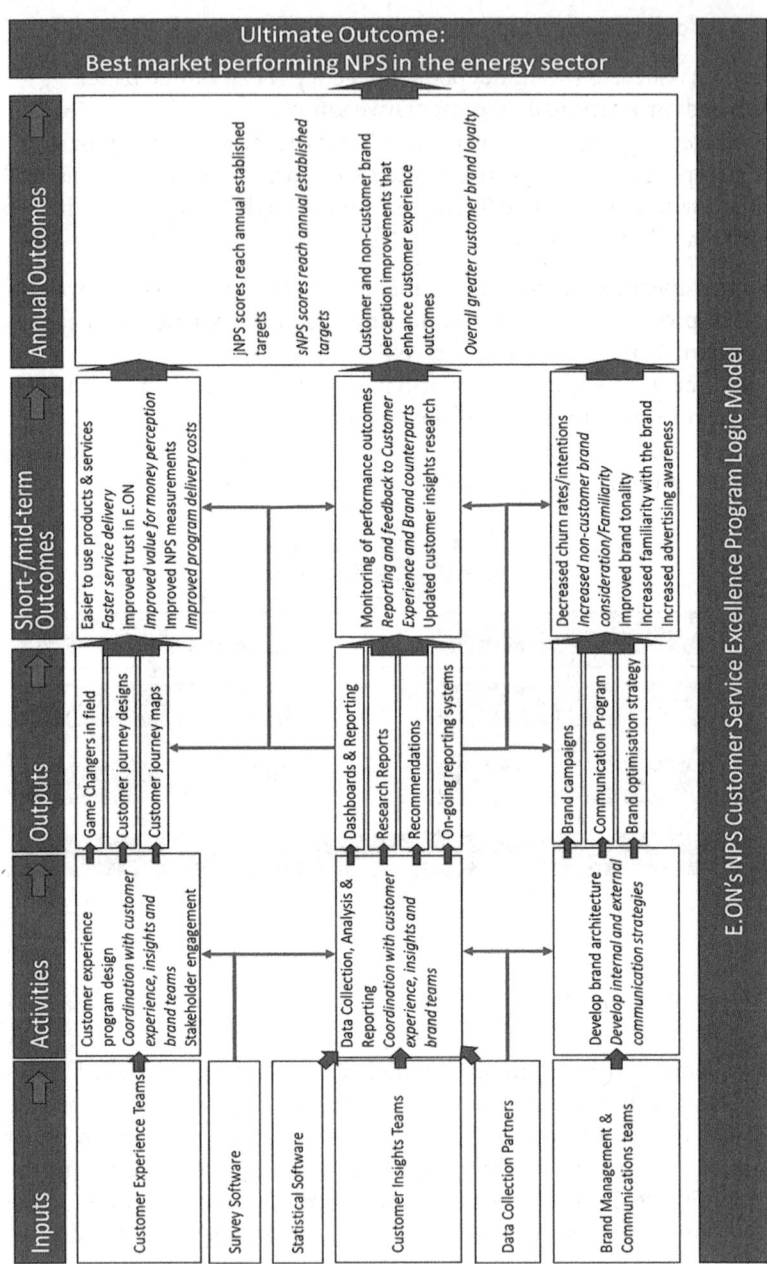

Fig. 2: Logic model underlying E.ON's NPS program

This CSEP Logic Model illustrates a high-level view of the expected relationships between financial and human inputs and desired outcomes, outlining three primary inputs to improve NPS performance: Customer Experience, Customer Insights, and Brand and Communications Activities. All three teams have different functions but the shared goal is to increase the likelihood of a customer recommending E.ON to a friend or colleague. Each group uses different methods to achieve these goals. Global Research and Insights acts as an interface between the teams, providing evidence-based recommendations to the Customer Experience and Brand and Communications teams to understand and optimize their activities to improve NPS.

1.2.2 *Implementation of the CSEP*

Implementing this system was no small feat. Funds were allocated to collect NPS measurements systematically, software was licensed to send out questionnaires, programs were purchased to perform statistical analysis and modeling that would be used to understand and report on program progress, and research and insight professionals were hired.

Dashboards were developed to provide employees and management with quick and easy access to key performance indicators, while an external partner was contracted to collect thousands of individual surveys of sNPS data every month across nine European markets. E.ON invested in employees to implement and leverage these new resources and to align the program with our ultimate goal of being the customer centricity leader in all our markets.

Guidelines were developed establishing the minimum requirements for all sampling and statistical methods, sampling structures, and survey frequencies to meet internal and external audit requirements.

In 2010, the E.ON SE Management Board incorporated the NPS program into its company-wide bonus structure. Since 2014, the achievement of specific NPS targets have been relevant to bonuses for all executives, and since 2016, as much as 20 percent of executive bonuses have depended on NPS performance.

2. How to increase NPS

Before giving examples of how E.ON improves NPS, it is necessary to be clear about what NPS can and cannot do. The assumption that a single key performance indicator can be used to manage a business must undoubtedly be critically questioned.

Keiningham et al. (2008) attempted to test the proposition that willingness to recommend is the best predictor of business success and attempted to replicate Fred Reichheld's research methodology as closely as possible. After testing several metrics across multiple industries, Keiningham et al. (2008, p. 88) concluded that,

> "... while it is quite tedious to have more variables and can sometimes convolute the picture of what you are researching, having too few variables introduces the possibility of peripheral blindness. And it would seem to us that this is exactly where NPS has fallen short: paring something complex down to a single number or a single metric."

Hayes (2010, p. 41) goes even further and states,

> "The NPS is not the best predictor of business performance measures. Other conventional loyalty questions are equally good at predicting revenue growth. Reichheld's claims are grossly overstated about the merits of the NPS. Reichheld and the other co-developers do not address these criticisms about the quality of the research (or lack thereof) behind their claims."

Of particular interest to E.ON is Reichheld's own statement identifying concern over the appropriateness of NPS for monopolies or near-monopolies (Reichheld and Markey, 2011). As noted above, this point was also crucial in the selection of the CSEP measure, given the uniqueness of the energy sector in Europe, the relatively recent liberalization in some markets, and the lack of liberalization in others.

Aware of the limitations of NPS, E.ON nevertheless decided to place this metric at the heart of the CSEP. More important than the score itself is to understand how to improve the results and how to show a clear relationship between activities and improved NPS performance.

2.1 Improving service excellence through research, insights, and experience

A fundamental concept in science is that measurements allow researchers to test theories and make predictions based on those measurements. In the case of E.ON's CSEP, a customer experience or brand activities that are expected to improve NPS must have testable and verifiable relationships to NPS performance improvement. The results of these tests form the basis for reporting and for deriving recommendations on which areas of action contribute most effectively to performance improvement.

Research and insight teams use multiple quantitative and qualitative data analysis methods to gain the insights needed to achieve program outcomes, focusing on gaps between actual service delivery and customer expectations, experiences, and perceptions. The intermediate goal is to obtain models that explain the relationship between these expectations, experiences, and perceptions and their ability to change NPS – these are called driver models.

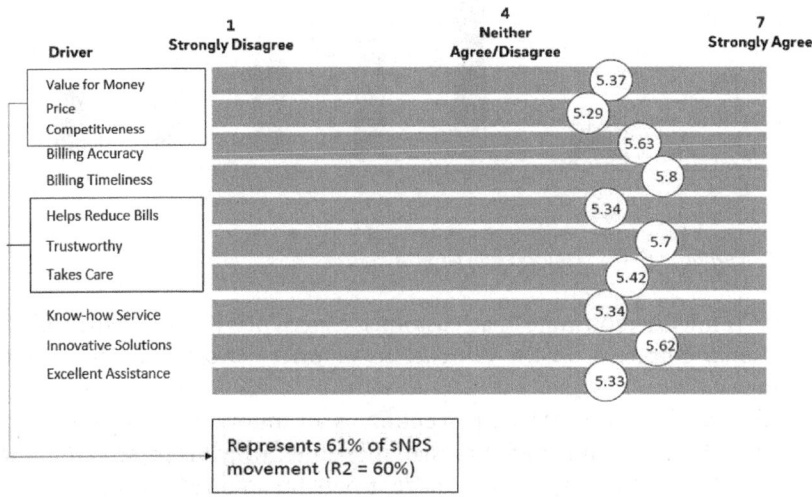

Fig. 3: Example of driver performance

Figure 3 shows a generic driver model with the importance of each driver in the boxes, using Shapley value regression modeling. These basic models form the foundations for performance dialogs and enable a better understanding of where to best allocate resources. This example model visualized that these specific drivers explain 60 percent of NPS movements. More importantly, this model illustrates the potential of each driver and its ability to improve NPS performance. In this example, "value for money" and "competitive pricing" are the strongest NPS drivers, but also perform the worst, providing a rich insight into how to allocate resources to maximize performance.

More detailed analysis through multinomial logistic regression allows the data to be further decomposed and us to understand the subtle perceptual differences between high-end detractors on the NPS scale (those who give a five or a six), passives, and promoters. Based on the driver performance shown in Figure 3, subgroup analysis is performed to determine what would be most important for a customer to give an extra NPS point or two (see Figure 4).

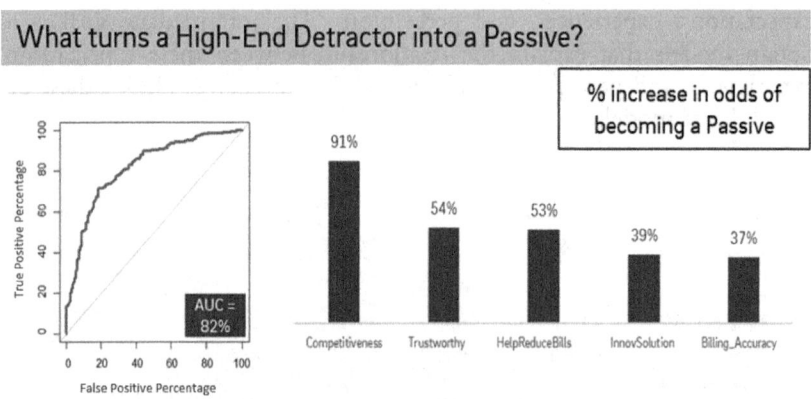

Fig. 4: Turning high-end detractors into passives

These results demonstrate that customer experience teams need to place additional emphasis on the dimensions of price-performance, trust, and billing.

Additionally, an improved perception as an innovative company offers potential for increasing NPS. Bayesian modeling, which is presented in the next section of this chapter, also made it possible to direct the activities of customer experience teams to contact channels that are most effective in guaranteeing price worthiness for subgroups such as high-end detractors.

While it may seem like digging too deep into the numbers, it cannot be stressed enough that this can never be the case. These data form the basis for recommendations on and insights into CSEP improvement and the results must be shared throughout the organization with corresponding intervention strategies taken accordingly. This requires that the information is easily accessible and communicated as simply as possible.

2.2 Bayesian networks

While driver models explain how much variance exists between specific service and brand experiences and NPS, the causal nature of the relationships is not fully understood by these models. Bayesian theory is used to address this blind spot.

Take, e.g., customer trust. Trust is a very abstract and complex construct. A research and insight team cannot simply make the recommendation: "You need to improve our customer trust." Moreover, trust is by far the most important driver of NPS/recommendation in many of our markets, with NPS and trust often being so highly correlated ($p > 0.8$) that they can act as sufficient proxies for one other. To understand how customer experience teams can better develop customer trust, Bayesian networks allow us to understand the fundamentals of trust and, by extension, the fundamentals of NPS (see Figure 5) based on the initial driver modeling.

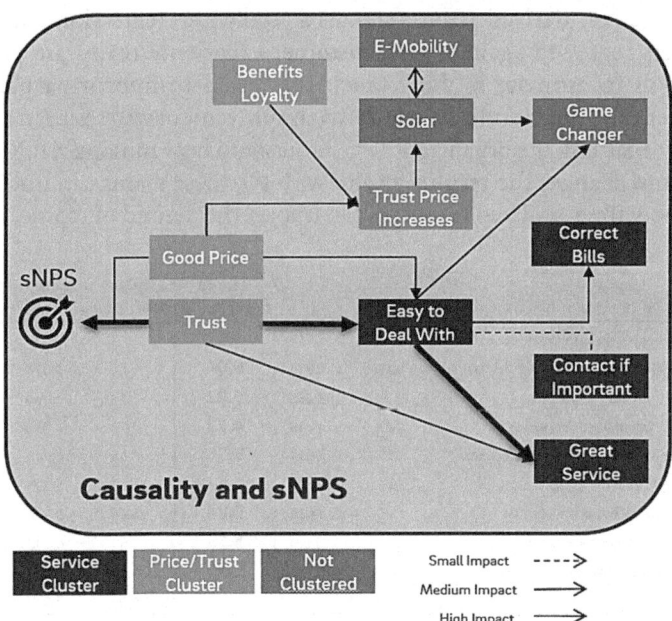

Fig. 5: Example Bayesian network

Within this network, one can see that simply meeting or exceeding basic service expectations leads to greater trust and a higher NPS. In this example, having a reliable power supply, being transparent and honest about price increases, rewarding loyalty, etc., all contribute to a higher perception of service quality and being perceived as barrier-free when dealing with customers. When these drivers of NPS are met, customers are much more likely to trust and recommend.

This type of analysis provides even more relevant information and recommendations for customer experience and service excellence teams, enabling them to follow the causalities between drivers.

2.3 Tools for the scenario model

While dashboards and reports bring data to life, data and research findings must also assist in how improving a driver can increase NPS. Here, Bayesian and regression modeling are combined in a scenario or "what if" tool (see Figure 6).

Using standard algebraic equations (NPS=B0+(B1*X1)+(B2*X2)+ (B3*X3)+... e) derived from standard multiple regression modeling of drivers regressed against NPS, customer experience teams are provided with tools to estimate by how much they need to improve a particular customer experience and how much that improvement will result in a higher NPS. By enabling the organization to understand how moving X1, X2, or X3 and so on, changes the resulting value of NPS, these teams can understand better how the associated resources can impact the desired outcome.

Driver	Shapley	β	Desired Driver Scores	Actual Driver Scores	% Change	Predicted NPS
How satisfied are you with the prices of energy?	18%	0.11911	4.67	4.67	0.00%	14%
Information provided is relevant to me	11%	0.05885	5.04	5.04	0.00%	
Is easy to deal with	12%	0.05455	5.52	5.52	0.00%	
Understands my needs	13%	0.05266	4.73	4.73	0.00%	
Gives me easy and clear instructions	11%	0.03594	5.36	5.36	0.00%	
Provides brilliant customer care	9%	0.03261	5.67	5.67	0.00%	
Has high-quality service	9%	0.03034	5.84	5.84	0.00%	
Meets my Needs	11%	0.02819	5.53	5.53	0.00%	
Is a trustworthy company	8%	0.02717	5.97	5.97	0.00%	
R^2 = 39%	100%		5.37	5.37	0.00%	

Predicted NPS = -2.134238 + (0.11911*4.67) + (0.05885*5.04) + (0.05455*5.52) + (0.05266*4.73) + (0.03594*5.36) + (0.03261*5.67) + (0.03034*5.84) + (0.02819*5.53) + (0.02717*5.97) + e

Fig. 6: Scenario model tool

By simply changing the mean value of the desired driver in the tool, one can see how much the NPS would increase due to the corresponding driver improvement. This is particularly important for achieving targets, as it allows managers and stakeholders to estimate the amount of resources required for this improvement.

2.4 Brand and marketing communication activities as a prerequisite for changing perceptions

As already mentioned, around 30 to 60 percent of customers report having no contact with E.ON for six months or longer. This poses a problem from the point of view of service and customer experience managers. If a customer has no contact for an extended time period, it is impossible to shape their opinion of the company positively through a direct experience. This gap must be filled by branding and communication activities. To paraphrase the tree falling in the woods thought experiment: If you have an outstanding customer experience or initiative but no one is there to experience it, does the experience really exist?

Answering this question emphasizes the importance of cross-departmental coordination when it comes to a CSEP. It is challenging for customer experience teams to improve awareness of specific offers or initiatives through contact channels alone. Brand and marketing communications can engage customers more broadly and educate them about available products and services, which will increase customer awareness.

More importantly, through regression and Bayesian statistics, it was found that product offers act as a cornerstone for improved service and trust perceptions on the part of customers, in addition to driving improved price perceptions.

It may also come as no surprise that a more positive brand perception is highly correlated with the likelihood of a customer recommending E.ON to others.

From corresponding models, insights and recommendations can be derived for brand and marketing communications teams to arrive at the messages best suited to increasing the likelihood that a customer will recommend E.ON to others. As seen in other models, value for money stands out as a strong predictor. In an industry where most customers are unable to name the exact price they pay, this presents challenges, as typical responses include "we will lower our price," which completely misses the point of this type of analysis. The imperative is to clarify the value of the service to customers. In E.ON's case, this value must either be demonstrated through a direct customer experience or meaningfully communicated to customers who have had little to no direct experience over extended periods of time.

3. Conclusion

This chapter provides a broad overview of why and how E.ON implemented its CSEP and gives a summary of how insights from data are used to develop strategies and activities aimed at improving NPS performance.

In summary, let us again mention the key elements discussed in developing, implementing, and monitoring a CSEP. First, it is essential to create a plan. This plan must describe the need for such a program, the resources required, and their potential to influence the achievement of the program's intended goals. This requires consultation with a wide range of stakeholders, and when this planning is done well, it greatly facilitates the program's implementation and allows for greater stakeholder buy-in and support.

Second, the program must be focused, measurable, and have clear goals and outcomes which are outlined in well-developed and detailed logic models. In developing the Program Profile and Logic Model, these essential criteria can be ensured insofar as they are supported by all stakeholders and, most importantly, by management and customers.

A CSEP is a never-ending journey. We enjoy our successes and learn from our failures. We see that some activities did not produce the desired results, while others performed surprisingly well. It is vital to understand the causes of both our successes and failures better and maximize the performance of a CSEP. Even a poor result does not automatically mean that the underlying premise was wrong – perhaps there was a flaw in the implementation of a sound strategy. Research and insights gained from our activities help us understand when a good idea was simply poorly executed and provide recommendations for improvement.

Bibliography

Delia, V. (2013). A glance at the European energy market liberalization, CES Working Papers, ISSN 2067–7693, Alexandru Ioan Cuza University of Iasi, Centre for European Studies, Iasi, 5(1), pp. 100–110.

Hayes, B.E. (2010). Beyond the ultimate question: A systematic approach to improve customer loyalty, American Society for Quality, Milwaukee.

Johnston, R. (2004). Towards a better understanding of service excellence, Managing Service Quality, 14(2/3), pp. 129–133.

Keiningham, T., Aksoy, L., Cooil, B. and Andreassen, T. (2008). Linking customer loyalty to growth, MIT Sloan Management Review, July 1, 2008.

McLaughlin, J. and Jordan, G. (1999). Logic models: a tool for telling your program's performance story, Evaluation and Program Planning, 22, pp. 65–72.

Morgan, N. and Rego, L.L. (2006). The value of different customer satisfaction and loyalty metrics in predicting business performance, Marketing Science, 25(5), pp. 426–439.

Reichheld, F.F. (2003). The one number you need to grow, Harvard Business Review, 81(12), pp. 46–54, 124.

Reichheld, F.F. and Markey, R. (2011). The ultimate question 2.0 (Revised and Expanded Edition): How net promoter companies thrive in a customer-driven world, Harvard Business Review Press, Boston.

Outlook

Outlook: New developments in service excellence

Matthias Gouthier

Management summary

Anyone who thinks that they know everything there is to know about service excellence after reading this edited volume will be disabused of this notion in this concluding article. The longer and more intensively one deals with service excellence as an expert, the more aware one becomes that there are still many unchartered areas on the economic and scientific map of service excellence. This article concludes by addressing seven developments that are currently emerging and will shape the development of service excellence in the coming years.

1. Service excellence – a book with seven seals

In the present case, the perception, evaluation, and selection of these developments are not based on empirically validated study results but are owed to the author's subjective assessment. However, this personal judgment is based on many years of scientific research, consulting, and various transfer activities. In particular, acting as the chairman of the technical committee ISO/TC 312 "Excellence in Service" and active participation in its working groups and task forces provide well-founded and up-to-date knowledge of where the journey will lead in the coming years. Thus, seven developments are currently emerging within the framework of the discussions that are continuously being held within the technical committee ISO/TC 312 "Excellence in Service," which will be discussed in more detail below:

1. Certifying service excellence
2. Measuring service excellence (performance)
3. Implementing service excellence
4. Qualifying for service excellence
5. Internal service excellence
6. Digital service excellence
7. Industry-specific differentiation of service excellence

The order in which the developments are listed is purely random and should not be interpreted in relation to relevance.

1.1 Certifying service excellence

The topic of certification has increasingly arisen since the publication of ISO 23592:2021. Inquiries are coming in from Germany but also from abroad as to whether companies can be certified based on the standard. However, several certification companies have also offered certification for service excellence on the (German) market before. For example, TÜV SÜD, TÜV NORD CERT, and DQS, to name just three well-known German certification bodies, currently offer service excellence certification. However, these are still based on the previous standards, DIN SPEC 77224:2011 and CEN/TS 16880:2015. While these standards were "only" technical specifications in both cases, the market now has an official, global ISO standard. This leads to the two consequences that, on the one hand, the attractiveness of getting certified has increased. On the other hand, both specifications will be taken off the market in the foreseeable future. Companies that want to be certified accordingly soon and certification bodies that want to offer such a certificate should therefore adapt to the new ISO standard now.

1.2 Measuring service excellence (performance)

One element, or more precisely, the ninth element of the service excellence model, is dedicated to measuring service excellence activities and results. This calls for an organization to systematically develop and apply a set of internal and external metrics that focus on all model elements. However, the comments in this regard are rather general and are limited in total to just under two pages. This is not particularly surprising, since a standard such as ISO 23592:2021 is intended to be kept short and concise. Of course, this is countered by the desire of users to receive the most factual information possible on what precisely measures service excellence and how.

This was the trigger for developing a further document in the form of a technical specification, the ISO/TS 23686 "Service excellence – Measuring service excellence performance." It provides companies with a more concrete plan of action for measuring service excellence or, more precisely, service excellence performance. After a brief introduction, the document first defines the key terms. This is followed by a description of the principles that are intended to guide the measurement of service excellence performance. The actual performance measurement or performance measurement system for service excellence is based on the OKR approach.

OKR stands for "Objectives and Key Results" and is currently a popular approach used to break down strategies into operational objectives and measurable results (see, e.g., Doerr, 2018). Consequently, this approach is suitable for operationalizing a service excellence strategy into measurable objectives, activities, and results. Following this, the measurement approaches for each of the four dimensions of the service excellence model are presented in four chapters on this technical specification that focus on the methods used and the metrics to be applied. This standard will most likely be published in Fall 2022.

1.3 Implementing service excellence

Suppose a company or its top management has decided to align the company (or parts of the company) with service excellence. In that case, the particular challenge arises as to how service excellence can be established in the company. Here, we are not talking about the introduction of one or more individual measures, but about introducing service excellence as a holistic and, above all, sustainable approach (Asif and Gouthier, 2015; Börnsen and Gouthier, 2019). Accordingly, in addition to observing the principles and realizing the four dimensions of the service excellence model and its nine elements, it is necessary to consider which steps are required to implement the concept permanently. Generally speaking, around 70 to 75 percent of all transformation programs in companies fail (see, e.g., Blanchard, 2010; McKinsey, 2020). Accordingly, a change management or transformation concept must be set up and implemented as an accompanying measure. The change management model, according to Kotter (2012), e.g., which consists of the following eight steps, is useful:

1. Within the organization, create a sense of urgency and importance for establishing service excellence.
2. To implement service excellence, a management coalition that accompanies and supports the process from start to finish must be established.
3. In addition, a vision, mission, and strategy of service excellence that have the traction to move the company in the desired direction must be developed.
4. To ensure all employees are on board, the vision for change must be communicated to them.
5. In support of this, employees are to be empowered on a broad basis to achieve service excellence.

6. Quick wins are needed to avoid discouraging employees and to solidify the service excellence approach.
7. To ensure that the establishment of service excellence does not fizzle out in the long term, the successes must be consolidated and further changes initiated in the direction of service excellence.
8. Finally, new service excellence approaches must be sustainably anchored in the organization's culture.

According to Kurt Lewin, these eight steps can be attributed to the three phases of a fundamental change process. Steps 1 to 4 are assigned to the "unfreezing" phase, steps 5 to 7 to the "changing" phase, and step 8 to the "anchoring" phase.

A standard is also planned for implementing service excellence, which is to be developed in one of the working groups of ISO/TC 312. However, more detailed information on this is not available at the time of writing.

1.4 Qualifying for service excellence

Excellent services are not always, but very often, characterized by delightful interaction between the customer and an employee. While a high level of professional competence can sometimes trigger customer delight, in many cases, it is the social skills of the employees and their commitment that characterize a five-star service and delight customers instead. As described in the article "Employee engagement requires motivation and qualification: The use of blended learning to implement service excellence" by Prof. Dr. Matthias Gouthier and Matthias Raquet, various skills and attributes are required to be able to delight the customer at the end of the day. These essential prerequisites include the right mindset and attitude toward the customer. In addition, it is crucial to accurately understand the customer and their needs, wishes, problems, and so on. Furthermore, the correct handling of critical situations is part of the required repertoire of actions. In addition, the employee should know how to offer a personal touch in interactions. And finally, the employee should have ideas on creating surprising wow moments for the customer.

However, there is no general standard for such a competence framework for excellent service interactions. Accordingly, a goal of ISO/TC 312 could be to develop a suitable competence framework in the future, which refers to the necessary non-technical skills of employees.

1.5 Internal service excellence

The services delivered to customers can ultimately only be as good as the sum of the inputs, activities, and processes conducted in a company. If a company's overall performance on the market is to be increased, it is also necessary to optimize the performance of the company's internal departments. To systematically achieve excellent services, a company's internal processes should run optimally and be understood in terms of an internal customer–supplier relationship. This task is the focus of internal service excellence (Hays, 1996). This is an approach that helps companies measure and develop the performance of departments as internal service providers and thus raise it to a higher level. Although many companies have already aligned their goals with achieving customer delight, a large proportion of service activities are carried out by internal company units. They, too, must internalize the idea of service excellence.

Therefore, the central question for companies is how internal departments can be systematically developed in terms of their performance quality to internally deliver excellent services. One way of doing this is to use maturity models. Maturity models in this context aim to make internal service excellence measurable. In addition, the current situation of a department must be assigned to a specific maturity level. If both the content dimensions of internal service excellence and the maturity levels are combined, a maturity model of internal service excellence is obtained.

This challenge could also be dealt with in a working group of the technical committee ISO/TC 312 and a corresponding standard or technical specification could be developed.

1.6 Digital service excellence

This is one of the most exciting, but at the same time, most challenging areas of service excellence. It is undisputed that digitalization is one of the most important developments and challenges for companies offering excellent service. However, the unanswered question is what is meant by "digital service excellence," what content or elements it comprises, and how it can be mapped. In principle, there are references to the ISO/IEC 20000 series of standards in this respect, which is being developed or refined by ISO/IEC JTC 1/SC 40 "IT service management and IT governance," with working group 2 being responsible in particular. ISO/IEC 20000 represents an internationally recognized series of standards for IT service management (ITSM), whereby the standard proclaims that not only an

ITSM but also a service management system (SMS) in general is described. In this context, ISO/IEC 20000 Part 1:2018—"Service management system requirements" contains the requirements for an SMS that an organization must establish, implement, maintain, and continuously improve to obtain certification. In contrast, ISO/IEC 20000 Part 2:2019—"Guidance on the application of service management systems" provides guidance on the application of an SMS based on ISO/IEC 20000–1:2018. This document provides examples and recommendations to enable organizations to correctly interpret and apply ISO/IEC 20000–1:2018, including references to other parts of ISO/IEC 20000 and different relevant standards.

Whether the two worlds of (IT) service management and service excellence will continue to grow together remains to be seen. The initial approaches look promising. There is already continuous exchange between ISO/TC 312 "Excellence in Service" and ISO/IEC JTC 1/SC 40 "IT service management and IT governance."

1.7 Industry-specific differentiation of service excellence

Before 2010, the term of service excellence already existed. However, there was neither a uniform understanding of service excellence, nor a uniform concept of what is meant by service excellence and which elements a service excellence approach contains. What did exist were company-specific concepts propagated to a greater or lesser extent in public. It was not until DIN SPEC 77224:2011, initiated and coordinated by the editor of this book, that the first standard describing a uniform service excellence model was created. This model was transferred into a European standard, CEN/TS 16880:2015, at the request of international companies that participated in creating DIN SPEC 77224:2011. This specification, in turn, formed the basis of the development of the current ISO standard 23592:2021.

While the strength of such a so-called horizontal standard lies in providing a generally applicable model of service excellence for all kinds of organizations, this is also one of its weaknesses. A generic service excellence model cannot reflect the specifics of individual industries or sectors, such as contact centers (Dharamdass and Fernando, 2018), facility management, financial services (Al-Marri et al., 2007; Dobni, 2002; Kim and Kleiner, 1996), retailing (Padma and Wagenseil, 2018), industrial services or public services (Hunt and Ivergård, 2015). However, what can be done is to adopt a general service excellence model to the specifics of an industry or sector. This is also evident, e.g., in the current discussions among the technical committee ISO/TC 312. A new working group to apply the service excellence model to the public sector is being discussed and supported.

There will undoubtedly be further such branch specifications in the future. In 2016/2017, e.g., Deutsche Bank played a leading role in developing DIN SPEC 77231:2017, which describes the requirements for the "Process and competence framework for the implementation of excellent service in branch banking." Against the background described above, it is entirely conceivable that more specific standards, such as those for industrial companies in terms of industrial service excellence, will also be developed at the international level in the future.

2. Conclusion

The further development of service excellence is far from finished today. It will not come to an end in the foreseeable future, as there will be permanently new developments, be it on the part of customer requirements, competitive developments, and technological developments, to name only a few, which will define new requirements for excellent service in the future. It, therefore, remains exciting to see where the topic of service excellence will continue to develop in the future.

Bibliography

Al-Marri, K., Ahmed, A.M.B.A. and Zairi, M. (2007). Excellence in service: An empirical study of the UAE banking sector, International Journal of Quality & Reliability Management, 24(2), pp. 164–176.

Asif, M. and Gouthier, M.H.J. (2015). Developing a self-diagnostic framework for assessing service excellence, International Journal of Services and Operations Management, 20(4), pp. 441–460.

Blanchard, K. (2010). Mastering the art of change, Training Journal, January 2010, pp. 44–47.

Börnsen, S. and Gouthier, M.H.J. (2019). TeamBank uses DIN SPEC 77224 for the continuous development of service excellence to delight customers permanently, Case study TeamBank AG.

CEN/TS 16880:2015 (2015). Service excellence — Creating outstanding customer experiences through service excellence, Brussels.

Dharamdass, S. and Fernando, Y. (2018). Contact centre service excellence: A proposed conceptual framework, International Journal of Services and Operations Management, 29(1), pp. 18–41.

DIN SPEC 77224:2011 (2011). Achieving customer delight through service excellence, Berlin.

DIN SPEC 77231:2017 (2017). Process and competence framework for the delivery of excellent service in branch banking, Berlin.

Dobni, B. (2002). A model for implementing service excellence in the financial services industry, Journal of Financial Services Marketing, 7(1), pp. 42–53.

Doerr, J. (2018). Measure what matters: How Google, Bono, and the Gates Foundation rock the world with OKRs, New York.

Hays, R.D. (1996). The strategic power of internal service excellence, Business Horizons, 39(4), pp. 15–20.

Hunt, B. and Ivergård, T. (2015). Designing service excellence. People and technology, Boca Raton.

ISO 23592:2021 (2021). Service excellence — Principles and model, Geneva.

ISO/IEC 20000–1:2018 (2018). Information technology — Service management — Part 1: Service management system requirements, Geneva.

ISO/IEC 20000–2:2019 (2019). Information technology — Service management — Part 2: Guidance on the application of service management systems.

ISO/TS 23686:2022 (2022). Service excellence — Measuring service excellence performance, Geneva.

Kim, S. and Kleiner, B.H. (1996). Service excellence in the banking industry, Managing Service Quality, 6(1), pp. 22–27.

Kotter, J.P. (2012). Leading Change, Boston.

McKinsey (2020). The changeable organization, McKinsey Quarterly Five Fifty, Feb. 25, 2020, https://www.mckinsey.com/business-functions/transformation/our-insights/five-fifty-the-changeable-organization, accessed 09/05/2021.

Padma, P. and Wagenseil, U. (2018). Retail service excellence: Antecedents and consequences, International Journal of Retail & Distribution Management, 46(5), pp. 422–441.

About the authors

Dr. Ferri Abolhassan

Dr. Ferri Abolhassan holds a doctorate in computer science and is editor of numerous specialist books. After holding positions at Siemens, IBM, IDS Scheer, and SAP, he joined Deutsche Telekom AG in 2008. He, e.g., headed the production unit and the IT division at T-Systems. In 2016, he became a member of the Management Board of Telekom Deutschland GmbH and is now the leader of its service business department with around 30,000 employees. Since May 2021, he has also been responsible for Telekom Deutschland's Privatkunden Vertriebsgesellschaft mbH, which includes the Telekom Shops.

Dr. Björn Becker

Dr. Björn Becker is responsible for launching new products for intercontinental flights at Lufthansa Group Airlines as well as all customer-related issues during the relaunch phase in the COVID-19 crisis.

Until 2020, he was responsible for the ground product and digital services of Lufthansa, Swissair and Austrian Airlines, including check-in & baggage drop-off, lounges, premium services, boarding, embarkation and disembarkation services, and services in digital channels (app, website, etc.). Dr. Becker has over 20 years of experience in different areas of the airline industry, a Ph.D. in revenue management, and numerous publications in journals and conferences.

Sabine Börnsen

Sabine Börnsen has held various management positions at TeamBank AG since 2012. She is currently responsible for two major digitalization projects.

After studying Business Administration in Germany and England, she obtained a Bachelor of Arts degree with honors in Business and Management in the U.K. in 2006 and a business school Master's degree with honors in Business Administration in 2008. Subsequently, she worked as a project manager for the management consultancy team of the E.ON Group throughout Europe.

She then moved to TeamBank AG and, as Head of the Organization, Process and Quality Management department, she was, e.g., responsible for its service excellence audits and certification.

Philippe D. Clarinval

Philippe D. Clarinval (MBA) is a hotelier who has managed many illustrious luxury hotels worldwide before taking over the Carlton Hotel St. Moritz as General Manager.

His unique approach to leadership has made him successful because he believes that people and purpose lead strategies to success. He is doing his Ph.D. at the University of Liverpool. He has studied in several executive education programs at the University of Oxford, Harvard University, and the Massachusetts Institute of Technology.

He is a member of the European Hotel Managers Association, a former President of the Cornell Hotel Society AlpAdria & Eastern Europe Chapter, and a passionate mentor and coach of CEOs and executives.

Svenja Daniel

Svenja Daniel started her professional career at Brenntag SE after studying economics. She wrote her master's thesis on the topic of customer experience in the B2B environment and subsequently led the rollout of service excellence in EMEA from 2018. In June 2021, she took over the company's global management as "Global Project Manager Service Excellence."

Brenntag SE is the global market leader in distributing chemicals and ingredients, playing a key role as a link between customers and suppliers in the chemical industry.

Prof. Dr. Matthias Gouthier

Prof. Dr. Matthias Gouthier holds the Chair of Marketing and Electronic Services, is Head of the Institute of Management in the Department of Computer Science, and Director of the Center for Service Excellence (CSE) at the University of Koblenz-Landau. Prof. Gouthier initiated the DIN SPEC 77224, the world's first official standard on service excellence. Following this, he took over the leadership of the European committee that transferred the German standard into a European standard (CEN/TS 16880). Since March 2018, he has headed the ISO/TC 312 "Excellence in Service" as Chairman, which developed the ISO standard 23592 "Service excellence." To bring the topic of service excellence continuously and more broadly into practice, he has been organizing the Excellence in Service conference series EXIS for ten years, an exchange and transfer platform dedicated to annually changing topics relating to service excellence. As a sought-after expert, he lectures at renowned universities and associations, ministries, management consultancies, and companies from various industries. As a management consultant, he has accompanied numerous companies on their way to service excellence. Finally, he co-founded oneservice AG in 2017. As Academic Director, he is jointly responsible for its Service Excellence Academy.

Enrico Jensch

Service visionary Enrico Jensch is responsible for international operations as the COO at Helios Health. He is also the COO at Helios Germany and, since July 2019, managing director of the two Helios divisions "Outpatient Care" and "New Business Models," which were founded in 2018. Jensch previously worked at Helios as Managing Director International and, until 2018, as Regional Managing Director of the Central-North Region. From 2007 to 2010, he managed the Helios Hospital Bad Saarow and in 2011 the Hospital Schwerin. Together with Carsten K. Rath, he has been establishing the "6 Chefs, 12 Stars" project at Helios Hospitals since 2020.

Juliane Köninger

Juliane Köninger studied international business at the Technical University of Nuremberg in Germany and spent a semester abroad at the Science University Malaysia. She then completed her master's degree in management and marketing at the University of Hohenheim. In addition to her studies, she was employed in the International Customer Training Department at Siemens AG and Marketing Communications at Mercedes-Benz AG. Since July 2018, she has been working in Customer Experience Management at Mercedes-Benz Mobility AG. Besides that, she researches as an external doctoral candidate at the Chair of Marketing and Electronic Services at the University of Koblenz-Landau.

Michael Moritz

Michael Moritz is Managing Director of WISAG Facility Service Holding GmbH, one of Germany's leading real estate service providers. The engineering graduate started his career at WISAG in 1994 as a project manager – after twelve years in the service of the German Air Force. Two years later, he was appointed to the management board of a regional company, after which he managed the business of WISAG Facility Management Holding for many years. Since 2001, he has been responsible for WISAG Facility Service Holding.

Christian Polenz

Christian Polenz has been a member of Team-Bank AG's Management Board since 2010. As deputy Chief Executive Officer (deputy CEO) and as Chief Customer Officer (CCO) of TeamBank, he is responsible for all matters relating to customers, specifically the customer dialog center, the customer bank, and marketing. Besides this, he is responsible for all data, IT, and product-related issues.

In addition to his training as a banker, Christian Polenz completed a part-time course of study. He then worked for Deutsche Bank AG and Bayerische Hypo- und Vereinsbank, among others. At TeamBank AG he started his career in various management positions and was appointed General Representative in 2006.

Matthias Raquet

Matthias Raquet has been CEO and co-founder of oneservice AG since 2017. He also holds the position of Vice Chairman of the Board of Directors at oneservice AG. Matthias Raquet had previously held a wide variety of management positions in the biotech industry for more than 30 years. Most recently, he was Vice President — Head of Global Service Solutions & Global Customer Management at QIAGEN, where he was responsible for global service.

Christopher J. Rastin

Christopher J. Rastin was born in Chatham, Canada, in 1979. He studied criminology and psychology at the University of Ottawa from 1998 to 2002, followed by graduate studies in Counseling Psychology. Between 2001 and 2013 he conducted research and evaluation projects for the Correctional Services of Canada, focusing on offender treatment programming and offender profiling. He further conducted research on culturally appropriate policing services for Indigenous populations by the Royal Canadian Mounted Police through the First Nations Policing Program. In 2013, he moved from Montréal to Düsseldorf and joined E.ON SE in 2018. He leads the Global Research and Insights team and is responsible for NPS and Brand research. Christopher has driven data/evidence-based decision-making at E.ON for the NPS program.

Carsten K. Rath

Entrepreneur Carsten K. Rath is the "No. 1 service expert in Germany" (n-tv). His principle of uncompromising service excellence is all about customer delight. As a grand hotelier, Carsten K. Rath has opened legendary luxury hotels. Today, the speaker, consultant and coach supports companies across all industries on their way into the digital future – because it is a part of service. Carsten K. Rath is passionate about passing on his experience and knowledge to the next generation. He currently works as a university lecturer in marketing and service excellence at various international universities and colleges. Rath is also COO at the Center for Service Excellence at the University of Koblenz-Landau. The Handelsblatt calls him "The international service authority."

Dr. Kristina Rodig

Dr. Kristina Rodig was born in Oranienburg in 1963. Since 2016, she is Head of Global Insights and Customer Experience Management at E.ON SE in Essen. After completing her studies in Potsdam, Smolensk, and Berlin with a doctorate in Russian literature and a master's in Business Marketing, she held various positions in the energy industry. She has worked as a press officer, key account manager, and in different senior marketing and customer service roles. She established the first customer insights unit for E.ON in Germany and played a key role in shaping the NPS program at E.ON. Her areas of expertise include customer loyalty strategies, complaint management, customer experience management, and market research and analytics.

How to implement Service Excellence and get officially certified

The solution is delivered by the Service Excellence Academy!

The management of the Service Excellence Academy initiated and coordinated the three official standards on Service Excellence:

DIN SPEC 77224, CEN/TS 16880 and **ISO 23592**.

We use our expertise to live our internal service excellence program.
And we support companies in successfully implementing Service Excellence.
You can't get more official expertise than this!

Get support from the specialists:

· Establish the right attitude and mindset for Service Excellence in your organization.

· Get your people trained to create outstanding customer experience
  and deliver an excellent service.

· Assessing the Service Excellence maturity level of your organization
  or service units.

· Auditing your company based on ISO 23592.

· Preparing your company to get officially certified on ISO 23592.

· Become ISO 23592 certified by SECERT GmbH

For further information, please visit our website: service-excellence-academy.com
or get in direct contact with us: info@service-excellence-academy.com

We want you to be delighted with us!

Service Excellence is more than a competitive advantage – It is a game changer!

www.service-excellence-academy.com